Music, Culture, and Society

Music, Culture, and Society

a reader

edited by

DEREK B. SCOTT

OXFORD
UNIVERSITY PRESS

OXFORD
UNIVERSITY PRESS

Great Clarendon Street, Oxford OX2 6DP

Oxford University Press is a department of the University of Oxford.
It furthers the University's objective of excellence in research, scholarship,
and education by publishing worldwide in

Oxford New York

Athens Auckland Bangkok Bogotá Buenos Aires Cape Town
Chennai Dar es Salaam Delhi Florence Hong Kong Istanbul Karachi
Kolkata Kuala Lumpur Madrid Melbourne Mexico City Mumbai Nairobi
Paris São Paulo Shanghai Singapore Taipei Tokyo Toronto Warsaw

with associated companies in Berlin Ibadan

Oxford is a registered trade mark of Oxford University Press
in the UK and in certain other countries

Published in the United States
by Oxford University Press Inc., New York

© Introduction and commentary, Derek B. Scott, and contributors, 2000

British Library Cataloguing in Publication Data

Data available

Library of Congress Cataloging in Publication Data

Music, culture, and society: a reader/edited by Derek B. Scott.
p. cm.
Includes index.
1. Music and society. I. Scott, Derek B.
ML3795.M784 2000 780—dc21 99-44502

ISBN 0-19-879012-0 pbk.
ISBN 0-19-879011-2 hbk.

10 9 8 7 6 5 4 3 2

Typeset by Best-set Typesetter Ltd., Hong Kong
Printed in Great Britain
on acid-free paper by
Biddles Ltd
Guildford and King's Lynn

Preface

When I embarked upon this Reader in 1991, I little thought what a nearly impossible task putting it together would prove to be. Indeed, it was originally to be edited jointly but, after two years, frustration with its progress drove my collaborator away. The fees for permissions that some publishers now demand are a major stumbling block to projects of this kind, so I must begin by expressing my sincere gratitude to those authors and publishers who reduced costs or allowed me to reproduce their work gratis. Another seemingly intractable problem was deciding what to include and exclude. Here, I would like to pay tribute to advice given in half a dozen anonymous reports supplied to Oxford University Press, and to the suggestions of those attending Critical Musicology sessions in the UK over the past few years. This book, then, has been a long time in preparation. Originally, sections were planned on ethnomusicology, music psychology, and film music studies. These were dropped as costs began to mount. Nevertheless, if I were beginning afresh, I would now wish to see a whole section on the impact of digital technology on music, in recognition of the growing scholarship in this area.

There is by no means a party line to be found in the succeeding pages. In truth, many of the writers included, and sometimes placed side by side, would argue vociferously with each other in the flesh. Texts have been selected either because they present significant new arguments, or because they have sparked off a wider debate. These readings cannot be grouped conveniently under the umbrella of either Critical Musicology or New Musicology as if those terms referred to a homogeneous body of thought or a consistent line of reasoning. All that can be said is that many of them have offered alternatives of one kind or another to the musicological mainstream. I have tried, in the main, to focus on texts that show evidence of a paradigmatic shift taking place in musicological thought in the 1980s. For that reason, too, I have chosen to reprint as an introduction an article of mine published in 1990 that explored these changes in critical perspective. In retrospect, I am intrigued that I did not use the term postmodernism once. In 1991, Joseph Kerman sought evidence of a paradigm shift by scrutinizing the content of meetings of the American Musicological Society during 1980–90. Compiling a list of 'key words' (*meaning, value, criticism, literary theory, deconstruction, narrative, canon, women, gender, sexuality, feminism, society, culture, politics, ideology*), he found a marked increase in their use in titles for sessions in the second half of that decade ('American Musicology in the 1990s', *Journal of Musicology*).

Those with a deep-seated interest in matters of music, culture, and society are certain to miss some of their favourite texts or to lament the absence of some important scholars. However, these omissions have in many cases been due to the following reasons. First, as already mentioned, permission costs restricted the overall size of the book (and sometimes ruled out a particular extract). Second, for a variety of reasons a permission was withheld or could not be granted. Third, a difficulty occasionally arose in obtaining English rights in certain countries. Fourth, it was my editorial choice, for which I take full blame, to opt for a diversity of issues, rather than a wide range of perspectives on just a few issues. Fifth, I wanted to appeal across a broad spectrum of readership and, as a consequence, steered away from heavily technical and analytical treatment of music.

In conclusion, I must emphasize that many authors feel justifiably uneasy about having their work represented in this way. It should be borne in mind that these excerpts take their ideas out of context, providing little sense of how they fit into a larger argument. To draw a musical analogy, no one listening to two minutes of a Mahler symphony could expect to gain an adequate impression of what the movement as a whole might be like (let alone the entire work). Perhaps the present book might be likened to a compilation album of 'juicy bits'; in which case, one of the best things that could come of it is that readers may be stimulated to seek out the fuller work of the authors concerned.

I owe gratitude to many, but wish to give particular thanks to the following for offering me ideas and advice: Sara Dodd, Lucy Green, Dai Griffiths, Stan Hawkins, Ralph Locke, Allan Moore, Charlotte Purkis, Simon Shaw-Miller, Helen Simpson, Steve Sweeney-Turner, and Sheila Whiteley.

Acknowledgements

While every possible care has been taken to trace ownership of the excerpts used in this reader and to obtain the correct permissions, it has not been possible in all cases. Please contact the publisher if you have any inquiries concerning copyright.

D. B. Scott, 'Music and Sociology for the 1990s', *Musical Quarterly*, 74:3 (1990); H. S. Powers, 'Language Models and Musical Analysis', *Ethnomusicology*, 24:1, © 1980 by the Board of Trustees of the University of Illinois; D. Cooke, *The Language of Music*, © Oxford University Press, 1959; L. Bernstein, *The Unanswered Question: Six Talks at Harvard* (Cambridge, Mass.: Harvard University Press), © 1976 by the President and Fellows of Harvard College; P. Tunstall, 'Structuralism and Musicology: An Overview', *Current Musicology*, 27 (1979); E. Tarasti, *Myth and Music: A Semiotic Approach to the Aesthetics of Myth in Music, especially that of Wagner, Sibelius and Stravinsky* (The Hague: Mouton, 1979), © E. Tarasti; G. Stefani, 'A Theory of Musical Competence', *Semiotica*, 66:1/3 (1987), © G. Stefani; S. Frith and A. McRobbie, 'Rock and Sexuality', *Screen Education*, 29 (1979); J. Taylor and D. Laing, 'Disco-Pleasure-Discourse', *Screen Education*, 31 (1979), © J. Taylor and D. Laing; C. Ford, *Così? Sexual Politics in Mozart's Operas* (Manchester: Manchester University Press, 1991), © C. Ford; E. Wood, 'Sapphonics', in P. Brett, E. Wood, and G. C. Thomas (eds.), *Queering the Pitch: The New Gay and Lesbian Musicology* (London: Routledge, 1994); D. Hatch and S. Millward, *From Blues to Rock: An Analytical History of Pop Music* (Manchester: Manchester University Press, 1987), © D. Hatch and S. Millward; P. Maultsby, 'Africanisms in African-American Music', in J. E. Holloway (ed.), *Africanisms in Amerian Culture* (Bloomington: Indiana University Press, 1990); J. Blacking, *How Musical Is Man?* (London: Faber, 1973); R. Leppert, *Music and Image: Domesticity, Ideology and Socio-Cultural Formation in Eighteenth-Century England* (Cambridge: Cambridge University Press, 1988); R. P. Locke, 'Constructing the Oriental "Other": Saint-Saëns's *Samson et Dalila*', *Cambridge Opera Journal*, 3:3 (1991); T. W. Adorno, *Introduction to the Sociology of Music*, translated by E. B. Ashton (New York: Seabury Press), © 1976 by The Continuum Publishing Company; D. Harker, *Fakesong: The Manufacture of British 'Folksong' 1700 to the Present Day* (Milton Keynes: Open University Press, 1985); D. B. Scott, *The Singing Bourgeois: Songs of the Victorian Drawing Room and Parlour* (Milton Keynes: Open University Press, 1989); P. E. Willis, *Profane Culture* (London: Routledge, 1978); R. Middleton, *Studying Popular Music* (Milton Keynes: Open University Press, 1990); D. Griffiths, 'Genre: Grammar Schoolboy Music', *Critical Musicology Newsletter*, 3 (July 1995) (Oxford: Oxford Brookes University), © D. Griffiths; G. Vulliamy, 'Music and the Mass Culture Debate', in J. Shepherd, P. Virden, G. Vulliamy, and T. Wishart, *Whose Music? A Sociology of Musical Languages* (London: Latimer, 1977), © G. Vulliamy; L. Green, *Music on Deaf Ears: Musical Meaning, Ideology and Education* viii **Acknowledgements**

(Manchester: Manchester University Press, 1988), © L. Green; A. F. Moore, *Rock: The Primary Text* (Buckingham: Open University Press, 1993), © A. F. Moore; M. Foucault and P. Boulez, 'Contemporary Music and the Public', translated by J. Rahn, *Perspectives of New Music* (Fall–Winter 1985); R. R. Subotnik, 'Toward a Deconstruction of Structural Listening: A Critique of Schoenberg, Adorno, and Stravinsky', in E. Narmour and R. Solie (eds.), *Explorations in Music, the Arts, and Ideas: Essays in Honor of Leonard B. Meyer* (Stuyvesant, NY: Pendragon Press, 1988); L. Kramer, *Music and Poetry: The Nineteenth Century and After* (Berkeley and Los Angeles: University of California Press, 1984), © L. Kramer; S. Sweeney-Turner, 'Resurrecting the Antichrist: Maxwell Davies and Parody—Dialectics or Deconstruction?', *Tempo*, 191 (1994); P. Scannell, 'Music for the Multitude? The Dilemmas of the BBC's Music Policy 1923–1946', *Media, Culture and Society*, 3 (1981); E. Eisenberg, *The Recording Angel: Music, Records and Culture from Aristotle to Zappa* (London: Pan Books, 1988); L. Goehr, *The Imaginary Museum of Musical Works: An Essay in the Philosophy of Music* (Oxford: Clarendon Press, 1992), © L. Goehr; P. Wicke, *Rock Music: Culture, Aesthetics and Sociology*, translated by R. Fogg (Cambridge: Cambridge University Press, 1990); P. Martin, *Sounds and Society* (Manchester: Manchester University Press, 1995); J. Attali, *Noise*, translated by Brian Massumi (Minneapolis: University of Minnesota Press) © 1985 by the Regents of the University of Minnesota; J. Shepherd and J. Giles-Davis, 'Music, Text and Subjectivity', in *Music as Social Text* (Cambridge: Polity Press, 1991); A. Goodwin, 'Popular Music and Postmodern Theory', *Cultural Studies*, 5:2 (1991).

Contents

x **Contents**

Introduction
Music, Culture, and Society: Changes in Perspective

DEREK B. SCOTT

The importance of sociological and cultural theory to music-historical studies has grown significantly in recent years. A distinguishing feature of the sociology of music during the 1980s which marked a departure from previous sociomusicological discourse was the erosion of the idea of mass culture, once a theoretical mainstay both of elitists and of Marxists who were concerned with distinguishing between mass culture and the Leninist proletarian 'second culture'. The new cultural theorizing has resulted in a crisis in music aesthetics, a collapse of modernist idealism, and a questioning of the method by which music history is interpreted. On the positive side, much work has been done on the social significance of music; and the prevailing climate of cultural relativism has been of particular benefit to our better understanding and appreciation of non-Western cultures.

The Mass Culture Debate

The idea of mass culture, of a mass audience passively consuming the mass-produced commodities of a 'culture industry', has spawned a selective interpretation of what is and is not important to music history. Jimi Hendrix is not in the *New Grove*; if you look for Charlie Parker in the *New Oxford History of Music*, you find Horatio Parker instead. Is the latter more 'important' than the former, of more significance musically to the twentieth century? That, clearly, is the implication.

The underlying assumption is that mass production, in which everything runs according to a commercially successful formula, is opposed to 'real' art in which problems and solutions are different for each work. Even craftsmanship per se is not art: 'natural forms and products of craftsmanship are not aesthetic objects, because they are not formally unique' (Jones 1955: 52). According to Adorno, the 'star' system preserves the aura of uniqueness for products of the culture industry. But was not Karajan a superstar? Is not Pavarotti a superstar? The failure to see 'art music' as involved in the marketplace has been a surprising omission even in the arguments of perceptive critics like Boulez (see

'Music and Sociology for the 1990s', *Musical Quarterly*, 74:3 (1990), 385–410.

e.g. Foucault and Boulez 1985). Explanations have to be found so that 'true art' remains commercially untarnished. Accordingly, although Mozart appears to be the most popular of all composers if judged by the number of different recordings available of his music, we should not conclude that Mozart belongs to mass culture for the simple reason that Mozart did not compose his music in order for it to be turned into a commodity; and if Stravinsky composed his *Serenade in A* for piano (1925) so that each of its four movements would fit onto a single side of a ten-inch disc, we must interpret this not as a concession to the requirements of the commercial medium of recording but as an example of the composer's delight in self-imposed limitations, an enthusiasm illustrated by his statement, 'The more constraints one imposes, the more one frees one's self of the chains that shackle the spirit' (Stravinsky 1942: 31).

Of course, we can understand why a modern composer would wish to be dissociated from the marketplace. Penderecki's *Threnody for the Victims of Hiroshima* forces us to confront the problem head-on: how is it possible to write anything which might be perceived as making financial profit from such a horrific event? Yet, in the nineteenth century it was an accepted practice to reconstitute gory events into merchandise for the drawing-room pianist, an example being John Pridham's descriptive fantasia, *The Battle March of Delhi* (1857). Artistic sincerity may not be enough; the musical style itself needs to be dissociated from commercialism. The modernist quest for novelty and exclusivity, related to the ever-present fear of art's being standardized and turned into a commodity, has parallels within jazz and rock, which, though regarded as mass culture, have produced their own modernists, such as John Coltrane and Pink Floyd. It must be remembered, too, that exclusivity can in itself create consumer demand, as has been shown by the booming multimillion-dollar market for modern art in the 1980s (*False Start* (1959) by Jasper Johns fetched the highest price ever paid for a painting by a living artist ($19 million)).

The argument over high and low art, a familiar component of elitist and mass-culture views, is, ironically, repeated within the very areas of music which are so often attacked as being low. In jazz, the debate concerns the difference between true jazz and dance band music (Vulliamy 1977). In rock, there is an attempt to distinguish between serious rock and brash, commercial pop. There is also the concept of 'cultural fall' to take into consideration. People commonly complain that culture has deteriorated within their own lifetime. Richard Hoggart, in his pioneering study of working-class culture (1957), is typical in this respect; he thinks that popular culture went downhill after the Second World War. The notion of cultural fall seems to pervade the *New Grove*. Did jazz finally merit consideration as art and was coverage given to jazz musicians only because rock was available to replace it as commercial junk? Jazz does not figure at all in the older *New Oxford History of Music*, and the *Everyman Dictionary of Music* deigned to improve upon its long-reprinted and utterly inaccurate definition of the blues only in 1988; jazz is still defined here as 'American dance music'!

The Collapse of Modernist Idealism

Among other things, modernism has been an attempt to create a universal culture. A collapse of modernist idealism—the end of the enterprise that sought to create an individual universe which speaks to all humanity under the terms of the Beethoven legacy (Scott 1981)—spells an end to the Western 'art music' tradition and makes aesthetic values problematic. The nineteenth-century belief in music as a humanizing force (Scott 1989: 194–7) was already shattered, along with other Arnoldian ideas about the civilizing power of high art, after the discovery of the atrocities committed by 'civilized' Nazi officers during the last world war (Steiner 1970).

Modernism, for all its theoretical incoherence, has been offered as the ortho-dox model of artistic change in this century. The modern period is defined by reference to the innovations of individual composers like Schoenberg, Messiaen, and Stockhausen, the implication being that social factors such as class, ethnicity, and patriarchy are of little importance to the history of music and only of marginal relevance in accounting for musical change. The mod-ernist composers march beneath the nineteenth-century banner proclaiming 'art for art's sake'. Taken to extremes, this doctrine, born of distaste for indus-trialization, proves an insuperable obstacle to the production of music which satisfies widespread social needs. In Debussy's words, 'art is of absolutely no use to the masses' (Debussy 1962: 66); or, as Schoenberg put it, 'If it is art it is not for all, and if it is for all, it is not art' (Schoenberg 1946: 124; he also makes clear his commitment to 'art for art's sake' in this article). It becomes a matter of concern that the new music should not win *too many* admirers: what dis-turbed Stravinsky about Berg's *Wozzeck* was 'the level of its appeal to "ignorant" audiences' (Stravinsky 1968: 124). Simultaneously, there was a concern about the appeal of the new music to conservative academics; witness Ravel's offended pride at being awarded the *Prix de Rome* (though Debussy had been a previous prizewinner). Conditions for membership in the select band of 'real' composers became ever more stringent; those who failed to accept that music was capable of an autonomous evolution, or did not feel the necessity of twelve-tone composition, were told emphatically by Boulez that they were useless ('Since the discoveries made by the Viennese, all compositions other than twelve-tone are *useless*': 1952*a*: 21; and 'tout musicien qui n'a pas ressenti . . . la nécessité du langage dodécaphonique est INUTILE': 1952*b*: 119).

The charge that composers were now working in a vacuum was countered in part by the argument that they were writing for posterity; of course, for this future audience to be of any size at all, the education and conversion of a large number of the 'ignorant' masses would have to be carried out. Still, the belief in future recognition became an abiding faith among modernists, a faith nour-ished by the myth of the unappreciated composer. Philistines of yesteryear had called Beethoven mad—to the everlasting comfort of any composer smarting from the insults of a hostile audience. Schoenberg went so far as to say: 'Nearly all the works nowadays generally acclaimed . . . met, when still new, with a cold or even hostile reception' (Schoenberg 1904: 38; this statement was made a few years before he enjoyed the very successful première of *Pierrot Lunaire*). Time and again we are told of the existence of modern masterpieces that lovers of music have perversely refused to take to their hearts, but that the day will surely come when these works receive their just recognition. However, the question being asked now is, when indeed will that day come? One reads calmly Wilfrid Mellers's assurance in 1968 that *Pli selon Pli* 'will establish itself as a crucial masterpiece of our time' (Mellers 1968: 115). Yet, Slonimsky's law of the forty-year gap between the arrival of a masterpiece and its general acceptance already has had to be doubled in the case of *Erwartung*, the work Robert Craft thought Schoenberg's masterpiece (the myth of the unappreciated composer is comprehensively attacked in Henry Pleasants 1955: 47–82, and 1961: 15–28). This creates a paradox for those who see longevity as a valuer of 'great art', for while *The Mikado* manages to survive despite high-minded scorn, *Erwartung* survives largely as a result of special pleading.

While literary and art historians were chronicling the decline of modernism during the 1980s, the same effort was not expended by music historians. This is not to say that modernism has been at any time without its critics, but earlier attacks on modernism, such as Constant Lambert's *Music, Ho!* (1934) and Henry Pleasants's *The Agony of Modern Music* (1955), rarely show much in the way of sympathy for their subject. Modernism is usually seen as wilfulness, an indulgence of the composer's ego, or a quest for romantic stature which inclines composers to forsake their public. In contrast, Shepherd, Virden, Vulliamy, and Wishart's *Whose Music?* (1977) was a markedly different critique, informed by a new sociomusicology. Criticism of modernism has since then increased even among those who were once its devotees; mention should be made of defectors from the avant-garde like Penderecki. It now seems evident that modernism has failed to achieve, or even point the way to, a cultural rebirth. As the year 2000 approaches, *Erwartung* once more springs to mind and prompts the question: Can anyone imagine a piece written in 1909 being thought too 'advanced' for the next century?

Throughout the 1980s criticism was mounting from the political right and left, from sociologists, ethnomusicologists, and anthropologists. The feeling that Western 'art music' was in crisis pervaded many of the decade's articles: the title, for example, of Michael Kowalski's article, 'The Exhaustion of Western Art Music' (Kowalski 1982) speaks for itself. Eric Gans in 'Art and Entertainment' (Gans 1985) takes a structural-anthropological stance, and is concerned with the complicity rather than the contrast between art and entertainment; he argues that the dominance of high culture has now been overturned by the popular. It became pointless to debate whether Boulez, Cage, or Tippett represented the way ahead for high culture since, to echo a well-known song, those taking the high road had been overtaken by those taking the low road. Even among the middle classes and the 'educated'—and among 'serious' musicians—attention has been drifting away from contemporary high culture to popular culture. The attention which a television arts programme would have given to a major new work by Tippett in the 1970s was more likely to be directed toward a new album by Elvis Costello in the 1980s. Equally significant has been the amount of 'crossover' between high and popular, which has been increasing since the late 1950s. A full-length study of the links between contemporary fine art and popular music has been undertaken by John A. Walker (1987). If we look to music alone for examples of the bridging of the high/low divide, we find the 'classical' violinist Nigel Kennedy trying his hand at rock, while the blues guitarist Eric Clapton presents us with a *Concerto for Electric Blues Guitar and Orchestra*. The Kronos string quartet has an arrangement of

Jimi Hendrix's *Purple Haze* in its repertoire. Placido Domingo and Kiri Te Kanawa have ventured into the popular arena, and José Carreras has hailed Andrew Lloyd Webber as 'an amazing composer' (on ITV's 'Music of the Night: The Songs of Andrew Lloyd Webber', broadcast 23 Dec. 1989). It has to be noted, however, that some would regard Carreras singing Lloyd Webber as the worst of popular music and, say, the Sex Pistols as the very best. The argument used to justify such an opinion would perhaps involve a contrast between what is interpreted as pretentious schmalz and what is identified as a genuine space for an expression of opposition within the dominant culture. Such a view, however, would not be entirely free from a mass-culture perspective itself. For a last example of the widening influence of popular music, we can compare the music chosen for film sound tracks over the past fifty years: in the cinemas of the 1940s Flash Gordon conquered the universe to the strains of Liszt, whereas in the 1980s his crusading was accompanied by the music of the rock band Queen.

The Romantic/Modernist Interpretation of Music History

Music history has been interpreted since the nineteenth century according to distinctively romantic and modernist tenets, with the emphasis being on formal and technical values, on novelty and compositional 'coups', on the composition in itself and its place in an autonomous musical process, and on internationalism—or, more precisely, on internationalism defined by the idea of a *single* culture with *universal* values. This method of interpreting music history, though nineteenth-century in origin, affects the way we understand the music and composers of earlier periods. Hans Keller, for example, sometimes wrote as if Mozart was groping towards serialism. A well-known example of how Mozart's life and music may be reinterpreted through this reading of history is offered by Peter Shaffer's *Amadeus*, in which art is seen as a reflection of life (a corruption of the distinction between romantic self-expression and baroque 'affect'); art is perfection, the artist is a visionary (Salieri cannot understand Mozart's unique vision in the 'confutatis' of his *Requiem*), and social and political issues are cast aside (Mozart, a member, it seems, of the republican Illuminati, says he is 'not interested in politics', and *The Magic Flute* is described as a vaudeville). It is all too easy when constructing the history of a cultural tradition to assume one is dealing with facts and not interpretation. The *New Grove*, for example, offers no definition of modernism; hence, there is no discussion of what this term means when it is used to label a particular body of music, nor explanation of how modernist theory rests upon an abstracted linear account of music history.

Raymond Williams pointed out how lines are drawn to link together ancestors within a cultural tradition; these lines will last 'often for as long as a century, and then suddenly with some new stage in growth these will be cancelled or weakened and new lines drawn' (1961: 69). To see how lines have been weakened in this century, one has only to consider who were the great figures at the close of the nineteenth century. There is a print dated 1902 containing six portraits by Haskell (this print was spotted in a Cambridge public house) entitled 'Great Musicians'; the composers represented are Mozart, Beethoven, Liszt, Gounod, Chopin, and Wagner. Gounod, along with Spohr, Borodin, Grieg, and others whose reputations were high at the turn of the century, has since fallen from grace. A mere twenty years after Haskell's portraits the compositions of Liszt were said to 'smite us with both admiration and aversion' (Rosenfeld 1922: 73). Some may presume that the reputation of Beethoven is unassailable; yet who could have predicted the assault upon Milton in the 1930s, first by F. R. Leavis, then by T. S. Eliot? And the 1990s have begun with an assault upon Shakespeare's stature by Gary Taylor. During the 1960s the line connecting Hindemith to modernist developments was weakened, and in some linear accounts he disappeared altogether; Mellers omits him from the linear 'chart of relationships' in *Caliban Reborn* (Mellers 1968: 183; Hindemith is also omitted from the linear chart in Bray 1974: 13).

To see where lines have recently been strengthened, one can turn to the writings of the late, erudite Carl Dahlhaus, who claimed in the 1960s: 'The art of Machaut, Josquin, and even Monteverdi is petrified; the attempt to revive this art beyond small circles is likely to be futile, unless remoteness in history is enjoyed as an esthetic titillation and archaic austerity is accepted as picturesque, and this means accepted by mistake and misunderstanding' (Dahlhaus 1982: 98). This statement is all the more astonishing for its having been made by someone who hoped to discover continuity in aesthetic criticism and who died before seeing Monteverdi's *Vespers* given prime-time transmission by BBC television on Christmas Eve 1989. To move on to twentieth-century composers, Robert P. Morgan complained in 1973 that Ives and Varèse had been 'treated as isolated figures outside the musical mainstream' by the music historians of the 1950s and early 1960s (1973: 95). He maintained that these composers needed to be relocated from periphery to mainstream following the failure of attempts to establish a common practice (total serialism) and the ensuing openness of composers to the kind of experimental eclecticism associated with Ives and Varèse. Now we are asked to recognize that they 'initiated an important *line* [my emphasis] in twentieth century musical developments' (Morgan 1979: 105). Interestingly, this important line enables the United States to take its place in the history of modernism: a line drawn from Varèse to Cowell to Cage can be used as an illustration of progressively radical exploration of timbre.

It is important to understand that a linear paradigm works to exclude or marginalize certain figures. Literary theorists have devoted much time to attacking the literary canon on these grounds: Alan Sinfield, for example, argues that 'the centralizing of the modernism of the first half of the twentieth century serves to marginalize the (relatively) rationalist work of Wells and Shaw. Once the canon has become established (in the full range of that word) it seems "natural"' (1983: 1). The 'standard repertoire' in music is not an equivalent of the 'literary canon'; Dahlhaus, for example, thought works like Tchaikovsky's Violin Concerto and Dvořák's Cello Concerto had an 'institutional basis for survival' (1982: 98); i.e. they served the demands of the music business (the marketing of classics); other works serving the same function would, he thought, replace them. Canons imply an autonomous cultural development, and those who fail to participate in that particular development, or who seek alternatives, are marginalized, as were Weill and Eisler for rejecting modernism. Someone who is seen to be part of a line, like Mussorgsky, is moved up, while anyone not part of the line, like Rimsky-Korsakov, is downgraded. The linear paradigm is a means of defending a single authentic culture. However, the development of a single culture requires a common practice, and modernism failed to establish one. Figures like Bartók and Stravinsky are not accommodated comfortably in Mellers's 'chart of relationships': Bartók links Beethoven and Debussy but his line leads nowhere, and it is significant that the influence of Richard Strauss on Bartók is ignored. Stravinsky links Debussy to Satie and Orff, and the latter is a dead end. Shostakovich, Britten, and Tippett are absent altogether.

Paul Griffiths has attempted to rehabilitate Shostakovich and Britten to the modernist canon, following their expulsion by Adorno and Boulez, by maintaining that their music admits the 'corruption' of diatonic harmony by irony subsequent to Schoenberg's 'revelation of an atonal universe' (1978: 84). But could this theory be applied to jazz? Does diatonic harmony appear, to use Griffiths's words, 'only within quotation marks' (ibid. 84) in Armstrong and Ellington? Even in the case of Kurt Weill, it is no longer convincing to claim, as does Elaine Padmore, that his success was due to a combination of 'vacuous triteness and Teutonic solemnity' (1973: 102). The view that Weill used the idiom of Berlin cabaret jazz to depict the moral decay of the Weimar republic is embarrassingly in accord with Hitler's own opinion of the decadence of jazz. As a result, admirers of Weill are often found wriggling around definitions of 'real' as opposed to 'commercial' jazz (suggesting the latter as a target for Weill's parody), even though Weill's attitude to cabaret music is complex and ambivalent. It may have been a recognition of this ambivalence that caused Schoenberg, who believed the quality of musical composition could be judged by objective aesthetic criteria, to make the extreme statement: 'His is the only music in the world in which I can find no quality at all' (quoted by Virgil Thomson; see Kowalke 1979: 3 n.).

Modernist artists, in the words of Charles Harrison, value their practice 'in terms of its power to generate a sense of the need for progress, where progress is measured by the victory of one "paradigm" of practice, one "hypothesis", one "concept of art", one manner over another less novel' (1981: 18). He was speaking of the visual arts, but the same holds true of music. One has only to think of the importance attached to the threefold revolution of 1912: Debussy's liberation from thematicism in *Jeux*; Schoenberg's liberation of the dissonance in *Pierrot Lunaire*; and Stravinsky's liberation of the bar line in *Le Sacre du Printemps*. At that time, the idea of a surfeit of major and minor was accepted by such varied modernists as Debussy, Busoni, Bartók, and Russolo (for example: 'We are tyrannized by Major and Minor', Busoni, *Outline of a New Aesthetic of Music*, 1907; 'the tonal scale must be enriched by other scales', Debussy, *Conversations with Ernest Giraud*, 1889–90; 'studying [peasant music] freed me from the tyrannical rule of major and minor keys', Bartók, *Autobiography*; Luigi Russolo in *The Art of Noises* (1913) stated his belief in the evolution toward 'noise sound', however else they might differ in their opinions about the road ahead. Jazz was, in complete contrast, dominated by major and minor until the 1960s.

Histories of modernism continually see works as 'pointing forward' to others, thus reinforcing a sense of self-determining progress in the arts. But can *Tristan und Isolde* really be said to point forward to the sudden and rapid developments of 1908–1909, such as Strauss's *Elektra* and Schoenberg's *Erwartung*? If a fifty-year gap is possible, why not concede a three-hundred-year gap and allow the idea that Gesualdo pointed forward to Debussy? Perhaps this would be acceptable to some; it has been suggested, after all, that the disintegration of language into its component noises in Stockhausen's *Gesang der Jünglinge* is 'an ultimate form of the process that was manifest, in the twilight of the Middle Ages, in the late Gothic motet' (Mellers 1968: 120). The destruction of a linear development in Stravinsky's style, when he turned to neoclassicism, was the main reason for the outrage felt by modernists like Boulez; it seemed as if style had been downgraded to capriciousness. Yet, it could be argued that Stravinsky, far from ditching the modernist obsession with progress, was suggesting fusion as a way ahead. Indeed, Schoenberg was satirizing Stravinsky as 'Modernsky' at this time (*Der neue Klassizismus*, Op. 28, 1925). Besides, where did Stravinsky's modernism come from in the first place? In his later years, he asserted that 'very little tradition lies behind *Le Sacre du Printemps*' (Stravinsky and Craft 1959: 147), and explained, 'I am the vessel through which *Le Sacre* passed' (ibid. 148). The last remark is typical of the ideas of the Russian formalists who flourished in the 1920s and thought that art existed in some form independently of the artist: Osip Brik, for example, maintained the *Eugene Onegin* would have been written even if Pushkin had not lived (Eagleton 1983: 3). The formalists, who seem to have influenced Stravinsky's own ideas, were, however, very keen on the use of novelty as a means of ensuring genuine aesthetic perception: the familiar, they considered, was merely *registered* by the brain. Moreover, novelty has to be distinguished from fashion, which has to establish itself immediately as convention in order to be fashionable (Dahlhaus 1982: 96). Nevertheless, novelty which guards against imitation tends towards a private symbolism or means of expression.

A major problem for 'linear modernism' is that, while Beethoven and Wagner appear to follow an evolutionary 'progress' in their music, many otherwise impeccable modernists, like Debussy and Schoenberg, do not. What is more, modernist composers are not even reliable in their tastes: Debussy admired Gounod and Richard Strauss but not Schoenberg; Stravinsky admired Weber and Tchaikovsky but loathed Wagner. Even such a fundamental principle as order, the relationship of parts to the whole, which provided the basis of St Augustine's aesthetics in *De Ordine*, is a contentious matter for modernism. On the one hand we have the fetishizing of order, such as Webern's use of concentrated thematicism as a substitute for the tonal hierarchy (fetishizing of numbers—see Boulez's criticism of this trend in 1954—and private coding are related developments), while on the other hand we have the polar extreme in the ideas of John Cage. In his article on Satie, for example, Cage asserts that the necessary requirements for an interest in Satie, and a recognition that this composer is 'indispensable' to twentieth-century music, is that we must 'give up all illusions about ideas of order, expression of sentiment, and all the rest of our inherited aesthetic claptrap' (1958).

Deterministic historiography has been attacked for many years; Leo Treitler complained, in several impassioned articles in the 1960s, about the tendency to search for influences and anticipations while neglecting cultural and historical context (e.g. 1967). Since musicologists have in the main left twentieth-century music to the analysts and theorists, it is easier to demonstrate the pitfalls of this approach by pointing out the way Bach cantata research was thrown into confusion with the discovery that the accepted chronology was incorrect (see Kerman 1985: 51–2). Another problem arises when important works by major composers—for example, the late quartets of Beethoven—do not immediately connect to others. It is always possible to argue for uniqueness or, indeed, for similarity by selecting empirical evidence for use in historical interpretation and analysis. Dahlhaus was aware of this when he chose to rely upon Max Weber's analytic instrument, the 'ideal type', to decide what was a historical fact. However, since the ideal-typical view is also constructed by the historian, it inevitably remains a theoretical construct even when empirical data is offered as verification (for some criticism of Dahlhaus's method see Gossett 1989). If Beethovenian sonata form is an ideal type, then Schubert's fusion of sonata and song is open to criticism; but then the latter could equally well be chosen as an ideal type for the purpose of criticizing, say, Dvořák's use of sonata form. If certain ideal types are bound up with notions of race, they can serve nationalist ends. Pfitzner, whose theories were taken up by the Nazis, attacked modernism as a symptom of the decadent 'Jewish-international spirit' alien to the German (Hans Pfitzner, 'Die neue Aesthetic der musikalischen Impotenz'; see Franklin 1989: 85). The theoretical assumptions of modernism itself rejected jazz as decadent and regarded the new music of Western Europe and the United States as superior to that of Eastern Europe and the Soviet Union. Empirical data can be used to demonstrate that most 'great' works were baffling to contemporaries; it can also be used to show the opposite. Empirical data can be used to show that Rimsky-Korsakov was in fact more important than Mussorgsky, by focusing on certain features which connect to the music of Stravinsky and Prokofiev. Schoenberg claimed that serialism grew out of necessity (1941: 216), yet this necessity was itself born of a set of particular cultural assumptions. Empirical data can be used to demonstrate that the change from extended tonality to atonality was an evolution, but it can equally well show that this was a qualitative leap. A belief in the historical necessity of atonality has led to the neglect of many areas of twentieth-century music history, such as the importance of Vienna to Hollywood (Korngold) or of Puccini to 'The Generation of the 1880s' in Italy. Worst of all, perhaps, has been the total neglect until recent times of the history of jazz.

The Social Significance of Music

The music-historical problem for jazz has been its resistance to assimilation into the Western 'art music' tradition because of fundamental aesthetic conflicts. The criteria for determining what is a beautiful or 'legitimate' style of singing and playing in jazz, for example, are frequently at odds with the criteria which prevail in 'art music'. Yet, the 'art music' tradition claims its aesthetic values are all-embracing and transcend social and cultural context. In 1922 Paul Rosenfeld wrote that 'the music of Wagner descended with the formative might of the perfect image. Men of every race and continent knew it to be of themselves' (1922: 3). The belief in universal values lies behind the internationalist aspirations of modernism: 'In ten years every talented composer will be writing this way,' Schoenberg remarked in 1910 (letter to Karl Wiener, 19 Mar. 1910; in 1964: 28). Composers of different nationalities and different musical traditions are shown to be moving towards the same end. Lines again prove a useful means of demonstrating this movement. The German line extending from Wagner to Richard Strauss to Schoenberg (representing the breakdown of the major-minor key system) and the Russian line from Glinka to Mussorgsky to Stravinsky (representing the development of concise, angular, and repetitive practices) begin to merge in the music of the French composer Debussy. Act 3, scene 2, of *Pelléas et Melisande* serves to illustrate a harmonic style reminiscent of *Parsifal* joined to a vocal style reminiscent of *Boris Godunov*. A further international dimension may be added to Debussy by stressing the influence of the Javanese music he heard at the World Exhibition in Paris in 1889. (It may be remarked that the by-no-means negligible influence of the harmony and cyclic devices of the now 'unimportant' Norwegian composer Grieg is rarely given as much attention in this analysis!)

Today, after all the efforts expended by ethnomusicologists, it would appear impossible to avoid the conclusion that music is no more international than other forms of cultural expression. Indeed, Jean Jenkins goes so far as to say, 'Every linguistic, geographical or social grouping down to its smallest unit usually possesses several distinct musical traditions' (1983: 5). The acceptance of modernism's international ambitions has led to distortions and contradictions in the way we interpret music history. For example, the supposed poor state of English music during the first half of the twentieth century is blamed on cultural insularity; yet the English musical renaissance of the late nineteenth century is usually credited to composers' acceptance of 'Englishness' instead of 'Germanness'. In fact there is no concrete evidence that cultural insularity is damaging: the musical renaissance in modern Zaire, for instance, is attributed to the cultural blockade of the 1970s. Modernism, an attempt to defend one universalist culture, is forced to attack localism as parochial or nationalist chauvinism, popular music as entertainment not art, and ethnic music as primitivism or ghetto culture.

The alternative would be to accept that we are living in an age of cultural relativism. Cultural relativism, a perspective taken from modern anthropology, has been the key to sociomusicological interpretation during the last decade. The argument that cultural values can be historically located was already familiar and was expanded by the recognition that significance could also be socially located. The last idea fuels the main argument against mass culture theory: that meaning can be made in the act of consumption—consumption is not always simply passive. It also renders questions of 'superior and inferior minds' redundant, for, as John Shepherd remarks: 'Difference in cultural values is due not so much to questions of inherent intelligence as to the existence of socially constructed and different cultural criteria which not infrequently display a mutual incompatibility' (1987: 64). The mutual incompatibility of jazz and Western 'art music' in this respect has already been noted. For a nineteenth-century example one could point to the incompatibility of Beethoven's classical Viennese style to the Scottish airs he arranged (see Scott 1989: 192–3). Cultural relativism is not to be confused with the pluralism Boulez so despises, nor with the patronizing approval Schoenberg gave to Gershwin; it calls for a recognition of cultural distinctions, not for a blanket disregard of values. Nor is it a plea for peaceful coexistence between art and entertainment, a dichotomy which, in any case, it challenges; the division between art and entertainment is, in fact, an assumption of mass culture theory.

It has taken a long time for a theory of musical relativism to gain ground. A major reason for the delay has been the amount of time consumed in the futile search for an underlying coherent theory by which modernism could be rationally explained and understood when there should have been a recognition that modernism had disintegrated into irrationality, failure, and irrelevance. These may seem strong words, but they represent accusations which are now commonplace in the visual arts and, particularly, architecture. The ambitions of modernist music towards internationalism have been overtaken by rock, which has already become a more widely accepted international musical language. The social history of our time is inseparable from rock, as the BBC television series *The Rock 'n' Roll Years* made evident with its apt juxtapositions of rock and contemporary newsreel. Measured in terms of social significance, the twelve-bar blues has been of greater importance to twentieth-century music than the twelve-note row. The stylistic crisis in the arts was, and remains, at root socio-economic—the need to find an art untainted by commercialism. Raymond Williams has pointed to the separation of art and thinking about art 'by ever more absolute abstraction, from the social processes within which they are still contained' (1977: 154). Williams argues that aesthetic theory is the main instrument of this evasion. Yet, aesthetics cannot always be divorced from social significance. Can anyone listen to those old recordings of castrati who survived into the present century with an aesthetic sensibility unmoved by the knowledge that these singers were mutilated as children? Is the division of music into commercial and non-commercial categories really an aesthetic or ethical distinction?

In social terms, modernism as a broad artistic movement has failed. As long ago as 1955 Henry Pleasants wrote, 'The final test of a language is: do people use it? Applied to music this test emerges: Is it a people's music? Exposed to this test, atonality collapses' (1955: 94). Schoenberg certainly did expect people to whistle atonal melodies in his lifetime. Atonality has achieved at most a limited social significance—as sound track music for horror movies. Cultural theorists sought in the past to find other kinds of social significance for modernist developments: Adorno drew a parallel between Stravinsky's neoclassicism and fascism (individualism sacrificed to collectivism in an increasingly authoritarian conformism) and viewed atonality as a rebellion against bourgeois mass culture. Thomas Mann, on the other hand, saw a connection between Schoenberg's music and the rise of Nazism. While it looks as if it was tempting to see the composer whose music you did not like as a Nazi collaborator, this was a search for social significance at a highly abstracted level.

Stravinsky, as is well known, ignored cultural context as important for meaning; 'music expresses itself' was his final thought on the subject (Stravinsky and Craft 1959: 101). Of course, Stravinsky's ideas are inevitably part of a particular stage in the history of cultural theory. The Russian formalists claimed that a text was made of *words*, not feelings, and therefore could be examined as a material fact—in other words, as a structure. The novel *Don Quixote*, for example, may be regarded not as being about its eponymous character; instead, the character is a device that holds the narrative together. A concentration on form leads to the structuralist idea that each field of creative activity enjoys a relative autonomy within its own sign system. The notion that each sphere of art should be true to itself is a modernist orthodoxy: for example, the label 'literary painter' was thrown at Magritte as a criticism because his canvases were not their own subjects, unlike, say, the paintings of Kandinsky. Cultural theorists have spent a great deal of effort modifying, deconstructing, and socially contextualizing all this. Here is Williams again: 'The formal quality of words as "signs" . . . was rendered as "arbitrary" by a privileged withdrawal from the lived and living relationships which, within any native language . . . make all formal meanings significant and substantial in a world of reciprocal reference which moves, as it must, beyond the signs' (1977: 168). The referential means of *Pacific 231* are arbitrary in a purely musical sense, and Honegger's description 'mouvement symphonique' suggests musical autonomy. But could this piece have been written before the advent of the steam locomotive? Indeed, what would boogie-woogie piano or much of the characteristic style of blues harmonica have been without trains? Referential devices develop in tandem with society. The opening of Vivian Ellis's *Coronation Scot* uses no musical technique or dissonant vocabulary which would have surprised Beethoven, yet it is meaningless unless one is familiar with the sound of a steam train pulling away. Continuing this line of thought, I would claim that, contrary to Stravinsky's opinion that expressive devices are established by convention with an autonomous musical practice, they are established as conventions through social practice and may be related to social changes. Musical meanings are not labels arbitrarily thrust upon abstract sounds; these sounds and their meanings originate in a social process and achieve their significance within a particular social context. Some of Stravinsky's own formal innovations are probably the result of extramusical considerations rather than an abstract development of musical language: for example, the novel bitonal motive for the eponymous character in *Petrushka* serves to express his duality as puppet and real person, and the use of overlapping meters in the Shrovetide Fair scene springs from the familiar fairground experience of hearing overlapping tunes. Schoenberg's free atonal period can be related to the new science of psychoanalysis and Freudian investigations into the inner reaches of the human psyche. Expressionist artists envied the supposed power of music to express the composer's 'internal life' (Kandinsky 1947: 40). Just as Kandinsky spoke of 'inner necessity', Schoenberg placed his trust in 'unconscious logic'; yet, if atonality was historically inevitable, this trust was as much a corollary as a cata- lyst to his adopting a new musical language. Even so, it would appear odd that the development of an extreme chromatic language should coincide merely by chance with an expressionist interest in extreme emotional states. We should also consider the historical parallel between Wittgenstein's investigations into the functions of language and those of Schoenberg into musical language. Wittgenstein was interested in the limits of language, and thought music capable of expressing what language could not. Schoenberg's comment in the published score of Webern's *Six Bagatelles* is clearly in accord with that idea: 'These pieces will only be understood by those who share the faith that music can say things which can only be expressed by music' (Webern 1913).

Social factors affect our response to music in a variety of ways. For example, French concern at the lack of an operatic tradition, which led to the unearthing of Rameau's *Hippolyte et Aricie* early in this century, developed in the context of nationalism arising from political defeat. French hostility towards Wagner at this time is as much politically as musically motivated; similarly, in nineteenth- century North America, the success of Wagner was affected by sociopolitical factors, and his works were much more easily assimilated than might have been expected (Peretti 1989: 28–38). The social significance of music extends from the broad political arena to the intimacy of the dance floor where a song like Chris De Burgh's 'Lady in Red' functions as a signal that the evening is drawing to a close and that couples should seize the opportunity provided by this sentimental ballad to move into a clinch. Changing social factors affect our response to works which may have previously provoked quite different reac- tions: *Così Fan Tutte* is not the same after the cultural impact of modern femi- nism, and *Peter Grimes* has become problematic due to present concern about child abuse; we are no longer so ready to accept Grimes as a tortured idealist.

Developments in technology also affect our response to music and our inter- pretation of music history. Debussy's *Jeux* was taken up by 1950s modernists because its fluidity of tempo and rhythm, its fragmentary melodic material, and its significant use of timbre enabled it to be seen as both ancestor and model for electronic composition. A technological development which has had a major impact on music in this century is sound recording. Over the past seventy years the concert audience has been transformed from musical ama- teurs to a large number of potential record buyers. This has had noticeable side effects. There is, for example, a tendency for professional performers to take heed of records which have been praised by critics or which have achieved high sales figures, and as a result there is not the variety of interpretation that existed even thirty years ago. There is also a tendency to think of certain old record- ings as part of a line terminating in the approved interpretations of the present. In the 1930s, according to this view, the clean approach of the Busch Quartet looks forward, whereas the Léner Quartet points backward because of its exces- sive 'scooping'.

What, then, of social changes taking place now? Green issues will obviously affect the arts, as in fact they are already doing. Modernism has usually allied itself with the latest technology; now technology is perceived as inhuman and polluting. Hip-hop was a reaction against the mechanics of the disco. The New Acoustic Roots movement was, to a great extent, born out of a rejection of electronic, acid-rain-producing, energy-consuming, urban/industrial society by espousing a type of music which joined hands with the developing world in the newly emergent category of 'World Music'. New artistic departures have arisen as a result of the shift in perspective by which nature is viewed as an ally rather than something to be opposed or subjugated in the interests of human progress. The enormous success of the film *Crocodile Dundee* (1986), in which a hunter from the Australian outback in tune with nature serves as a critique of urban artifice and angst, is a clear indication of a social mood which will soon demand some rewriting of cultural history, insisting on giving added prominence to the philosophy of Rousseau, perhaps, or fighting for a place for John Clare in the literary canon. The re-evaluation of Percy Grainger is already taking place; can Cyril Scott, Colin McPhee, Peter Warlock, and Alan Hovhaness be far behind?

Areas of Neglect

Some areas of neglect in music historiography have already been suggested, such as the marginalizing of composers and works which do not fit into a linear modernist account of the dissolution of tonality. There has been a lack of weight accorded to the historical, social, economic, psychological, or other circumstances which bear upon a composer's music, and insufficient attention has been paid to the commissioning body or audience for which it was composed. Surely no one doubts the importance of these areas. To choose examples from the careers of major figures in the classical canon, one can show that Mozart abandoned a flute concerto in mid-composition because a commissioner failed to pay up; the same composer was persuaded by a concert promoter to change a movement of his Paris Symphony; and it was a publisher who persuaded Beethoven to replace the finale of his late B-flat quartet with something more conventional. And yes, someone as interested in music and society as Wilfrid Mellers has no room among all the high-flown phrases of *Caliban Reborn* for any words about publishers, the dissemination of music, how composers earn money to eat, or (with reference to the particular thesis of this book) *why* rather than *how* the Renaissance model for Western composition is giving way to non-Western influences.

For the past two centuries publication has been crucial to the dissemination of new music. Publications are often a useful guide to the shifting evaluations within the canon of 'great' music. Publication is of major importance in establishing a work: it was not Mendelssohn's famous revival but Novello's cheap edition of many years later which established Bach's *St Matthew Passion* in the choral repertoire. To take another example, we were told on a recent television arts programme that Haydn's symphonies 'are a major part of the classical canon' and Christopher Hogwood made it clear that he regarded every single one as a masterpiece (Melvyn Bragg, *South Bank Show*, Thames

Television, 28 Jan. 1990); this assessment of Haydn can be historically located by reference to the fact that published scores to all the symphonies became available only in the 1950s. If Haydn's Symphony No. 50 never appeared in print before 1951, and might not unfairly be described as unknown before that time, then it can only have become part of the classical canon during the past forty years. There is a dislike of talk of publication perhaps because it links art to the marketplace, but it is impossible to ignore the fact that a published piece of music is a commodity to be sold. Conceptual art arose partly from the desire to escape commodification; but even John Cage's *4'32"* does not avoid being commodified, since C. F. Peters publishes a 'score' containing instructions for performance.

A publisher may act as a patron; Debussy's first revolutionary work, *Prélude à l'Après-midi d'un Faune*, was not written until 1894 when he had been made financially secure by an allowance from the publisher Georges Hartmann. A publisher may promote a particular style of music: for example, Universal and the Second Viennese School. When a war of ideas started between Berg and Pfitzner, Universal appointed the former as editor of its house journal, a tribute to his robust defence of modernist aesthetics. Universal Edition maintained a keen (and, it has to be said, profitable) association with modernism after the Second World War by offering contracts to Boulez and Stockhausen. The ideas circulating at Darmstadt in the 1950s were disseminated by the publication of the periodical *Die Reihe*, English translations of which were soon produced. In the 1960s *Perspectives of New Music* became the leading pro-modernist journal. The fact that this is a North American publication adds weight to a well-worn contention that there is a link between power and cultural value. Is it by chance that the emergence of the United States as a superpower coincides with a participation in the promotion of modernism—most obvious in the visual arts but also significant in music?

After the United States, France pours the most money into modernism, but here support comes from the state rather than wealthy businessmen, foundations, or multinational corporations. There is perhaps a desire to establish France as the cultural leader of post-1992 Europe. Whether that happens or not, benefits have already accrued to the state as a result of government funding of IRCAM, which in the mid-1980s was running at an equivalent of $3.5 million a year. In 1980 Berio recruited Peppino di Guigno, who invented the 4X, a digital signal processor, the following year. Jean-Pierre Armand, the head of the 4X team, used it to simulate aircraft noises and designed a programme for pilot training. In 1985, according to a news report, Armand conceived 'a pattern of underwater noises so realistic that it has been protected as classified defence information and prompted the French navy to order its own 4X' (Lebrecht 1985: 48). The writer of this report adds wryly, 'Even if it fails to make great music, IRCAM may yet win the next world war.' And so, while the question of what Boulez has done for twentieth-century music may still be a matter for debate in some quarters, what he has done for the French armed forces is not.

In contemporary musical life, the recording company is more important than the music publisher. There is a remarkable similarity in marketing techniques used for the classical repertoire and for music of the popular cate-gory, but it is little noticed or remarked upon because the distinction between 'commercial pop music' and 'non-commercial art music' begins to grow cloudy when these techniques are examined. A Deutsche Grammophon advertise-ment of 1989, encouraging the purchase of a boxed set of the Beethoven sym-phonies, proclaimed that the conductor, Karajan, was 'the greatest exponent of Beethoven', that he 'must surely be the world's greatest conductor', that the Berlin Philharmonic's delivery was 'surely the nearest to musical perfection', and that the Beethoven symphonies are 'unsurpassed masterpieces'. If this is not the star system so despised by Adorno, then what is? Furthermore, these 'ultimate' and 'essential' recordings were only available on CD or cassette; therefore, those still hanging on to old-fashioned vinyl must 'surely' feel the necessity to buy more up-to-date equipment.

Though there has been a serious neglect of socio-economic issues in music historiography, equally worrying has been its ethnocentricity. Before Peter Brook's stage and film versions of *The Mahabharata*, most 'cultured' people in the West were completely unaware of the existence of this two-thousand-year-old Indian epic; is it surprising, then, that the 'classical' music from the Indian subcontinent receives so little attention? There is no need to travel so far around the globe in order to discover a highly developed and neglected music; there is the unique cultural form of *piobaireachd* which originated among the Gaelic communities of the Scottish Highlands and Islands. *Piobaireachd* may be used as an illustration of the way meaning depends on sociocultural context rather than on universally valid musical devices. The interval of the tritone con-veyed emotional anguish to seventeenth-century Venetians, yet it evidently did not carry this meaning to a seventeenth-century Highlander (Scott 1984: 41–4). There is even an old *piobaireachd* of uncertain date bearing the title 'Praise of Marion' (*Guileagag Moraig*) which, in one variation alone, contains twenty-nine tritones within thirty-two bars.

It is a disregard for cultural distinctions coupled with a belief in a single 'authentic' culture which allowed Alfred Einstein to claim that there had been no genuine Czech music before Smetana (Einstein 1947: 296). If there are few who go so far as that nowadays, how many are there still who fail to notice or comment upon the contradictions in Bartók's use of peasant songs? Was Bartók so very deeply absorbed in peasant song, one is entitled to wonder, when so much of his own output is not vocal but instrumental? Did he value this mater-ial for the possibilities it opened up for him tonally and rhythmically? In other words, was he interested in the opportunity to mix nationalist sentiment with modernist progress? Of course, this is an unfair oversimplification, but it does touch upon matters which ought not to be ignored. Relevant to the subject of folk song, for instance, is the once firmly held Marxist-Leninist theoretical posi-tion that perceives two cultures in capitalist society, a bourgeois culture and an emergent socialist culture with roots in the working class (Lenin 1913). This position was taken up with only slight modification by Ian Watson in the early 1980s in a book on folk song in Britain. (Watson 1983). Watson adopts a mass culture perspective: popular culture for him is that which he considers to be the emerging proletarian culture; the rest of what is commonly termed popular, he calls 'anti-class-culture'. His ideas are similar to those of Christopher Caudwell and others in the 1930s (Caudwell 1937). By viewing rock as a means of defusing opposition, however, Watson fails to explain why rock has been found subversive in all totalitarian societies.

If some Marxists have shuddered at the thought of being labelled revisionists, so have those at the other end of the political spectrum who have clung with equal fervour to their own mass culture assumptions. Often, and paradoxically, these assumptions accord with Adorno's idea of the debasing effects of a 'culture industry'. The traditional right and left unite in opposing the use of rock music and other elements of popular culture in the schools. Schools play an important role in initiating children into the dominant cultural values, the educational strategy being to ask *what* rather than *why*. Until there is an acknowledgement of the social significance which underpins cultural values, this is scarcely likely to change.

Nevertheless, there have been many changes which make one optimistic for the future. In December of 1989 the Hayward Gallery in London for the first time devoted an entire exhibition to the work of black artists; it was entitled 'The Other Story' and seemed to be a recognition at long last of the increasingly multicultural society of post-Second World War Britain. The close of the 1980s also brought with it a separate two-volume *Dictionary of Jazz* taken from the *New Grove*. Praise, too, should be given to the excellent ethnomusicological articles in the *New Grove*. How long will it be before the appearance of a *Dictionary of Rock* from the same prestigious stable?

I feel I should end by paying tribute to the wealth of research now being carried out by a new breed of sociomusicologists, many of whom would undoubtedly wish, in turn, to pay their respects to Weber's pioneering work *Music and the Middle Class* (Weber 1975) and Shepherd, Virden, Vulliamy, and Wishart's *Whose Music?* Academic study of popular musics has been well served by the *History of Popular Music in Britain* series from the Open University Press (edited by Richard Middleton and Dave Harker) and the annual multidisciplinary journal *Popular Music* from Cambridge University Press (edited by Middleton and David Horn). Cultural relativism will certainly not provide the key to all problems, but it has opened the door to a method of interpretation which seems in keeping with the late twentieth century. One of the biggest problems for the cultural relativist is finding a satisfactory explanation for artistic distinction; how do we explain why we feel that Weill's German period is better than his American, or that some rock is better than others? However, those who wish to dismiss cultural relativism should be warned: since we hold that all values are relative and that there are no independent standards of truth, we refuse to accept that there is any way of establishing the validity of cultural relativism itself.

References

Boulez, Pierre (1952*a*), 'Schoenberg Is Dead', *The Score* 6, 18–22.

—— (1952*b*), 'Éventuellement', *La Revue musicale*, 212, 119.

—— (1954), 'Recherches Maintenant', *Nouvelle Revue Francaise*, 23.

Bray, Trevor (1974), 'Twentieth-Century Music 1900–1945', in *The Development of Instruments and their Music*, A304 Units 23–5 (Milton Keynes: Open University Press).

Cage, John (1958), 'Eric Satie', in *Art News International*; repr. in *Silence* (Cambridge: MIT Press), 76–82.

Caudwell, Christopher (1937), *Illusion and Reality* (London: Lawrence & Wishart, 1946).

Dahlhaus, Carl (1982), *Esthetics of Music* (orig. pub. as *Musikästhetik*, Cologne, 1967), trans. William Austin (Cambridge: Cambridge University Press, 1982).

Debussy, Claude (1962), 'Monsieur Croche Antidilettante', in *Three Classics in the Aesthetics of Music* (London: Dover).

Eagleton, Terry (1983), *Literary Theory* (London: Blackwell).

Einstein, Alfred (1947), *Music in the Romantic Era* (London: Dent).

Foucault, Michel, and Boulez, Pierre (1985), 'Contemporary Music and the Public', *Perspectives of New Music*, Fall–Winter, 6–12.

Franklin, Peter (1989), 'Audiences, Critics and the Depurification of Music', *Journal of the Royal Musical Association* 114:1, 80–91.

Gans, Eric (1985), 'Art and Entertainment', *Perspectives of New Music*, Fall–Winter, 24–37.

Gossett, Philip (1989), 'Carl Dahlhaus and the "Ideal Type"', *19th Century Music* 13:1 (Summer), 49–56.

Griffiths, Paul (1978), *A Concise History of Modern Music* (London: Thames & Hudson).

Harrison, Charles (1981), *English Art and Modernism 1900–1939* (London: Allen Lane).

Hoggart, Richard (1957), *The Uses of Literacy* (Harmondsworth: Peregrine Books, 1984).

Jenkins, Jean (1983), *Man & Music*, exhibition catalogue (Edinburgh: Royal Scottish Museum).

Jones, Daniel (1955), 'An Attempt to Formulate General Aesthetic Principles through Music-Aesthetics', *The Score and IMA Magazine* 11 (Mar.), 35–52.

Kandinsky, Wassily (1947), *Concerning the Spiritual in Art* (London: Wittenburn).

Kerman, Joseph (1985), *Musicology* (London: Fontana).

Kowalke, Kim H. (1979), *Kurt Weill in Europe* (Ann Arbor: University of Michigan Press).

Kowalski, Michael (1982), 'The Exhaustion of Western Art Music', *Perspectives of New Music*, Fall–Winter, 1–14.

Lebrecht, N. (1985), 'Boulez and the Well Tempered 4X', *The Sunday Times Magazine*, 17 Feb., 48.

Lenin, Vladimir I. (1913), 'Critical Remarks on the National Question'; repr. in *Collected Works*, 20, trans. Bernard Isaacs and Joe Fineberg, ed. Julius Katzer (Moscow: Progress Publishers, and London: Lawrence & Wishart, 1964), 24.

Mellers, Wilfrid (1968), *Caliban Reborn* (London: Gollancz).

Morgan, Robert P. (1979), 'Rewriting Music History—Second Thoughts on Ives and Varèse' (orig. pub. in *Musical Newsletter*, 1973), repr. in Ian Bonighton and Richard Middleton (eds.), 'Ives and Varèse', *The Rise of Modernism in Music 1890–1935*, Units 22–4 (Milton Keynes: Open University Press).

Padmore, Elaine (1973), 'German Music in the Twentieth Century', in Frederick Sternfeld (ed.), *A History of Western Music, V: Music in the Moderm Age* (London: Weidenfeld & Nicolson), 95–133.

Peretti, Burton W. (1989), 'Democratic Leitmotives in the American Reception of Wagner', *19th Century Music* 13:1 (Summer), 28–38.

Pleasants, Henry (1955), *The Agony of Modern Music* (New York: Simon & Schuster).

——(1961), *Death of a Music* (London: Gollancz).

Rosenfeld, Paul (1922), *Musical Portraits* (London: Kegan Paul).

Schoenberg, Arnold (1904), 'Pamphlet of the Society of Creative Musicians', in *A308 Documents, The Rise of Modernism in Music 1890–1935* (Milton Keynes: Open University Press, 1978), 38–9.

—— (1946), 'New Music, Outmoded Music, Style and Idea', in Leonard Stein (ed.), *Style and Idea: Selected Writings of Arnold Schoenberg*, trans. Leo Black (London: Faber, 1975), 113–24.

—— (1941), 'Composition with Twelve Tones', in Leonard Stein (ed.), *Style and Idea: Selected Writings of Arnold Schoenberg*, trans. Leo Black (London: Faber, 1975), 214–44.

—— (1964), *Letters*, ed. Erwin Stein (London: Faber).

Scott, Derek B. (1981), 'Platonis Orpheus', *Composer*, Spring, 11–15.

—— (1984), 'The Tritone in Piobaireachd', *Piping Times*, May, 41–4.

—— (1989), *The Singing Bourgeois* (Milton Keynes and Philadelphia: Open University Press).

Shepherd, John (1987), 'Towards a Sociology of Musical Styles', in A. L. White (ed.), *Lost in Music: Culture, Style and the Musical Event* (*Sociological Review* Monograph, 34; London: Routledge & Kegan Paul), 56–76.

Sinfield, Alan (1983) (ed.), *Society and Literature 1945–1970* (London: Methuen).

Steiner, George (1970), *Language and Silence* (London: Faber).

Stravinsky, Igor (1974), *Poetics of Music* (1942) (Cambridge: Harvard University Press).

—— (1968), *Dialogues and a Diary* (London: Faber).

—— and Craft, Robert (1959), *Expositions and Developments* (London: Faber).

Treitler, Leo (1967), 'On Historical Criticism', *Musical Quarterly* 53, 188–205.

Vulliamy, Graham (1977), 'Music and the Mass Culture Debate', in John Shepherd, Phil Virden, Graham Vulliamy, and Trevor Wishart (eds.), *Whose Music? A Sociology of Musical Languages* (London: Latimer), 179–200.

Walker, John A. (1987), *Cross-overs: Art into Pop/Pop into Art* (London: Methuen).

Watson, Ian (1983), *Song and Democratic Culture in Britain* (London: Croom Helm).

Weber, William (1975), *Music and the Middle Class* (London: Croom Helm).

Webern, Anton (1913), *Six Bagatelles*, Op. 9 (Vienna: Universal Edition).

Wiliams, Raymond (1961), *The Long Revolution* (Harmondsworth: Penguin).

—— (1977), *Marxism and Literature* (Oxford: Oxford University Press).

Part I

Music and Language

Introduction

This section begins with an overview from Harold Powers, who summarizes three fields of study that embrace what he calls the metaphor of music as language: musical semantics, phonology and musical shapes, and musicology and linguistics. The reader is also encouraged to peruse three more recent articles by Powers (1995, 1996, and 1998) that deal with meaning more particularly.

The excerpt that follows is from a book cited by Powers, *The Language of Music* (1959), in which Deryck Cooke attempted to show that Western composers had long associated the same melodic phrases or degrees of major and minor scales with the same emotions. He was at pains, later, to stress that he had used the term 'language' not to suggest that music functioned like a verbal language, but to describe 'a means of communication' (1974: 215). He also claimed that he had not been trying to explain exactly *what* music communicated, but to show that music 'did express something which could be loosely characterised as "emotion" or "feeling"' (216). Cooke wanted to prove 'that music was expressive of emotion' (219); thus, his project is one of humanist idealism, an attempt to show how a transcendent human nature expresses itself in music.

His later position was not significantly different; it was summed up by a Schopenhauerian quotation from Wagner to the effect that music does not express this or that particular passion (for example, love or longing) but passion in itself, and in a way inexpressible in any other language. Cooke does not consider what effect the cultural and historical experience of listeners may have on the way they interpret music: his schema for communication is straightforward: Composer → Composition → Listener. His work, nevertheless, can be used to fuel an argument that music is a symbolic order within which meanings are social and conventional. This could then lead to a poststructuralist argument that meaning in music is not the expression of an inner essence but discursively constructed (cf. the differing meanings of the tritone in two differing musical styles mentioned in the Introduction to this reader—Cooke never considers that musical meanings might be arbitrary, resting upon knowledge of a particular style). Some aspects of Cooke's work are not too remote from Frits Noske's discussion of semiotic devices in *The Signifier and the Signified* (1977)—see, for example, chapter 8, 'The Musical Figure of Death'. Noske, however, stresses the importance of convention in sign formation, rather than implying that it originates from a universal human essence.

Leonard Bernstein was invited to give the Charles Eliot Norton Lectures at Harvard in 1973. His third lecture, from which the next excerpt is taken, was on musical semantics. Until then, making links between Chomsky's ideas of transformational grammar and musical processes was the concern of a few scholars only, and credit is due to Bernstein for awakening a much wider interest in the subject. In this lecture, he considers analogies between nouns modified by adjectives and melody modified by harmony, and discusses the musical use of rhetorical devices such as antithesis, alliteration, anaphora, and chiasmus. His main concern, however, is to demonstrate that the linguistic concept of transformation can be applied to music, and that musical transformations can be understood as metaphors: 'A piece of music is a constant metamorphosis of given material, involving such transformational operations as inversion, augmentation, retrograde, diminution, modulation, the opposition of consonance and dissonance, the various forms of imitation (such as canon and fugue), the varieties of rhythm and meter, harmonic progressions, coloristic and dynamic changes, plus the infinite interrelations of all these with one another. These *are* the meanings of music. And that is as close as I can come to a definition of musical semantics' (1976: 153).

Yet, it may be argued that in music a distinction ought to be made between transformation and variation, reserving the former as a term for indicating radical changes in musical character, and the latter to suggest embellishment or changes in configuration that relate more closely to the original material. Bernstein's snappy definition of metaphor—'This-is-that'—is made to apply whether the 'transformation' is similar to or different from the character of the original. It may be wondered, also, whether there is not room for a theory of musical metonymy (identification with similarity) as well as musical metaphor (identification with difference). Do the fragments of introductory material that appear in the main body of the first movement of Beethoven's 'Pathétique' Sonata constitute, perhaps, a musical equivalent of a synecdoche, a part standing for a whole (as in 'a familiar face appeared at the meeting')? One of Bernstein's difficulties is that he conceives music as a metalanguage, whereas what he is actually doing is using linguistic discourse as a metalanguage for and about music. A more sweeping objection to Bernstein's method would be made by Deleuze and Guattari, however, who contend that we should think of music as a 'superlinear system, a rhizome instead of a tree' (1988: 95).

It should be noted that Bernstein marks his distance from structural linguistics by introducing a distinction between meaning and expression, speaking of the latter in terms that suggest a human essence lying behind the meaning ('expressing something'). Moreover, faced with his claim that if it were possible to collect, compare, and find consistency in sample 'feelings' from a concert audience '*then* we'd know something', Pierre Bourdieu would argue that all we would know is that the audience possessed similar cultural capital (see 1984: 11–18).

In the earlier part of the article from which the next excerpt is taken, Patricia Tunstall describes structuralism as a modern reformulation of Cartesian and Kantian theories of universal cognitive properties, the ultimate goal of the structuralist project being to uncover the formal properties common to all human minds. She distinguishes two models of structural analysis in musicology, the one semiotic and the other anthropological. The former is characterized by 'the assumption that artistic works are not so much acts of free and spontaneous individual creation as they are assemblages of socially meaningful signs' (1979: 57). The latter is influenced by Claude Lévi-Strauss's 'premise that music and myth are analogous because both are intelligible but untranslatable, and while each takes specific forms in specific cultures, both have fundamental structural characteristics that particularly illuminate cognitive principles of order' (57).

In the given excerpt, she advances the idea that musical structure may be 'an unmediated reflection of the formal operations of cognition'; but this raises questions for a poststructuralist about the possibility of musical choices being made for ideological reasons. For example, a desire to signify distinctions of gender or ethnicity in music may have a structurally disruptive impact or result in particular structural ramifications. It is also to be wondered whether music is quite as free of semantic associations as is suggested here.

According to Lévi-Strauss, music involves two levels of articulation. An example of the first level would be the major scale: Lévi-Strauss remarks that a scale has a hierarchical structure (1986: 22). An example of the second level would be the use of this scale for melody and harmony, subjecting it to rhythm, etc., and creating a musical form. This implies that there can be no *natural* expression in music, since 'culture is already present' (22) before the secondary code, containing the significant elements, is reached. Yet Lévi-Strauss believed that music, like myths, brought you face to face with 'conscious approximations . . . of inevitably unconscious truths' (18). Though Lévi-Strauss usefully identifies primary and secondary levels of articulation in tonal music, he has been accused by Umberto Eco of proposing the tonal system as a 'natural metalanguage' particularly in the context of Lévi-Strauss's criticism of atonal music. Eco points out that there are systems without double articulation and systems with interchangeable levels of articulation, and comments: 'To confuse the laws of tonal music with the laws of music *tout court* is rather like believing that if one has a pack of French playing cards (52 plus one or two jokers), the only possible combinations among them are those established by bridge' (1977: 230).

The impact of Lévi-Strauss's structuralism is evident in the writings of Gilbert Chase, John Blacking, and Steven Feld, among others. For example, Steven Feld declares his book *Sound and Sentiment* to be 'an ethnographic study of sound as a cultural system, that is, a system of symbols, among the Kaluli people of Papua New Guinea' (1982: 3). In his book *Myth and Music*, Eero Tarasti makes use of Lévi-Strauss's theory about mythical thought and A. J. Greimas's method of semeanalysis to analyse what he regards as musical reconstructions of myth. He labels the principal types of these reconstructions the 'hero-mythical', the 'nature-mythical', and the 'magic-mythical'. The given excerpt follows his initial movement from Lévi-Strauss's aesthetics of myth to the aesthetics of music. In his later work, especially *A Theory of Musical Semiotics*, Eero Tarasti has contributed perhaps the most sophisticated theoretical defence to date of the idea that music has an inner logic accessible to musical semiotics, and that this logic exists as a universal in all human practices. Some of those who follow this path are more concerned with structural analysis than the interpretation of socio-cultural meaning: Raymond Monelle, for example, clings to a notion that 'pure instrumental music' exists 'without any associative meaning', the analysis of which he intends 'as a demonstration of theory, not as providing critical insight' (1991: 73–4).

The Gino Stefani piece that follows comes from a special issue of *Semiotica*, entitled 'Semiotics of Music', with Eero Tarasti as guest editor. The same issue contains an insightful article by Philip Tagg: 'Musicology and the Semiotics of Popular Music'. Tagg has pioneered a hermeneutic-semiological analytic method for popular music, outlined in 'Analysing Popular Music: Theory, Method and Practice' (1982). Stefani's work has been selected to illustrate developments in the semiology of music, since access to Jean-Jacques Nattiez's work is now readily available with the publication of *Music and Discourse* (1990).

An enormous debt is owed to Carolyn Abbate for her translating of these writings of Jean-Jacques Nattiez, which are essential reading for anyone interested in musical semiotics. Abbate's own work, like Tarasti's, proves very resistant to being served up in small portions, but her arguments (1991) concerning musical narrativity and the idea of 'voices' in music have had considerable impact. Yet, her desire to protect the 'physical and sensual force' of music's 'voices' is not, despite her own doubts, incompatible with poststructuralist theory. A poststructuralist would readily acknowledge that such 'voices' are indeed perceptible, but go on to argue that they are produced as an effect of the music and/or performance, and not that they exist as a presence within the music.

Finally, mention should be made of the stimulating contribution to debates about music and language provided in Lawrence Kramer's productive fusing of J. L. Austen's speech act theory and the critique it drew from Jacques Derrida (see Kramer 1990: 6–9 and 1995: 10–12). Kramer demonstrates convincingly that language does not have sole claim to communicative acts. For example, a musical 'expressive act' can comfortably fit into the description of a communicative act that seeks to affect a flow of events (has *illocutionary force*) and yet is capable of functioning in new contexts (is *iterable*).

An Overview

HAROLD S. POWERS

The metaphor of music as language has three principal aspects, depending upon whether the focus is on semantics, on phonology, or on syntax and grammar.

Musical Semantics

First of all, music is often said to express or evoke something that might have been conveyed verbally. In certain restricted cases, like drum or whistle languages, something like music is even used as a referential coded substitute for language; the Tepehua 'thought' songs described by Boilès (1967) seem to be the extreme case. But many musical cultures recognize conventionally coded induced associations of specific musical entities with persons, events, or things, in real life as well as in ritual or drama. In the most familiar cases the something that might have been conveyed verbally is emotive/expressive rather than cognitive/ostensive, and sometimes a more or less systematic doctrine of musical affect or musical ethos is found. In high cultures musical entities are often systematically correlated with non-musical phenomena, many of which may have strong expressive associations of their own. In some of the medieval North Indian systems of melodic types six superordinate types are correlated with the six seasons, which have strong affective connotations. In some sources of medieval European theory a similar correspondence is found between the four Galenic humours, the four Aristotelian elements, and the four pairs of plainsong modes (Gerbert 1784: 218–19). Of course the linguistic metaphor need not be invoked in connection with musical ethos, but it often is. Individual affects, or whole classes of affect, are ascribed to musical entities like motives or tunes, or to musical features like rhythms or intervals, and these features or entities are then said to be units of discourse in a musical language of pure expression. The late Deryck Cooke's many times reprinted *The Language of Music* (1959) is an extended application of this aspect of the metaphor to Western music of the fifteenth to twentieth centuries.

Most musicologists, however, are a little embarrassed by the notion that music is a language whose message is something other than itself. For instance, I confess to some discomfort over attempts by Keil and Keil (1966) and by Deva and Virmani (1968, 1974) to use the Osgood/Suci/Tannenbaum 'semantic differential' method, with all its inductive paraphernalia of questionnaire

'Language Models and Musical Analysis', *Ethnomusicology*, 24:1 (1980), 1–4, 7–9.

and factor analysis, in order directly to find or confirm affective meaning to one or another individual North Indian *rāga*. There are simply too many uncontrollable variables. Not evaluative scales of good–bad, hard–soft, and active–passive, but rather paradigmatic scales of compatible–incompatible, same–different, and superordinate–subordinate seem to me the fundamental elements of a semantics of North Indian classical music, as I tried to show in 'The Structure of Musical Meaning: A View from Banaras' (1977). Musical semantics may establish systematic relationships of meaning in musical discourse, but musical-verbal dictionaries of specific affects must be compiled ad hoc from exterior non-musical contexts. Those contexts may be verbal text or dramatic situation (as in Cooke 1959), or any other cultural (or even natural) event. The experience and expectations of fully enculturated listeners might well serve as a source too, though only one of many.

In 'Language and Music: Areas for Cooperation' (1963: 28), William Bright recognized that

> it is widely felt that music, like language, conveys something—that a musical performance, like a linguistic message, contains something more than the physical properties of the individual sounds which make it up.

But Bright too seems to have regarded the 'content' of music as merely a function of what he called its 'endosemantic' structure (pp. 28–9). For Bright (p. 26),

> [the] two main types of link between language and music [are] their mutual influence in singing, and their structural similarity.

These are what I referred to at the outset as the phonological and the grammatical aspects of the music as language metaphor.

Phonological and Musical Shapes

Bright's own instance for the direct influence of linguistic phonology on musical sound was taken from South Indian classical music. He pointed out that there is a consistent pattern of correspondence between long and short syllables in a text and longer and shorter durations in its musical setting, and quoted a couple of lines from a Telugu *padam* to illustrate. I can confirm that the correspondences are exactly so in principle, though very much more complex in some circumstances. In Telugu compositions in South Indian classical *rāga*-s (melodic types) the relationships between text rhythms and musical rhythms are multiplex and heterogeneous, yet all musical rhythms can be derived in one way or another from Telugu prosody (itself multiplex and heterogeneous, incorporating both Dravidian and Sanskritic prosodic features at all levels, from syllable and foot on to stanza and beyond).

Of course, direct connection between phonological features in a language and basic features in the music associated with that language hardly constitutes a metaphor. But to the extent that the vocal music of a culture is the model for instrumental music as well, the indirect influence of language–music connection may be easily discernible in musical practices having no connection with text. It is patently the case that rhythmic patterns in modern South Indian instrumental music are largely an outgrowth of the vocal repertory, which until recently has dominated South Indian practice. But this is in large part true for North Indian instrumental music as well, and not just in those very recent '*gāyakī aṅg*' fashions modelling their art on the vocal *khayāl* style. The oldest traditions of Hindustani solo instrumental music are for plucked strings, and the performance styles of the *sitār* seem originally to have been essentially independent of vocal influence, as in most Middle Eastern plucked string styles today. But the plucking patterns—the *mizrāb*—of all traditional genres, improvised and memorized alike, now reflect the quantitative relation of long and short syllables of language in varying degrees. Except in the case of the *jhālā*, in fact, the contrast of long and short is very much more evident than the motor accents of hand and finger movement so characteristic of Middle Eastern plucked string playing, such as Persian *chār-mezrāb*. *Sitār* playing has become 'Indianized'. Onto an original quasi-Middle Eastern accentual style in rhythm have been grafted quantitative features. These appear most obviously in the several varieties of *joḍ*, which seems to have come in from vocal *nom-tom* via the *bīn*.

On a larger and more abstract scale too one can discern the connection of language forms and musical design in South Asia. Modern Indian performance practice in general is in considerable part connected with the mostly devotional post-classical literature of later Sanskrit poetry (beginning with the *Gītā Govinda*) and of the 'medieval' and modern vernaculars. This poetry is characterized by refrain and stanza design, quite unlike the older classical Sanskrit poetry in which every quatrain is an independent entity. Furthermore, the poems are normally designed *en rondeau* semantically, and often even grammatically, in that the beginning of the independent refrain comes as a logical or even syntactic continuation and completion of the last words of the stanza. Finally, there is usually a matching rhyme of stanzas with refrain, sometimes even the matching of a word or two; this ensures that not only the end of the stanza but also the end of the refrain itself will flow easily back into the beginning, for the repetitions as well as for the returns of the refrain.

These three characteristic textual features have exact musical correspondences, not only in performance but in the abstract background structures as well. As to performance, first, there is a fundamental part in contrast with a second responding part, musically as well as verbally. There is also continuous leadback, melodically as well as (often) syntactically, from the endings of both principal part and responding part to the beginning of the principal part. Finally, at the end of each of the two parts in the majority of cases there are sonically parallel passages, based on syllabic rhyming or identity in the verbal domain and on equivalence or identity of melodic contour in the melodic domain.

Here again, formal parallels between tune and text in themselves hardly constitute a metaphor. But the three features that correspond—contrast of two parts, use of leadback connections, and musical rhyme—mark not only the characteristic shape of performance but are also built into the still more abstract shape of the underlying musical substance. Almost every classical *rāga*—that is, melodic type—is itself structured in terms of these features: first, a clear contrast of two main registers, each defined thematically as well; second, linear connections at the boundaries from each register into the next, and especially in descent; third, parallelism between the nuclear motivic contours and/or intervallic contents of each register.

[. . .]

Musicology and Linguistics

Parallels between the formal patterns of sound and structure in text and music, whether concrete or abstract, are of course not unique to Indian music. I have myself used such structural parallels in dealing with the influences of word rhythm and textural form in seventeenth–eighteenth-century music composed to Italian texts (see especially 1962: 82–90, and 1968: 280–6, 308–9). Others will readily find instances from other areas, from Paris to Peking. It is an interesting area for study, with more subtleties than one might think. But nowadays the main focus of interest in the language–music connection is in the putative abstract structural similarities of language and music. Many have been encouraged to think that analytical models of linguistic structure may be heuristically relevant for the analysis of musical structure.

The new literature of linguistics-based analysis of music is growing fast. Analyses and programmatic theories have come out of both the Western theoretical and the ethnomusicological traditions, and even more significantly, some musically competent linguists have interested themselves professionally in the subject. It is in this structurally oriented literature that the most interesting insights on the language–music connection are to be found, and at the same time the most faddish foolishness. The harsh criticisms of the foolishness that make up the bulk of Steven Feld's 1974 article 'Linguistic Models in Ethnomusicology' seem to me thoroughly justified. But Feld seems not to have noticed the real insights available to musicology from a knowledge of the study of languages, or at any rate not to have valued them very much, because of his own strong theoretical bias against any consideration of 'music sound' outside of its cultural context. This bias comes from Merriam and Blacking (as expressed for instance in Merriam 1964: 26–32, or Blacking 1973: 25–7) and given the kind of parochial notions they were reacting against, the bias is a healthy one. But they overreact. It is of course true that (like language) no music can exist without people who make it. It is also true that (like some uses of language) some music may sometimes be more efficiently interpreted by discussing it as though it did have a life of its own. When and to what extent any particular music ought to be interpreted out of context depends in part, as it does in the study of linguistic phenomena, on the purpose of the investigation, and in part it depends on the role of that music in the culture in question— and of course this last question cannot be resolved by music-analytical methods of whatever origin. Some musics can be managed apart from cultural context more readily than others, Western and Indian art musics being two notorious examples, while other musics are so intimately tied in with a cultural or even material context as to be incomprehensible except in that context.

Ethnomusicologists need not therefore denigrate abstract musical analysis merely on principle, even abstract musical analysis inspired by linguistic models. Sociolinguists are not throwing out abstract linguistic analysis and abstract models, they are merely incorporating them in their broader field (Labov 1972: 186–7, 201–2).

To whatever extent methodological and theoretical imbalances in the new literature on music as language arise from insufficient attention to cultural factors in the societies being investigated, equal or greater imbalances arise from inattention to cultural factors in the society of the investigators. In the sequel I propose to illustrate three broad areas in which the reach of the new literature seems to be exceeding its grasp.

First, some of the more enthusiastic proponents of linguistics-based musical analysis have not seemed very familiar with the analytical musicology they find inadequate. It may be, as some have suggested, that musical analysis unaccountably or perversely lags behind other disciplines. It may also be that scholars working out of the by no means negligible existing traditions have long been dealing with many of the same kinds of problems as structural linguists, only in a more abstruse and intractable domain, where the linguist's handy tool of 'meaning', often used for rough work in the field if seldom acknowledged in fine print, has not been available.

Second, there is paradoxically little comparative basis for the new linguistics-based music-analytical literature, even though much of that literature comes from ethnomusicologists. Comparisons in ethnomusicology are seldom really cross-culturally multilateral but rather tend to be bilateral, and in a curious way. 'Ethnic' musics are matched one at a time against theoretical models derived from various sources: field experience with one of them, anthropological theory, linguistics, or the investigator's notions of 'Western' music or 'standard' music theory, in varying proportions. But modern synchronic linguistics did not grow out of bilateral comparisons of a language with a model, or of an alien language with some aspect of the investigator's language. The now enormously influential *Cours de linguistique générale* (1916) of Ferdinand de Saussure, posthumously compiled by two of his students from their lecture notes and those of other students, is a seminal work of European structural linguistics and semiology. Saussure began his career, however, with the at the time equally influential *Mémoires sur le système primitif des voyelles dans les langues indoeuropéennes* (1879), a landmark work of comparative linguistics in the *Junggrammatiker* vein, and what little else Saussure actually published in his own lifetime was also in this field. Modern linguistics began with multilateral comparisons of languages in families, from Indo-European to Athabaskan, and their individually described grammars were matched not against borrowed models but against each other. A theoretical musicology inspired by linguistics could do worse than look to the history of linguistics in this regard, as well as to its latest fashions.

Third, the new literature seems uninterested in older traditions of language models for musical analysis. Yet those traditions are of value not only in their own right but even more because they have left significant residues in our modern notions of what constitutes musical analysis and even music itself. As is well known, there is not always agreement about what 'music' is and about what is 'music', not just across cultures but even within them. The very notion that music is something that can be segmented and analysed, and the traditional terminology for doing so, have deep and particular roots in historical language models for musical analysis that are peculiar to Western European culture.

On Musical Inspiration

DERYCK COOKE

How does a musical work originate in the composer's mind? Normally as a *conception*. This can arise in four main ways. (1) From a *literary text* which the composer feels an urge to set to music (masses, anthems, songs, some operas and oratorios). (2) From a '*literary*' *idea* which the composer feels an urge to use either as a basis for a vocal and instrumental composition (some operas and oratorios) or as a programme for a purely instrumental work (symphonic poems, and programme-symphonies like Berlioz's *Symphonie Fantastique*). (3) From an *ideal or concept* which the composer feels drawn to use as the basis of a purely instrumental work without a specific programme (Beethoven's 'Eroica' Symphony, or Carl Nielsen's 'Inextinguishable'). (4) From a '*purely musical*' *impulse*—the desire, say, to write 'a great symphony' (Schubert's Ninth).

What motivates a conception? Why does a composer suddenly feel an impulse to write a work founded on a certain text, programme, idea, or musical genre? Something more than a passing whim, surely: it must be that he has something to say, whether he knows it or not. In other words, a certain complex of emotions must have been seeking an outlet, a means of expression, of communication to others; a state of affairs of which the composer may have been quite aware, or only half aware, or completely unaware. The moment of conception is the moment in which the nature of the complex of emotions becomes entirely clear to his conscious mind—except in the case of a 'purely musical' impulse: here the emotional stimulus of the conception often remains almost entirely unconscious right through the whole process of composition, and beyond it, since it is finding expression in the inexplicit language of music, which is emotionally unintelligible to the conscious minds of its most powerful exponents.

And what is meant by a conception? Usually a vague sense of the nature, mood, and shape of the work to be composed, with the separate parts and the actual material as yet unrealized, or only partly realized. Examples are Beethoven's conception of a great symphony in honour of Napoleon which resulted in the 'Eroica', and Wagner's decision to make Siegfried and the Nibelung myth the subject of a new type of opera—music-drama—which materialized in *The Ring*.

What is the next stage in the act of musical creation? The event known as *inspiration*—the sudden materialization of a musical idea in the composer's

The Language of Music (Oxford: Oxford University Press, 1959), 168–75.

mind. It has been called the 'next' stage, though it may in fact precede or accompany the conception. An example of the former is the *Hebrides* Overture of Mendelssohn. Writing home (7 August 1829) during his Scottish tour, he said: 'In order to make you understand how extraordinarily the Hebrides affected me, the following came into my head there'; and he noted down the opening theme of the work in his letter. The inspiration came first, then; but the conception (that of a 'seascape' overture) must have followed close. Conception and inspiration can be simultaneous: when Schubert read Goethe's poem 'The Erl King' and sat straight down and set it to music then and there, he must have experienced the conception (a tone-painting of a gallop through a stormy night) and the inspiration (the drumming accompaniment and expressive vocal line) more or less as a single mental event. But frequently, inspiration takes its time in following the initial conception. William Byrd and Hugo Wolf pondered over words, the latter sometimes waiting for years for inspiration to arrive; Wagner brooded deep and long over mythology; Haydn, in his later years, prayed; Beethoven wrestled; César Franck played other men's music; Stravinsky sits at the piano and probes. Ultimately, however, what eventually turns up, whether quickly or slowly, whether 'pure' or in connection with words and ideas, is musical inspiration.

And what is this 'inspiration'? Something which, in Mendelssohn's words, 'comes into our heads'—and apparently quite inexplicably. In Aaron Copland's words: 'The composer starts with his theme; and the theme is a gift from heaven. He doesn't know where it comes from—has no control over it. It comes almost like automatic writing' (*What to Listen for in Music*, ch. 3). William Byrd has described exactly how it happens, in the preface to the 1610 edition of his *Gradualia*, in connection with the setting of religious words: 'As I have learned by experience, there is a secret hidden power in the texts themselves; so that to one who ponders on things divine and turns them over carefully and seriously in his mind, in some way, I cannot tell how, the aptest numbers occur, as if of their own accord . . .'.

But inspiration does not come from nowhere: nothing can come out of nothing. Music as we know it could not be created at all but for the existence of a long tradition of past music; and every composer draws continually on his experience of this tradition—which cannot be anywhere else, for him, but in his own *unconscious mind*. In the composer's unconscious is stored all the music he has ever heard, studied, or written himself; some of it, to use the Freudian term, is 'pre-conscious', i.e. more or less accessible to the conscious faculty of memory, but most of it is forgotten, or half-forgotten. And it is from this storehouse that inspiration must come: any new musical idea which suddenly 'comes into the composer's head' must be created in some way or other out of his experience of the music of his predecessors and contemporaries (and of his own music), which belongs to the vast mass of life-experience retained in his unconscious. In other words, what we call 'inspiration' must be *an unconscious creative re-shaping of already existing materials in the tradition.*

This unconscious process has always been regarded as an ultimate mystery, but our identification of the basic terms of musical language . . . offers us a chance of coming to grips with the problem at last. For in the music examples [in an earlier chapter], we have a mass of detailed evidence to support the hypothesis that inspiration is an unconscious re-shaping of already existing material: all the 'inspirations' assembled there have quite obviously arisen out of the various composers' experience of the music of their predecessors. Our hypothesis is, in fact, already confirmed in one particular field—that of *melody*—and we may use this fact as a starting-point for our investigation of the problem of inspiration. No doubt the unconscious process of re-shaping must also occur in the fields of harmony and rhythm; but let us ignore these for the moment, and concentrate entirely on the melodic element, since we have the evidence at our disposal, and since melody, as we have tried to show, is the fundamental basis of musical language. We can begin from this undeniable fact: that the 'basic term' type of inspiration . . . is clearly a matter of reproducing certain well-worn melodic *formulae* in new guises.

At first sight, this would seem to be a bewildering state of affairs. Many of the inspirations . . . are of the highest order; yet how can there be anything 'inspired' about a process which merely reproduces, in slightly different form, something which has already been used many times before? How are we to reconcile this constant reliance on the same melodic material with the indisputable fact of the creative vitality of 'inspiration'? Before we can solve this problem, we must first answer the preliminary question . . . how is it that composers do return again and again to the same few scraps of melody?

There can be only three possible explanations of the fact that a handful of melodic phrases have been used over and over again: plagiarism, unconscious 'cribbing', and coincidence. The first of these may be ruled out straightaway since, apart from isolated examples like Handel and Bononcini, composers have not been guilty of intentionally stealing other men's themes as a basis for their own works; and in any case, we are concerned only with unintentional, unconscious resemblances.

Unconscious cribbing seems a fairly obvious explanation in certain cases, where the 'inspiration' is clearly a reproduction of another composer's idea in easily recognizable form: here 'inspiration' functions simply as the sudden return to consciousness of an actual theme by another composer, once heard, since forgotten or half-forgotten, and now no longer recognized when it reappears. How easily this can happen was experienced by Manuel de Falla. The opening theme of *Nights in the Gardens of Spain,* according to the biography by Pahissa, 'came to Falla spontaneously, without his having any idea that it might have originated in his subconscious, yet one day, he met Amadeo Vives, who told him that, oddly enough, he had written a *zarzuela* which began in exactly the same way. This coincidence troubled Falla until the explanation suddenly came to him—he and Vives lived on two different floors of the same house in the Calle Serrano in Madrid. On the pavement below, an aged blind violinist had every day come and played these notes on a badly tuned violin. Constant repetition had fixed the notes in their minds so that, without realizing it, they had both written them as their own'.

Similarly Wagner, rehearsing Act 3 of *The Mastersingers* one day, and arriving at Hans Sachs's words 'Mein Freund, in holder Jugendzeit', suddenly realized, and pointed out with a smile, that the melody was straight out of Nicolai's *The Merry Wives of Windsor*. And others have noticed that in *The Ring*, the Rhinemaidens' motive appears to be from Mendelssohn's *Melusine* Overture, the theme accompanying Sieglinde's dream from Liszt's 'Faust' Symphony, and the Nibelung motive from Schubert's 'Death and the Maiden' Quartet—but here we run up against an obstacle. Is the last of these three examples in fact a case of 'unconscious cribbing'? We are all too apt to jump to conclusions in these matters. It is not certain that Wagner ever heard any of Schubert's chamber music; this may be just as much a coincidence as is the resemblance between the tragic themes of *Parsifal* and Verdi's *Otello*.

When it comes to it, we shall find that any attempt to make a wholesale attribution of musical resemblances to unconscious cribbing will take us on to shaky ground, even when the composer points it out himself. Returning to the melody in *The Mastersingers* which Wagner recognized as belonging to *The Merry Wives of Windsor*, what is it in reality but one further variation of the sequence of falling fourths (major 6–3–5–2–4) which pervades the whole opera in different forms, and which originally appears in the Overture, the first part of the work to be composed, in a form quite unlike Nicolai's tune? Again, the Rhinemaidens' motive, when it first enters in *The Rhinegold*, acts as a derivative of the opening motive of the whole work, which is quite different from the *Melusine* melody. There can be no simple explanation of examples like these. In any case, unconscious cribbing can hardly be the explanation of the many resemblances.

The answer to our problem, then, can only be *coincidence*—which would seem to be no answer at all, unless we are prepared to believe that the world is ruled by blind chance. Yet it is in fact the correct and perfectly satisfying answer, if we despoil the word of its acquired connotation of chance, and understand it in its simple generic sense of a 'happening together' or a 'happening in the same way'. For it is clear . . . that, in tonal music, things just do happen over and over again in the same way, melodically—but for a very good reason. There are only twelve notes in the scale; and a tonal composer intent on expressing a certain emotion is limited to fewer; and there is not an infinite number of shapes into which he can weave the few notes at his disposal—in fact they will often fall quite naturally into those familiar patterns which we have called the basic terms of musical vocabulary. Given the structure of the scale, with its tonic and dominant, and that of the triad, with its third, these patterns were inevitable from the beginning: they might be described as *propensities* to group certain tonal tensions together in certain ways, which crystallized into *habitual propensities*, and were handed down unconsciously as elements of the musical heritage of Western Europe. Some of them, such as the 'wailing' minor 6–5, and the 'innocent' pentatonic (major) 1–3–5–6–5, must date back into prehistory; others, such as those involving the augmented fourth or the chromatic scale, are obviously of later date, and the process of their growth into habitual propensities could no doubt be accurately plotted by painstaking research into the history of expressive idioms in music.

It does not seem fanciful to suppose that, in the tonal composer's unconscious, a state of affairs exists which can be described metaphorically in the following way. (1) Memories of the innumerable expressive uses of each of the *tonal tensions* must attach themselves together in groups, by the association of ideas (or, rather, by the association of feelings); and each group of this kind must be attached to a kindred group of memories of sense-experiences, life-experiences, and literary and artistic experiences, also by the association of feelings. (2) These composite groups must contain within them certain sub-groups, each attached to a specific melodic use of the tonal tension concerned, i.e. to one of the *basic terms* of musical vocabulary: for example, of the vast number of associations connected with the major sixth, many will be attached to the major 6–5, or 8–7–6–5, or 1–3–5–6–5, or to other patterns involving the major sixth, no doubt, not identified in this book. (3) Memories of the expressive uses of certain *keys* must also attach themselves together, by the association of feelings, and these groups must also attract memories of life- and art-experiences, thereby forming the well-known associations in composers' minds between certain keys and certain moods. Owing to individual idiosyncrasies difficult to analyse, these associations tend to vary from composer to composer, but there is a large measure of agreement (owing to the historical development of key-signatures, instruments, etc.): the 'tragic' C minor, for example, the 'common light of day' C major, the 'brilliant' D major, and the 'luxurious' D flat major. Naturally, in view of this, the various basic terms will be attracted with greater or less intensity to the different key-areas.

Returning now to the question of inspiration, . . . we can see that 'inspiration' can often mean 'the breaking through into consciousness of a particular basic term, in a certain form, from a certain key-area'. This is obviously what happened to William Byrd when the inspiration came to him for some of the motets in his *Gradualia*. If we turn to the openings of *Gaudeamus Omnes* (Let us all rejoice—No. 29), or *Plorans Plorabit* (Weeping, mine eyes shall weep—No. 28), or *Beati Mundo Core* (Blest are the pure in heart—No. 32), we shall find it amusing to imagine the austere composer 'pondering' on the texts, 'turning them over carefully and seriously in his mind', until 'the aptest numbers occurred as if of their own accord'—as re-shapings of the basic terms 1–2–3–4–5 (in the traditionally 'simple' key of F major), 1–3–4–5 (in the 'melancholy' key of G minor), and 1–5–6–5 (again in the 'simple' F major). We should not be too amused, though, since without undergoing the experience of 'inspiration' we can do nothing with these dead patterns, whereas by doing so Byrd has turned them into living themes.

On Musical Semantics

LEONARD BERNSTEIN

A metaphor—or any comparative statement, even a simile—must function in terms of the two compared items being related to a third item, which is common to both. That is, we are comparing A and B, whether they are my dog and your dog, or Juliet and the sun—A and B, both of which must relate to a third factor, X, which is abstractable from both. If A is Juliet and B is the sun, then X is *radiance* (or any number of other things, but let's say *radiance*); A has X, and B has X, therefore A is like B. Juliet is like the sun. We then delete the *like* and Juliet *is* the sun. And what a deletion is there! Of such transformations are metaphors made, and of such metaphors is beauty born.

You remember I spoke of the mind having to go through a series of decision-making steps when confronted by a semantic incongruity—first seeking justification, and then either rejecting it or accepting it on a poetic level? Well, add to that a whole other series of steps, these very ones we've been describing—namely, the finding of an X-factor to which A and B can both relate. (My dog is your dog because they're both brown. But that can't be, says the mind; oh, I see, it *can* be, *in a poetic sense.*) Now all of that complex mental process takes place in a millisecond, a flash of time: such is the wonder of our cerebral computer. But the moment we come to deal with *musical* metaphor, even that millisecond is eliminated—because we don't have to deal with the problems of A and B being incompatible. Why not? Because the As and Bs of music are not burdened by literal semantic weights like my dog or your dog or even Juliet. If we call the first two bars of Brahms's Fourth Symphony A [Ex. 1], and the second two B [Ex. 2], we *instantly* perceive the musical transformation, with no time or effort needed to explain that relationship in terms of semantic meanings; the only time required is the time it takes to play the music.

In fact, when you think of the number of transformations taking place in the short space of those few bars of Brahms, it becomes almost incredible that all of them can be instantaneously perceived. What we've called A in itself involves a transformation [Ex. 3]: the descending major third transformed to its exact inversion, an ascending minor sixth. So A already contains a metaphor; and so does B [Ex. 4]. But in addition to that, B is itself a metaphor of A, being a comparative transformation of A [1], one degree of the scale lower [2]. And add to that the *harmonic* metaphor accompanying the melodic one [Ex. 5]: the A pro-

The Unanswered Question: Six Talks at Harvard (Cambridge, Mass.: Harvard University Press, 1976), 125–31, 133, 135.

Ex. 1

Ex. 2

Ex. 3

Ex. 4

Ex. 5

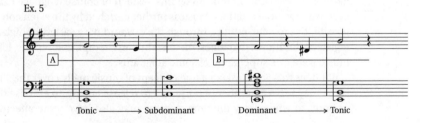

gression is tonic/subdominant, and the *B* progression is dominant/tonic; a beautiful parallelism, and a luminous example of this-is-that.

So in music as well as in poetry, the *A* and *B* of a metaphor must both relate to some *X*-factor—not radiance or brownness, but a common factor such as the rhythm [see Exx. 1 and 2] or those harmonic progressions [see Ex. 5]. You see there is still that triangular formation of *A*, *B*, and *X* to be reckoned with. And yet, with all this to be perceived, all these metaphors-within-metaphors, we still don't require even that one millisecond before perceiving it. There is no need to go through 'that-can't-be—oh,-I-see-it-can-be-in-a-poetic-sense'; because the music *already exists in the poetic sense*. It's all art from the first note on.

[. . .]

In the first lecture on phonology, we dealt with the ordering of phonemic elements out of the harmonic series so as to produce meaningful tonal relationships; *meaningful*, ergo *semantic*. In the second lecture, on syntax, we were dealing with the ordering of those tonal relationships so as to produce meaningful structures. So now that we come to consider musical semantics in general, what meanings are there left to deal with? Obviously, the musical meanings that result from the combination of both, of what we might call phono-semantics plus morpho-semantics—meanings derived by the various transformational procedures with which we've been playing.

'Playing': that's the word that leapt out, and precisely the world I want to use. It sounds frivolous, I know, but it is on the contrary essentially related to our semantic thinking. 'Play' is the very stuff and activity of music; we *play* music on our instruments just as the composer *plays* with notes in the act of inventing it. He *juggles* sound-formations, he *toys* with dynamics, he *glides* and *skips* and *somersaults* through rhythms and colours—in short, he indulges in what Stravinsky called 'Le Jeu de Notes'. The Game of Notes: a striking concept of what music is.

And why not? All music, even the most serious, thrives on its puns and anagrams. Where would Richard Strauss be without his musical puns, or Bach and Beethoven without their musical anagrams? One can almost think of a given piece of music as a continuing game of anagrams, in which there are, as it were, twelve 'letters' [Ex. 6] that can be juggled and rejuggled. The constant rearrangement and transformation of these 'letters' is made particularly rich by the combined possibilities of horizontal and vertical structures—melodic, harmonic, and contrapuntal anagrams—which of course language cannot do, even with twenty-six letters. Music is further enriched by the extension of these possibilities to near-infinity, through the extraordinary variety of high and low registers, durations, dynamics, meters, rhythms, tempi, colorations. It's as if all music were one supergame of sonic anagrams.

But does this Stravinskian game concept of music really cover the subject? A game may serve a number of purposes: to release energy, to exercise the mind or body, to while away the time. A game may also have more affective func-

Ex. 6

tions: to compete, to show off, to establish a shared intimacy with the opponent. All these may well be functions of music too, and frequently are; but nobody is going to assert that music stops there. There's got to be more to it than those merely pleasurable functions, even if they do go so far as to constitute a refreshment of the spirit. Music does more than that, says more, *means* more.

'Means': there's the problem. Means what? Sad? Glad? 'Moonlight' Sonata? 'Revolutionary' Etude? Bi-units of information? Significational sensory effects? Cybernetic feedback? What do we mean by 'mean'?

Well, the very first Young People's programme I ever gave on television, about fifteen years ago, was entitled 'What Does Music Mean?' Here I am still asking that question, and my answers haven't changed very much. But I think I can now present a more mature formulation of them, particularly since I have a more mature audience to tell it to.

As concisely as possible, this is it: music has intrinsic meanings of its own, which are not to be confused with specific feelings or moods, and certainly not with pictorial impressions or stories. These intrinsic musical meanings are generated by a constant stream of metaphors, all of which are forms of poetic transformations. This is our thesis.

I believe this thesis can be demonstrated, and in fact has already been partly demonstrated, even if not scientifically proved. The problem of proof stems, no doubt, from that very unscientific word 'metaphor', which I have already been using in a highly metaphorical way, and will no doubt continue so to do. But I should clarify this broad use of the term at least to the extent that we can distinguish one use from another.

There are three specific ways in which I want to use the term 'metaphor'. First, those intrinsic musical metaphors I have already mentioned, which are of a purely musical order, and operate rather like those puns-and-anagram games we were speaking of. All these metaphors derive from transformations of musical material—those very *Chomskian* transformations we investigated last week. By transforming any given musical material from one state to another, as I showed earlier with that bit of Brahms, we automatically arrive at the test equation of any metaphor: this-is-that; Juliet is the sun.

Secondly, we must define *extrinsic* metaphors, by which musical meanings relate to non-musical meanings. In other words, certain semantic meanings belonging to the so-called 'real world', the 'world out there'—the *non*-musical world—are assigned to musical art in terms of literal semantic values, namely extramusical ones. This form of this-equals-that is typified in Beethoven's 'Pastorale' Symphony (which we will be hearing after the intermission), in which certain notes are *meant* to be associated in the listener's mind with certain images, such as merry peasants, brooks, and birds. In other words, these notes equal those birds; *these are those*. It is a variation of the old formula.

And finally, we must think of metaphor in an *analogical* way, as we compare those intrinsic musical metaphors with their counterparts in speech, strictly verbal ones; and this comparison is in itself a metaphorical operation. It says: this musical transformation is like that verbal one; this is like that. Delete 'like', and you have the metaphor.

Now, having defined my usages of 'metaphor', I suppose I am committed to plunging into the perennial aesthetic debate. It's a debate I don't particularly wish to prolong. So many excellent and sensitive minds have wrestled with this problem of the Meaning of Music, to say nothing of the Meaning of Meaning: Santayana and Croce, Prall and Pratt, I. A. Richards, Suzanne Langer, Bergson, Beardsley, Birkoff, and Babbitt—and Stravinsky himself. One thing they have always agreed on, in one way or another, is that musical meaning *does* exist, whether rational or affective or both. As hard as they have all tried to be logical, to avoid romantic generalizing or philosophical maundering, they have all had to bow eventually to some nagging truth which insists that those innocent F sharps and B flats, however sportively juggled or played with, do emerge from a composer's mind meaning something, nay, expressing something—and expressing what may otherwise be inexpressible.

But wait: isn't there a difference between 'meaning' and 'expressing'? There is, if we are to be at all accurate. When a piece of music 'means' something to me, it is a meaning conveyed by the sounding notes themselves—what Eduard Hanslick called 'sonorous forms in motion' (a wonderful phrase), and I can report those meanings back to you precisely in terms of those forms. But when music 'expresses' something to me, it is something I am feeling, and the same is true of you and of every listener. We feel passion, we feel glory, we feel mystery, we *feel something*. And here we are in trouble; because we cannot report our precise feelings in scientific terms; we can report them only subjectively. If we could collect sample 'feelings' from a concert audience, lay them slide by slide on a lab table, compare them and find them consistent, *then* we'd know something, then science would smile on our endeavours. But alas, 'feelings', whatever they are, slither past the scientific laboratory, and we are left asking such pseudo-scientific questions as, 'Where does *affect* come into all this? Is it those intrinsic musical meanings that move us so deeply, or is there a transference of affect, via the notes, from the composer to the performer to the listener?'

On Musical Structuralism

PATRICIA TUNSTALL

For several theorists, the tools and concepts of semiology have been considered useful as a model for a musical structuralism. However, the reliance upon semiology as it has been developed in other fields of analysis raises central difficulties. As a rule, semiologists take from Saussure the definition of semiology as the science of signs, and the definition of a sign as the existence of a one-to-one relation between a signifier and a signified. The application of the latter definition to music reawakens a long-standing issue in music aesthetics: what kinds of things are 'signified' by the elements of music? Many hypotheses have been suggested by those interested in semiological research (see Subotnik 1978). David Osmond-Smith writes that the term 'semiotics' should perhaps be used in reference to the specific semantic meanings sometimes found in music, such as an instrumental imitation of a non-musical sound (1971). Sociological analyses offer a definition for the meaning of music closely allied with its social functions. (see Etzkorn 1974). The semiologist Roland Barthes claims that the elements of aesthetic objects carry connotations as well as denotations: the signifieds of such objects therefore include both semantic and ideological meanings (1967).

However, no agreement seems to exist among musical semiologists about the definition of music's signifieds. Nattiez, for example, rejects all the kinds of meanings cited above. He declares that semiology is not the study of 'the expressive, semantic aspect of music' (1974: 61); neither is it the determination of 'the connections between certain sonorous combinations and certain social structures' (71). In Nattiez's view, these purposes rule out the level of scientific rigour that, for him, is the distinguishing feature of semiological inquiry. The work of Roland Barthes he finds particularly unscientific: 'he gives the illusion of science to a procedure that is nothing other than the course of traditional hermeneutics' (67). According to Nattiez, semiotics must entirely disregard the question of music's meanings, and investigate only the internal arrangements of its elements.

If this is the case, however, the usefulness of semiological procedures as they have been developed in other fields is called into question. Semiological investigations of other art forms are usually undertaken with attention to the semantic as well as the syntactical properties of artistic elements. It is, in fact, precisely the existence of *both* kinds of properties that makes these investigations illuminating. A semiological analysis of a work of art or literature entails a structural reorganization of its formal elements, but that reorganization is accomplished with reference to semantic meanings; the reinterpretation of relations among elements depends partially upon the semantic associations of those elements. Works of literature or art are seen to involve meaning on several different levels—syntactical, semantic, connotative—and these levels must be considered in relation to each other. Semantic meanings may reveal implicit syntactical connections, for example; conversely, discovery of syntactical connections may reveal implicit semantic meanings. The analytic task is thus a charting of the structural relations among different levels of meaning. The organizational patterns of signifiers, in other words, are examined with reference to signifieds. The conclusions of semiological enquiries often rely upon such references.

Musical analysis, however, cannot rely upon a systematic reference to signifieds in its investigation of signifiers. Music seems to involve primarily syntactical, not semantic, relations; it does not exhibit a systematic one-to-one correspondence of each specific musical element with a specific non-musical meaning. According to Saussure's definition, then, music must be considered not a system of signs but a system of signifiers without signifieds. Therefore musical analyses can make only limited use of the particular virtues of the semiological approach.

This is not to say that musical structuralism is unviable, but that semiological models may not be its most useful tools. Although musical elements do not have semantic meanings, their organizational patterns may have extra-musical significance. The general goal of all structuralist endeavour is to examine the structural characteristics of objects in order to form hypotheses about the structural categories of cultures and the structural procedures of the human mind. Musical structuralism implies that such examinations do not necessarily have to involve semantic components; music's value for structuralism may lie precisely in the fact that it is *not* semantic. Its unique feature is that it lacks the kinds of meanings that semiological techniques are designed to investigate, but does not lack the kinds of significance with which structuralism is ultimately concerned. Its elements are not signs, but the relations between them are coherent and meaningful. It is these relations themselves, the formal operations performed upon sonorous elements, that are the essence of musical structure. Perhaps, then, that structure is a uniquely lucid and unmediated reflection of the formal operations of cognition.

Lévi-Strauss was one of the first to suggest that music's 'intelligible but untranslatable' nature makes it especially important for structuralism. As a sensuous manifestation not of concepts but of operations, music provides an unusually clear demonstration of the basic ordering processes of the mind. Unclouded by semantic associations, the procedures of music reflect not the mind's ideas but only its activities. It is thus an eminently appropriate object for an enquiry concerned with the nature of mental activity itself.

It is perhaps significant that Blacking does not invoke specifically semiological concepts and models; his work allows for the potential development of new concepts and models suited for the analysis of the uniquely abstract kinds of meaning found in music. Like Lévi-Strauss, Blacking finds that music involves a synthesis of immanent, untranslatable structuring activity with culturally particularized forms. The analysis of musical structure may therefore be most fruitful for an understanding of mental structures and for the ways such structures emerge within specific cultures. Suggests Blacking, 'Music may express the quintessence of a society's socio-conceptual structure and hence serve as a kind of litmus paper for structuralist analysis' (1972: 6). Blacking enriches structuralist thought with a new formulation of the concept of 'transformation', suggesting that musical transformations reveal the precise connections between universal logical processes and culturally specific ones. Musical transformations occur, argues Blacking, in relation to social experience: the capacity for transformation may be universal, but is only activated under the stimulation of social phenomena. 'By observing the patterns of social interaction which mediate between the innate structure of the mind and its extensions in culture, ethnomusicology can demonstrate the affective, social basis of musical transformations' (1972: 9).

In conclusion, musical analysis may be most enlightened by those structuralist principles that are *not* specifically borrowed from semiological endeavours in other fields. The application to music of a science of signs may eventually yield disappointing results: this science is oriented towards a kind of extramusical significance that music may not have and, when divorced from that orientation, may not yield substantially enlightening analyses. The structuralist interest in basic logical processes, on the other hand, invites a search for other kinds of extramusical significance, and this search may prove more rewarding. By bringing to musical analysis a desire to illuminate the rational character of musical processes, and to speculate upon the extramusical implications of those processes, a structuralist musicology will link its premises and goals to the traditions of its philosophical antecedents. This emphasis upon the cognitive dimensions of musical activity may provide new insights both about cognition and about music.

On Music and Myth

EERO TARASTI

In the last chapter, 'Finale', of *Mythologiques*, Lévi-Strauss discusses the place of music in the field of structural studies, which include four impor-tant spheres, those of mathematics, language, music, and mythology (1971: 578).

When comparing these spheres one will notice that mathematical structures are lacking all concreteness and in this respect are opposed to linguistic facts. Linguistic structures on the contrary are, as is shown by Saussure, doubly con-crete because their fulfilment implies sounds as well as meanings, Musical structures are composed of sounds but on the other hand they are detached from meanings, according to Lévi-Strauss. Mythical structures, on the other hand, consist of meanings, but their phonetic manifestation is irrelevant; in other words, the same myth could be told in different ways with the mythical value remaining unchanged. The relations among these cultural phenomena can be outlined with the following schema:

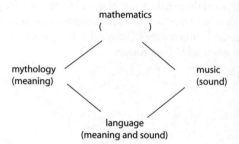

Accordingly, music and mythology are like two offshoots of language, each branching off in its own direction. They both are languages lacking in something. As Lévi-Strauss says, (1971: 579), music is language without meaning (*La musique, c'est le langage moins le sens*) and therefore it is easy to explain why a listener to music feels an irresistible need to fill this gap with meanings provided by himself. In an analogous way myths, i.e. systems of meanings, can detach themselves from their verbal foundation to which they are not as strictly bound as ordinary messages. Consequently, it is valid to con-

Myth and Music: A Semiotic Approach to the Aesthetics of Myth in Music, especially that of Wagner, Sibelius and Stravinsky (The Hague: Mouton, 1979), 29–32.

sider myth and music as closely related when observing their specific sign structure.

However, Lévi-Strauss overlooks one possible relation between myth and music: he does not discuss a case in which music could acquire meaning or content from mythology, just as mythology could in part acquire sound from music, as it does in a ritual, for example, where myth may be performed with a song melody.

Although the tonal structures may be imbued with many different semantic contents in the minds of listeners, this does not prevent the firm interweaving of myth and music in a given cultural context. The listeners would then, with instinctive sureness (which, of course, would none the less be conditioned by cultural conventions) associate certain mythical figures with musical forms. This fact could hold true especially for cultures in which a strong and coherent tradition prevails. Consequently one might conclude that music in some cases could entirely replace a mythical text. Charles Boilès (1973) has been able to show in his study about music in the ritual life of the Tepehua Indians that this may occur at least in the so-called primitive musical cultures. He has observed that the Tepehuas associate certain meanings with their instrumental melodies so that there exist fully prescribed equivalences between melodic phrases and semantic meanings. These meanings are mythical, because it is the task of music to establish communication between man and the spirits. But what is remarkable is that the Indians even outside the ritual can explain precisely the mythical meanings of any tune. Do such associations take place in the field of Western art music, too?

This might well be the case if it happens in a cultural context sufficiently strong and homogeneous. Since music 'in the first place is an expression of man's spiritual, psychical life', as Hugo Riemann has stated (1928: 7), one might presume that in such a culture music and its aesthetic contents would reflect also the world-view and mythology characteristic of that culture. This would simply once again emphasize the relationship between the mythical sphere and what in the Western civilization is called an 'aesthetic' imagination and fantasy.

Resting on this hypothesis, a model can be constructed in order to make the nature of such musical communication more precise. Furthermore, this diagram presupposes that a musical work is placed on two levels, technical and aesthetic, as Rudolph Reti (1961: 136) has proposed (or translated into a 'structuralist' language on the levels of 'signifier' and 'signified') (see Ducrot and Todorov 1972: 132; Nattiez 1975: 52).

(In this context it would be superfluous to discuss whether this kind of articulation of a musical sign system is legitimate or not, which certainly constitutes an essential problem for music aesthetics.)

	Form	Substance
Expression (composer) technical level	A musical work created by a composer while setting a form upon the substance of music expression	The first articulation of culture whereby a culture yields the musical substance among other acoustics codes i.e. scales, rhythms, dynamics, timbres, etc.
Content (listener) aesthetic level	The second articulation of culture whereby a culture determines the patterns and symbols which permit a listener to interpret his responses to a musical work	The associative responses aroused by the composition in a listener

This model presents a musical communication where a composer functions as the sender of the message and a listener as its receiver.

Besides the aspects of expression and content, the form and substance of the composition are involved. The intervention of culture is also displayed in the form of double articulation. The first articulation affects the substance of musical expression and the second one the form of content. Consequently two different structures determine a musical communication: the first is manifested in the form which a composer sets upon the musical substance afforded by culture, while the latter is in the form which a culture gives to the individual listener's musical experience.

In addition to this the existence of a third structure or code can be assumed. It is not shown in the model, but it would connect the two forms which are set apart on different levels of expression and content. As will be later affirmed, the whole present study will be focused on this code since it refers to the very problem of interaction between myth and music.

One might thus ask whether this sort of code can be determined universally and conclusively regarding the music of a given period or whether it varies according to composer and audience. Later some variants of just this connecting code will be discussed, particularly their regulation of the interaction between myth and music in the history of Western music since Romanticism, and their determination of its modality during each era. In the second part of the study one will also see how this code varies according to different musical styles, as exemplified by Wagner, Sibelius, and Stravinsky.

Earlier, in dealing with Barthes's theory, one possible variant of this code was touched upon, namely that in which myth subsumes other sign systems and forces them to relinquish partially their meaningfulness.

The foregoing model approaches this situation from the opposite viewpoint, namely that of music, where music in turn may profit from myth, deriving complementary content from it. The influence of myth is then manifested within the second articulation of culture.

As to the function of culture in the chart, one may observe that a given musical culture provides a composer with substance for composition; in other words, scales (established by a tuning system), rhythms, dynamics, harmonic progressions, etc. which are given a form by a composer in his composition. Concerning the listener, culture operates in the opposite direction establishing a form for his experiences, and it is due to this form that the meaning discovered in a musical work by a listener is the 'logical expression' of his internal feelings and not merely an emotional stimulant, as Susanne Langer has remarked (1951: 185). These forms are in the nature of universal patterns, 'archetypes' which arise from the subconscious of the listener and thus constitute a part of the stock of symbols common to every music listener of the period. Sometimes these patterns even include entire myths, as does the Finnish Kullervo-myth in the symphony of Sibelius, or a collection of myths as in Wagner's *Ring* tetralogy. Occasionally a mythical pattern is reduced to a mere 'nature-mythical' or 'psychic-mythical' element (to use the terminology of Jaspers 1919: 139–41, 156–8) as it often is in the symphonic poems of Liszt and of other Romantic composers.

On the other hand, it sould be obvious that, regarding the content of his own composition, a composer himself is not in any privileged position but is only one of numerous listeners, who experience a musical work in various ways. One might even claim that it is just this fact which renders some compositions 'immortal' master works: they are no longer dependent on their composer's historical position or era for they represent their content in such a general and universal manner that even the listeners of highly disparate eras or cultures can provide their own 'mythical' interpretation of the contents and consequently experience them always as subjective and timely. In such cases it would be difficult to assign any concrete mythical pattern to music since one is now confronted with pure structures of musical, as well as mythical thought.

On the Semiotics of Music

GINO STEFANI

Musical experience is obviously ruled by a great number of codes. What criteria does our choice meet? In brief, our model has been found, by trial and error, to be the most economical one to represent simultaneously both common and specialized competence—that is, to put artistic projects into the general framework of social projects in sounds and music. This is also a good approach for the evaluation of both popular music and contemporary art music.

Our Model of Musical Competence (MMC) consists of a set of code levels articulated as follows:

General Codes (GC): perceptual and mental schemes, anthropological attitudes and motivations, basic conventions through which we perceive or construct or interpret every experience (and therefore every sound experience).

Social Practices (SP): projects and modes of both material and symbolic production within a certain society; in other words, cultural institutions such as language, religion, industrial work, technology, sciences, etcetera, including musical practices (concert, ballet, opera, criticism).

Musical Techniques (MT): theories, methods, and devices which are more or less specific and exclusive to musical practices, such as instrumental techniques, scales, composition forms, etcetera.

Styles (St): historical periods, cultural movements, authors, or groups of works; that is, the particular ways in which MT, SP, and GC are concretely realized.

Opus (Op): single musical works or events in their concrete individuality.

Let us see now all these levels of musical sense in an interpretation of a popular item, the beginning of Beethoven's Fifth Symphony.

GC. In the famous theme:
we hear two sets of sound impulses, of medium strength and consistency, well marked, relatively short, in a medium-low register, neither dry nor soft. These sound events can easily be interpreted as two sets of 'strokes'.

'A Theory of Musical Competence', *Semiotica*, 66:1/3 (1987), 9–15.

SP. From the GC, as well as from the overall form of the sequence—three short strokes followed by a longer one; then a short silence followed by a repetition of the pattern—we easily get the idea of something or somebody striking in a somewhat ritualized and conventional way, as if knocking at the door. In this we identify a signal of beginning, which creates a sense of suspense and expectation—like an announcement, or an entry in a ceremony, or the introduction of a speech.

MT. The phrase begins with the sequence G–G–G–E flat—our set of 'strokes' is 'musically' structured. These sound impulses (at least the first three of them) have a precise duration and a metrical position, a definite height on the staff, and a certain tonal function. The technical code also presents us with ambiguity, suspense, and expectation. This strange motive is not a 'melody'; its key is uncertain (C minor? E flat major?); it would be very difficult to foresee what follows these two short segments of notes.

St. However, every 'native speaker' of our main Western musical language is able to hear this beginning as a gesture of command and drama. Many of us perceive in it, more precisely, something like that 'titanic heroism' or 'heroic titanism' which traditional criticism ascribes to Beethoven's music, and we all recognize the style and content of the Fifth Symphony as a whole as Beethoven's.

Op. The beginning of this work—the motive dramatically bursting in, introducing and anticipating in a generative synthesis the whole 'history' of the first movement—was interpreted by its author as a good metaphor for 'fate knocking at the door', and it has been recognized as such everywhere, by both the public and the critics, since 1808.

Obviously we do not assert here that Beethoven's work is nothing but 'the symphony of fate'; many other interpretations would be pertinent. What we intend to do here is simply to indicate how our model can function when applied to the production of sense about a concrete piece of music.

The Levels

We have looked at our model as a whole. Now let us examine its individual levels more closely.

General Codes (GC)

At the root of any production of sense upon sound and music events we find the general codes through which we perceive and interpret every experience. They are first of all the sensorial-perceptual schemes (spatial, tactile, dynamic, thermic, kinetic, etcetera) which enable us to classify a sound as high/low, near/remote, hard/soft, clear/dark, warm/cold, strong/weak, etcetera. At the same level we find the logical schemes (that is, more or less elementary processes and mental operations) by means of which we apply to everything—and therefore to sound as well—such categories as identity, similarity, continuity/discontinuity, equivalence, opposition, symmetry, transformation, etcetera.

We also include in this basic stratum of general codes those more complex categories which *homo faber, ludens, loquens* elaborates from everyday experience, both natural and cultural. We mean those common categories by which we describe an object or events as 'made this way'—for example, granular, compact, flowing, in a rounded or pointed form, like a constellation, growing slowly or by a set of explosions, in a wave form; in short, any one of the processes of which everyday life gives us countless examples. How many processes of this kind have given an explicit model for musical composition since 1950?

The competence level, which itself can be divided into many sub-levels, is the most basic and common. One might call it the 'anthropological level' of musical competence, were the term not so full of implications. We find here sound as matter or material, and the interaction between sound and sense, sound and mind. Most pedagogical projects, clinical practices, and the poetics of Cage (1961) are primarily founded upon this stratum of sense production. But the example from Beethoven has shown us that it can *never* be regarded as a parenthesis. Another important point is that everybody may exercise this stratum of codes with music.

Intertextuality?

Social Practices (SP)

Sense production in music then proceeds through codes pertaining to certain social practices. It is in this way, for instance, that the beginning of a piece of music is built and/or interpreted as a ceremonial entry or the introduction to a speech; that the articulation of a melody is described as a 'phrasing' as if it were a verbal discourse, that the curves and inflections in a melody reflect the intonations of speech, or that so many musical rhythms and meters immediately recall similar or identical features of poetry and dance, and so on. It is by this network of sense that one eventually manages to build up, more or less systematically, the relationships between music and society or, rather, between the various social practices of a culture.

As for the past, 'musical genres' give us evidence of social practices in music—think of marches, hymns, berceuses, serenades, entratas, preludes, dances, operas, and ritual forms. The practices of language, ritual, theatre, and spectacle are still important codes for both producing and interpreting musical events. Since the 1950s scientific practices have also provided musical 'inspiration', for instance mathematics with combinatorial and stochastic models.

This competence level, though vast, does not have the anthropological application of the former. In fact, many social practices are limited to a certain human group, sometimes very small. Within this group, however, it is something which is codified and recognizable by every member, according to the degree of their socialization or 'general culture'.

At the bottom, this level is close to general codes; at the top, we find a set of social practices related to musical codes, and therefore called 'musical practices': singing, playing, and composing, as well as social institutions such as concerts, opera, theatre, music schools, music laboratories, criticism, and musicology. As one can see, both musical and non-musical practices contribute to sense production in music in different but equally important ways. Take for instance Ligeti's *Lux aeterna*: the meaning it gained from Kubrick's

2001: A Space Odyssey is probably as important as that given to it by a musico-logical approach. Besides, many contemporary experiences (Cage and computer music, for instance), having apparently little relevance in such a musical practice as the concert, may become more relevant in a non-musical practice such as theatre or lecture.

Musical Techniques (MT)

In our culture—throughout the history of the world—there is a place for codes which are more specifically 'musical', being connected with techniques, instruments, systems, and devices specially designed or employed for music-making. This is what usually is viewed as 'musical competence' with no further qualification, whereas in our model it is only one of the competence levels.

Let us recall our introductory comment about codes: they are not only supporting structures but also significant correlations. In this perspective, musical systems as codes mean musical 'languages'. Musicians and musicologists have a tendency to neglect or even to deny the semantic thickness of techniques; thus they consider music essentially as the production of objects or events. But for our society as a whole, for its general competence in music, music is always the production of signs. It is therefore particularly important here to consider ordinary people, what they think and feel about musical 'language', and what they do with it.

According to a widespread opinion, 'laymen' are ignorant about musical techniques; they do not 'understand' musical language (Karolyi 1965: preface). As one can see, confusion reigns here between *linguistic* competence and *grammatical* competence. Speaking and understanding a language is different from studying its written grammar and theory. Now, the 'language' of our traditional music belongs to common culture; therefore the psychologist Robert Francès (1958) spoke of a 'musical mother tongue of Western people'.

We do not intend to describe this language here. We only want to recall two main features pertinent to our model: (1) its heterogeneous character, and (2) its functioning as a code in the full semiotic sense—that is, as a rule for correlating *expression* and *content*. Its heterogeneity strikes us immediately when we think of the different 'qualities' or 'parameters' constituting music: pitch, duration, dynamics, timbre, articulation, types of attack, etcetera. In fact, each of them is organized by codes which are disparate, independent, and of different strength. Even the code appearing to be the strongest one, the tonal code, is in fact a 'hypercode' which is built with the contribution of different syntactic-semantic layers, among which we may indicate: the octave pattern (expression of emphasis); the scale and individual intervals (Cooke 1959); major/minor modes with their bipolar 'ethos' still persisting in every kind of hearer; tonal syntax with its 'embodied meaning' (Meyer 1956, 1973; and Francès 1958); chordal features (consonant/dissonant); etcetera. Even more heterogeneous are the 'rhetoric' codes regulating the organization and perception of polyphonic devices, melodic structures, and musical 'forms'.

In view of this complexity it is easy to see the inadequacy of the current idea of a 'musical language' as something coherent, composed of many 'elements' hierarchically linked by a single principle—which in fact remains unstated.

diverse in character or content (OED)

What advantage does our model offer, then, by describing musical language as a stratification of levels which are more or less 'coalescent', as Boulez (1963) would say? Perhaps the most prominent is the fact that, by embedding 'pre-musical' levels, our model allows us to embody not only systems of morphology, syntax, and rhetoric, but also those 'speech acts' or 'communication acts' which explain—to a certain extent—the constitution and working of these 'technical' levels.

In fact, all the various techniques and rules for intervals, dynamics, timbre, and rhetoric embodied in a Sonata, or a Fugue, or a Concerto do not provide unity themselves; unity comes rather from projects and modes of behaviour which stand before or beyond techniques—that is, at GC and SP as well as St and Op levels.

Besides, depending on the technical competence of musicians, one can make music by means of any system or device; the result would automatically be a musical 'language' with as much right to be so termed as the tonal one. Actually, this idea was widespread for some decades concerning twelve-tone technique and enlarged seriality, which were considered a historically necessary evolution of the traditional musical 'language'.

The relativity of this perspective, which neglects the social aspect of language with its semantic and pragmatic implications, appears clearly in the light of our model. In this light twelve-tone technique takes on two meanings: (1) an extension of MT from inside (as in musicians' and theorists' views), and (2) an integration into the MT level of processes which originate from SP or GC levels. This integration, of course, is not at all in the nature of things, but requires motivation again to be found in previous competence levels.

It is at the MT level that one usually begins to find applicable the definition of music as 'the art of sounds', which in a narrower sense can be reformulated as 'the art of notes'. In the frame of our model this definition shows itself to be inadequate. In fact, on the one hand artistic projects with sounds can be realized outside the specific MT level (for instance, with elementary sound events); on the other, MT serve also for SP (signalling, rites, therapy, etcetera) where the artistic project is not primary or relevant.

Styles (St)

Both Corelli and Beethoven employ certain musical systems, but each in a different way and with different meanings; that is, in a different style. 'Style' is a blend of technical features, a way of forming objects or events; but it is at the same time a trace in music of agents and processes and contexts of production. Stylistic competence is, therefore, the ability to form and/or interpret both aspects.

In normal cases, the distinction between these two aspects passes unnoticed. So when speaking of baroque, romantic, Beethovenian, or expressionist style we may mean, simultaneously or separately, both the musical signifier and the historical and cultural signified. Style codes are thus rooted on the one hand in MT, and on the other in SP. To MT the new competence adds an inventive way of using systems; to SP it adds the experience of precise contexts and circumstances.

According to some scholars (for example, Nattiez 1975), when dealing with music one should not speak of 'systems' or languages, but only of styles (tonal, twelve-tone, etcetera). From our point of view, this approach privileges the construction of sound objects as well as the autonomy of artistic projects, at the expense of the social functions and practices which give sense to those projects and objects. Pursuing this idea to its logical conclusion, we should here speak only of idiolects—that is, styles peculiar to single works and not susceptible to generalization into common schemes. In that case, no language could exist.

Opus (Op)

In a minimal sense, competence at opus or work level is the trivial fact of recognizing a piece; for example, 'this is Beethoven's Fifth Symphony'. Recognizing in this way is normally the lowest degree in sense production, an exercise of repetition and reproduction of identity. Only in particular cases can it become a valuable exercise requiring a considerable amount of intelligence (such as when guessing some piece which is not so very well known).

As we have said before, in our traditional highbrow culture Op level is the most pertinent to artistic projects and to the social practices which make them concrete. So in a concert, for instance, what we are directly confronted with are neither techniques nor style, but individual works. In fact, criticism—which is the most typical act of highbrow musical competence—is usually a discourse about single works. However, this has not been the only perspective in our history, nor is it today. The absolute primacy of the work as a finished product has been denied in jazz, folksong, contemporary poetics, and musical life in general because of the manifold functions we recognize in music in so many contexts, especially through mass media.

Besides, creativity displays itself in several phases: projects, models, and programmes are often valuable in themselves and for their capacity to engender a great number of concrete realizations, independently of that particular realization which is called the 'opus'. After all, working with sounds does not always end in finished 'works'. Discovering and extending the processes of sense production with sounds can be as interesting musically as hearing a good piece of music.

References

Abbate, Carolyn (1991), *Unsung Voices: Opera and Musical Narrative in the Nineteenth Century* (Princeton: Princeton University Press).

Barthes, Roland (1967), *Elements of Semiology*, trans. Annette Lavers and Colin Smith (New York: Hill & Wang).

Bernstein, Leonard (1976), *The Unanswered Question: Six Talks at Harvard* (Cambridge, Mass.: Harvard University Press).

Blacking, John (1972), 'The Existence and Limits of Musical Transformations', paper delivered to the Society for Ethnomusicology Congress, Toronto.

—— (1973), *How Musical Is Man?* (London: Faber).

Boilès, Charles (1967), 'Tepehua Thought-Song', *Ethnomusicology* 11:3, 267–92.

—— (1973), '*Les Chants instrumentaux des Tepehuas*', *Musique en jeu* 12.

Boulez, Pierre (1963), *Penser la musique aujourd'hui* (Paris: Gonthier).

Bourdieu, Pierre (1984), *Distinction: A Social Critique of the Judgement of Taste*, trans. Richard Nice (London: Routledge).

Bright, William (1963), 'Language and Music: Areas for Cooperation', *Ethnomusicology* 7:1, 26–32.

Cage, John (1961), *Silence* (Middletown, Conn.: Wesleyan University Press).

Cooke, Deryck (1959), *The Language of Music* (Oxford: Oxford University Press).

—— (1974), 'The Future of *The Language of Music*', in *Vindications: Essays on Romantic Music* (London: Faber, 1982), 215–22.

Deleuze, Gilles, and Guattari, Félix (1988), *A Thousand Plateaus* (London: Athlone).

Deva, B. Caitanya, and Virmani, K. G. (1968), 'Meaning of Music: An Empirical Study of Psychological Responses to Indian Music', *Sangeet Natak* 10, 54–93.

———— (1974), *Semantic Descriptions and Synesthesic Relations of Raga-s*, Research Report II (New Delhi: Sangeet Natak Akademi).

Ducrot, Oswald, and Todorov, Tzetan (1972), *Dictionnaire encyclopédique des sciences du langage* (Paris).

Eco, Umberto (1977), *A Theory of Semiotics* (London: Macmillan).

Etzkorn, K. P. (1974), 'On Music, Social Structure and Sociology', *International Review of Aesthetics and Musical Sociology* 5, 43–9.

Feld, Steven (1974), 'Linguistic Models in Ethnomusicology', *Ethnomusicology* 18:2, 179–217.

—— (1982), *Sound and Sentiment: Birds, Weeping, Poetics and Song in Kaluli Expression* (Philadelphia: University of Pennsylvania Press).

Francès, Robert (1958), *La Perception de la musique* (Paris: Vrin).

Gerbert, Martin (1784) (ed.), *Scriptores Ecclesiastici de Musica Sacra Potissimum*, 3 vols. (St-Blaise).

Jaspers, Karl (1919), *Psychologie der Weltanschauungungen* (Berlin).

Karolyi, Otto (1965), *Introducing Music* (Harmondsworth: Penguin).

Keil, Charles, and Keil, Angeliki (1966), 'Musical Meaning: A Preliminary Report', *Ethnomusicology* 10:2, 153–73.

Kramer, Lawrence (1990), *Music as Cultural Practice: 1800–1900* (Berkeley: University of California Press).

—— (1995), *Classical Music and Postmodern Knowledge* (Berkeley: University of California Press).

Labov, William (1972), *Sociolinguistic Patterns* (Philadelphia: University of Pennsylvania Press).

Langer, Susanne (1951), *Philosophy in a New Key* (New York).

Lévi-Strauss, Claude (1971), *L'Homme nu* (Paris).

—— (1986), *The Raw and the Cooked: Introduction to a Science of Mythology* (orig. pub. 1964 as *Le Cru et le Cuit*, Libraire Plon), trans. John and Doreen Weightman (Harmondsworth: Penguin).

Merriam, Alan P. (1964), *The Anthropology of Music* (Evanston, Ill.: Northwestern University Press).

Meyer, Leonard B. (1956), *Emotion and Meaning in Music* (Chicago: University of Chicago Press).

—— (1973), *Explaining Music* (Berkeley: University of California Press).

Monelle, Raymond (1991), 'Structural Semantics and Instrumental Music', *Music Analysis*, Vol. 10, Nos. 1–2, 73–88.

Nattiez, Jean-Jacques (1974), 'Sur les relations entre sociologie et semiologie musicales', *International Review of Aesthetics and Musical Sociology* 5.

—— (1975), *Fondements d'une sémiologie de la musique* (Paris: Union Générale d'Éditions).

—— (1990), *Music and Discourse: Toward a Semiology of Music*, trans. Carolyn Abbate (Princeton: Princeton University Press).

Noske, Frits (1977), *The Signifier and the Signified* (The Hague: Nijhoff).

Osmond-Smith, David (1971), 'Music as Communication: Semiology or Morphology?', *International Review of Aesthetics and Musical Sociology* 5, 108–11.

Powers, Harold S. (1962), '*Il Serse* Transformato', *Musical Quarterly* 48:1, 73–92.

—— (1968), '*L'Erismena* Travestita', in H. S. Powers (ed.), *Studies in Music History: Essays for Oliver Strunk* (Princeton: Princeton University Press), 259–324.

—— (1977), 'The Structure of Musical Meaning: A View from Banaras', *Perspectives of New Music* 14:2/15:1, 308–34.

—— (1980), 'Language Models and Musical Analysis', *Ethnomusicology* 24:1, 1–60; reprinted in *The Garland Library of the History of Western Music* (New York 1985), 13:193–252, and in *The Garland Library of Readings in Ethnomusicology* (New York 1990), 5: 303–62.

—— (1995), 'Reading Mozart's Music: Text and Topic, Syntax and Sense', *Current Musicology* 57, 5–44.

—— (1996), '*A Canonical Museum of Imaginary Music*', *Current Musicology* 60/61, 5–25.

—— (1998), 'Music as Text and Text as Music', in *Musik als Text: Bericht über den Internationalen Kongreß der Gesellschaft für Musikforschung Freiburg im Breisgau 1993*, I (Kassel: Bärenreiter Verlag), 6–37.

Reti, Rudolph (1961), *The Thematic Process in Music* (Oxford).

Riemann, Hugo (1928), *Grundriss der Musikwissenschaft* (Leipzig).

Stefani, Gino (1987), 'A Theory of Musical Competence', *Semiotica* 66:1/3, 7–22.

Subotnik, Rose Rosengard (1978), 'The Cultural Message of Musical Semiology', *Critical Inquiry* 4, 741–68; repr. in *Developing Variations* (Minneapolis: University of Minnesota, 1991), 169–94.

Tagg, Philip (1982), 'Analysing Popular Music: Theory, Method and Practice', in D. Horn and R. Middleton (eds.), *Popular Music Yearbook* (Cambridge), 37–67.

—— (1987), 'Musicology and the Semiotics of Popular Music', *Semiotica* 66:1/3, 279–98.

Tarasti, Eero (1979), *Myth and Music: A Semiotic Approach to the Aesthetics of Myth in Music, especially that of Wagner, Sibelius and Stravinsky* (The Hague: Mouton).

Tarasti, Eero (1994), *A Theory of Musical Semiotics* (Bloomington: Indiana University Press).

Tunstall, Patricia (1979), 'Structuralism and Musicology: An Overview', *Current Musicology* 27, 51–64.

Part II

Music and the Body (Gender, Sexuality, and Ethnicity)

Introduction

This is neither a reader on diverse ethnic practices nor in feminist musicology; the excerpts in this section concern the need to develop a theoretical framework that returns music to the body and provides an understanding of cultural contexts, with all the ideological baggage that entails. For a recent survey of feminist musicology, see the collection of four articles headed 'Toward a Feminist Music Theory', in *Perspectives of New Music* 32:1 (Winter 1994), 6–85. Another overview is being written by Ruth Solie for the revised *New Grove*.

A caution is perhaps necessary at this point regarding the differing theoretical models that are applied in studies of culture and society. A cultural sociologist, for example, is inclined to emphasize the mediating role of cultural institutions, critics, and the media, and to support the idea of a self-expression varying according to social experience. A poststructuralist or semiotician, on the other hand, may be concerned to stress that meaning is discursively constructed, the link between signifier and signified is arbitrary, and that meanings rely solely on conventions. If this second paradigm is adopted, then it entails a reluctance to use a term like 'expression' since it implies that an inner human essence is being communicated. Instead, the focus is on the way meanings are constructed or encoded so as to produce a recognition of their validity, reality, or authenticity. For further information, see the Brief Explanatory Notes on Theory at the end of this book.

Until recently, musicology has steered away from questions of music's relation to the body. Symptomatic of this has been the neglect of dance (or of its removal from the discipline of Music to that of Performing Arts). It has been suggested that critics of Susan McClary's writings on music and sexuality have been disturbed most of all by 'the suggestion that, by losing control of one's body and by experiencing the sexual politics of music, one also loses control of the music itself' (Bohlman 1993: 431). In an openly polemical article (1991), McClary has argued that the typical nineteenth-century musical narrative of 'tonal striving, climax, and closure' (114) is phallic in character and not the value-free formal convention it is taken to be.

A pioneering article on sexuality in rock by Simon Frith and Angela McRobbie and a response by Jenny Taylor and Dave Laing appeared at a crucial time when what might be described broadly as a poststructuralist theoretical model was challenging the culturalist model. Two contending paradigms are displayed in these two pieces. The recurrent theme of the former article is of music as a means of sexual *expression*. The label 'cock rock' conveys neatly the phallic urgency of masculine representations in much rock and has entered the vocabulary of popular music criticism. It should be said that this excerpt does not, of course, represent Frith and McRobbie's last words on the subject; neither does it adequately indicate the theoretical richness of their later work. The reader is advised especially to seek out Frith's *Performing Rites* (1996), which confirms his status as one of the most important contributors to the criticism and theory of popular music.

The poststructuralist character of Taylor and Laing's critique is most clearly evident in their statement, 'what is at issue is not how much is revealed or expressed by a Frank Sinatra or a Thin Lizzy, but the radically different codes and conventions of representation involved in different genres'. They see the pitfalls of essentialism (the assumed communication of a 'natural' sexuality) in Frith and McRobbie's arguments. Ironically, the theory of the 'male gaze' that Taylor and Laing borrow from Laura Mulvey was, itself, later accused of essentialism (on the grounds of its being too biological) by gay and lesbian writers. It would now be preferable to state that the 'normatively masculine subject' is addressed rather than the 'male'. In analysing listening pleasure, the writers make reference to Roland Barthes's idea of the 'grain' of the voice (1977). Barthes defines the 'grain' as 'the body in the voice as it sings' (188), and insists elsewhere (185) that it is not merely the timbre of the voice. Barthes takes Julia Kristeva's terms 'geno-text' and 'pheno-text' and applies them to music as 'geno-song' and 'pheno-song'. In 'geno-song' the signified is ignored in favour of a sensually produced meaning Barthes calls *signifiance*. Barthes extends the idea of 'grain' to the impact of the performer's body in instrumental music, and concludes his essay by remarking that 'the simple consideration of "grain" in music could lead to a different history of music from the one we know (which is purely pheno-textual)'.

Charles Ford's critical and analytical study *Così*? (1991) locates Mozart's music firmly in its sociocultural and ideological context. He discusses both operatic masculinity and operatic femininity in this book, and is often concerned with uncovering representations of gender in phrase-grouping structures: he notes, for example, that typical 'feminine' groupings are accumulative, whereas 'masculine' groupings are hierarchic (see 181). According to Ford, a 'sense of a coherently hierarchised and dynamically closed field of presence . . . was as axiomatic for the Enlightenment's music as reasonable, individual male autonomy was for its literature' (150). As an example of its lack, he refers to the final 23-bar grouping of Dorabella and Fiodiligi's duet (*Così fan tutte*, no. 20, 'Prenderò quel brunnettino'). On a larger scale, he speaks of a rondo as being 'characteristically feminine, since relatively unstructured' (180). Ford also points to a variety of 'feminine' sub-styles, for instance, the 'diffuse and fluid sense of musical time' exemplified by 'Porgi amor' (150).

The emergence of gay and lesbian musicology has been of even more recent date. When the distinguished musicologist Philip Brett came out, enormous interest in this field was guaranteed. He and Elizabeth Wood are two of its best known scholars, and both feature prominently in an anthology of essays on gender and sexuality in musical scholarship edited by Ruth A. Solie (1993) as well as in the ground-breaking *Queering the Pitch* (1994), which they edited together with Gary Thomas. Wood develops a theory of the Sapphonic voice, by which term she means to suggest a voice that resonates 'in sonic space as lesbian difference and desire' (1994: 28). The voice type she has in mind is one with a wide compass embracing registers conventionally associated with other voice types. The Sapphonic voice refuses conventional categories, offering its own vocal construction of gender and sexuality.

In the next excerpt, David Hatch and Stephen Millward problematize the concept of black music. The intention is not to devalue the importance of black musicians to blues, jazz, and pop. Indeed, later in their book, they state: 'For many fans, the contribution of black musicians to pop is so overwhelmingly important as to be self-evident: this legacy therefore requires no defence. Notions such as "black music" may thus be seen to be counter-productive in that they call such a conclusion into question' (129). Though music itself cannot be labelled easily as 'black' or 'white', Portia Maultsby shows that black people have created, interpreted, and experienced music 'out of an African frame of reference', and that African retentions may exist 'as conceptual approaches—as unique ways of doing things and making things happen— rather than as specific cultural elements' (1990: 205).

John Blacking, coining his famous definition of music as 'humanly organized sound', posits the existence of universals in the *behaviours* that are particular to music. While this has similarities to the position adopted by Leonard B. Meyer (1960: 49–54), he is concerned to emphasize that only a 'context-sensitive analysis of the music in culture' (17–18) could lead to proper understanding of musical structure. This, he believed, would reveal a single valid explanation for each musical work. Nattiez disagrees (see 1990: 168). Blacking is also prepared to suggest the existence of 'universal structural principles in music', such as theme and variation, and binary form (112). He sees parallels between musical structures and Chomsky's ideas on deep and surface structures in language without, however, claiming that music is a kind of language (21–3). The apparent discovery of universals in cultural artefacts can usually be traced to an *etic* analysis (i.e. one based on the analyst's own epistemological standpoint and methodological paradigm) rather than an *emic* analysis (i.e. one informed by the participants in a particular culture). Blacking attempts to find a balance in his work between universal and cultural determinants.

Richard Leppert is an initiator of a new branch of music theory: his ambitious project has been to build a sophisticated theoretical model for understanding the connection between sight and sound in *non-theatrical* musical performance, particularly regarding the representation of such performance in fine art (his book *Music and Image* was a pioneering study). In *The Sight of Sound: Music, Representation, and the History of the Body* (1993), he presents the full spectrum of his perceptive ideas on the significance of the visual dimension of musical performance. However, in the given excerpt he is discussing the impact of upper-class ideology on the performance of country dances in eighteenth-century England. A discourse of bodily movement in these dances established a class hierarchy of the body.

Ralph Locke's article on Saint-Saëns's *Samson et Dalila* places the opera within 'an ideologically driven view of the East', and thus engages with theories of the cultural Other and of Orientalism. The latter term was coined by

Edward Said for his provocative study (1978) of the perceptions and treatment of the Arab world by Western scholars and politicians; this book provides useful information on the ideological context within which Saint-Saëns was working. *Samson* makes an intriguing object of study, since it is not typical of Orientalist operas, and Locke is concerned to avoid a reductive critique, such as an entirely negative reading suggesting covert racism. He offers, instead, a sense of the complexities and contradictions in the way ideology operates in this opera, and avoids a simplistic model for interpreting 'borrowings' from ethnic practices of the Middle East (for further discussion of such 'borrowings', see Locke 1998). Inevitably, however, some of the discussion has been curtailed in this excerpt, and characterization is not as deeply examined as in the full article where, for example, Locke explores Delilah's (feigned?) protestations of love and Samson's passive responses in their duet at the end of Act 2 ('Mon cœur s'ouvre à ta voix'). An intermediate-length version of the article (bearing the same title but incorporating more substantial revisions, especially within the opening) has appeared in Dellamora and Fischlin (1997: 161–84).

On the Expression of Sexuality

SIMON FRITH AND ANGELA MCROBBIE

Any analysis of the sexuality of rock must begin with the brute social fact that in terms of control and production, rock is a male form. The music business is male run; popular musicians, writers, creators, technicians, engineers and producers are mostly men. Female creative roles are limited and mediated through male notions of female ability. Women musicians who make it are almost always singers; the women in the business who make it are usually in publicity; in both roles success goes with a male-made female image. In general, popular music's images, values, and sentiments are male products. Not only do we find men occupying every important role in the rock industry and in effect being responsible for the creation and construction of suitable female images, we also witness in rock the presentation and marketing of masculine styles. And we are offered not one definitive image of masculine sexuality, but a variety of male sexual poses which are most often expressed in terms of stereotypes. One useful way of exploring these is to consider 'cock rock', on the one hand, and 'teenybop', on the other.

By cock rock we mean music-making in which performance is an explicit, crude and often aggressive expression of male sexuality—it's the style of rock presentation that links a rock and roller like Elvis Presley to rock stars like Mick Jagger, Roger Daltrey, and Robert Plant. The most popular exponents of this form currently are Thin Lizzy—their album *Live and Dangerous* articulates cock rock's values very clearly. Cock rock performers are aggressive, dominating, boastful, and constantly seek to remind the audience of their prowess, their control. Their stance is obvious in live shows; male bodies on display, plunging shirts and tight trousers, a visual emphasis on chest hair and genitals—their record sales depend on years of such appearances. In America, the mid-west concert belt has become the necessary starting point for cock rock success; in Britain the national popularity of acts like Thin Lizzy is the result of numberless tours of provincial dance halls. Cock rock shows are explicitly about male sexual performance (which may explain why so few girls go to them—the musicians are acting out a sexual iconography which in many ways is unfamiliar, frightening and distasteful to girls who are educated into understanding sex as something nice, soft, loving, and private). In these performances mikes and guitars are phallic symbols; the music is loud, rhythmically insistent, built round techniques of arousal and climax; the lyrics are assertive and arrogant, though the exact words are less significant than the vocal styles involved, the

'Rock and Sexuality', *Screen Education*, 29 (1979), 5–8, 12–15.

shouting and screaming. The cock rock image is the rampant destructive male traveller, smashing hotels and groupies alike. Musically, such rock takes off from the sexual frankness of rhythm and blues but adds a cruder male physicality (hardness, control, virtuosity). Cock rockers' musical skills become synonymous with their sexual skills (hence Jimi Hendrix's simultaneous status as stud and guitar hero). Cock rockers are not bound by the conventions of the song form, but use their instruments to show 'what they've got', to give vent to their macho imagination. These are the men who take to the streets, take risks, live dangerously and, most of all, swagger untrammelled by responsibility, sexual and otherwise. And, what's more, they want to make this clear. Women, in their eyes, are either sexually aggressive and therefore doomed and unhappy, or else sexually repressed and therefore in need of male servicing. It's the woman, whether romanticized or not, who is seen as possessive, after a husband, anti-freedom, the ultimate restriction.

Teenybop, in contrast, is consumed almost exclusively by girls. What they're buying is also a representation of male sexuality (usually in the form of teen idols) but the nature of the image and the version of sexuality on display is quite distinct from that of the cock rocker. The teenybop idol's image is based on self-pity, vulnerability, and need. The image is of the young boy next door: sad, thoughtful, pretty, and puppy-like. Lyrically his songs are about being let down and stood up, about loneliness and frustration; musically his form is a pop ballad/soft rock blend; less physical music than cock rock, drawing on older romantic conventions. In teenybop, male sexuality is transformed into a spiritual yearning carrying only hints of sexual interaction (see Les McKeown's soft swaying hips). What is needed is not so much someone to screw as a sensitive and sympathetic soulmate, someone to support and nourish the incompetent male adolescent as he grows up. (See John Travolta's attraction to 'older women'.) If cock rock plays on conventional concepts of male sexuality as rampant, animalistic, superficial, just-for-the-moment, teenybop plays on notions of female sexuality as being serious, diffuse, and implying total emotional commitment. In teenybop cults live performance is less significant than pin-ups, posters, and television appearances; in teenybop music, women emerge as unreliable, fickle, more selfish than men. It is men who are soft, romantic, easily hurt, loyal, and anxious to find a true love who fulfils their definitions of what female sexuality should be about.

The resulting contrast between, say, Thin Lizzy fans and David Soul fans is obvious enough, but our argument is not intended to give a precise account of the rock market. There are overlaps and contradictions, girls put cock rock pin-ups on their bedroom walls and boys buy teenybop records. Likewise there are a whole range of stars who seek to occupy both categories at once—Rod Stewart can come across just as pathetic, puppy-like, and maudlin as Donny Osmond, and John Travolta can be mean and nasty, one of the gang. But our cock rock/teenybop comparison does make clear the general point we want to make: masculinity in rock is not determined by one all-embracing definition. Rather, rock offers a framework within which male sexuality can find a range of acceptable, heterosexual expressions. These images of masculinity are predicated on sexual divisions in the appropriation of rock. Thus we have the identity of the male consumer with the rock performer. Rock shows become a collective experience which are, in this respect, reminiscent of football matches and other occasions of male camaraderie—the general atmosphere is sexually exclusive, its euphoria depends on the absence of women. The teenybop performer, by contrast, addresses his female consumer as his object, potentially satisfying his sexual needs and his romantic and emotional demands. The teenybop fan should feel that her idol is addressing himself solely to her, her experience should be as his partner. Elvin Bishop's 'Fooled Around', a hit single from a couple of years ago, captures lyrically the point we're making:

> I must have been through about a million girls
> I love 'em and leave 'em alone,
> I didn't care how much they cried, no sir,
> Their tears left me as cold as stone,
> But then I fooled around and fell in love . . .

> (© Crabshawe Music, 1975)

In rock conventions, the collective notion of fooling around refers explicitly to male experience, falling in love refers to the expectations of girls.

From this perspective, the cock rock/teenybop contrast is clearly something general in rock, applicable to other genres. Male identity with the performer is expressed not only in sexual terms but also as a looser appropriation of rock musicians' dominance and power, confidence and control. It is boys who become interested in rock as music, who become hi-fi experts, who hope to become musicians, technicians or music businessmen. It is boys who form the core of the rock audience, who are intellectually interested in rock, who become rock critics and collectors. (The readership of *Sounds*, *New Musical Express*, and *Melody Maker* and the audience for the *Old Grey Whistle Test* are two-thirds male; John Peel's radio show listeners are 90 per cent male.) It is boys who experience rock as a collective culture, a shared male world of fellow fans and fellow musicians. The problems facing a woman seeking to enter the rock world as a participant are clear. A girl is supposed to be an individual listener, she is not encouraged to develop the skills and knowledge to become a performer. In sixth form and student culture, just as much as in teenybop music, girls are expected to be passive, as they listen quietly to rock poets, and brood in their bed-sits to Leonard Cohen, Cat Stevens, or Jackson Browne. Women, whatever their musical tastes, have little opportunity and get little encouragement to be performers themselves. This is another aspect of rock's sexual ideology of collective male activity and individual female passivity.
[. . .]

Rock Contradictions

The audience for rock isn't only boys. If the music tends to treat women as objects, it does, unlike teenybop romance, also acknowledge in its direct physicality that women have sexual urges of their own. In attacking or ignoring conventions of sexual decency, obligation, and security, cock rockers do, in some respects, challenge the ways in which those conventions are limiting—

on women as well as on men. Women can contrast rock expression to the respectable images they are offered elsewhere—hence the feminist importance of the few female rock stars like Janis Joplin, hence the moral panics about rock's corrupting effects. The rock ideology of freedom from domesticity has an obvious importance for girls, even if it embodies an alternative mode of sexual expression.

There are ambiguities in rock's insistent presentation of men as sex objects. These presentations are unusually direct—no other entertainers flaunt their sexuality at an audience as obviously as rock performers. 'Is there anybody here with any Irish in them?' Phil Lynott of Thin Lizzy asks in passing on the *Live and Dangerous* LP, 'Is there any of the girls who would like a little more Irish in them?' Sexual groupies are a more common feature of stars' lives in rock than in other forms of entertainment and cock rock often implies female sexual aggression, intimates that women can be ruthless in the pursuit of *their* sex objects. Numerous cock rock songs—the Stones' for example—express a deep fear of women, and in some cases, like that of the Stranglers, this fear seems pathological, which reflects the fact that the macho stance of cock rockers is as much a fantasy for men as teenybop romance is for women.

Rock may be source and setting for collective forms of male toughness, roughness, and noisiness, but when it comes to the individual problems of handling a sexual relationship, the Robert Plant figure is a mythical and unsettling model (in the old dance hall days, jealous provincial boys used to wait outside the dressing room to beat up the visiting stars who had attracted their women). Cock rock presents an ideal world of sex without physical or emotional difficulties, in which all men are attractive and potent and have endless opportunities to prove it. However powerfully expressed, this remains an ideal, ideological world, and the alternative, teenybop mode of masculine vulnerability is, consequently, a complementary source of clues as to how sexuality should be articulated. The imagery of the cheated, unhappy man is central to sophisticated adult-oriented rock and if the immediate object of such performers is female sympathy, girls aren't their only listeners. Even the most macho rockers have in their repertoire some suitably soppy songs with which to celebrate true (lustless) love—listen to the Stones' 'Angie' for an example. Rock, in other words, carries messages of male self-doubt and self-pity to accompany its hints of female confidence and aggression. Some of the most interesting rock performers have deliberately used the resulting sexual ambiguities and ironies. We can find in rock the image of the pathetic stud or the salacious boy next door, or, as in Lesley Gore's 'You Don't Own Me', the feminist teenybopper. We can point too at the ambivalent sexuality of David Bowie, Lou Reed, and Bryan Ferry, at the camp teenybop styles of Gary Glitter and Suzi Quatro, at the disconcertingly 'macho' performances of a female group like the Runaways. These references to the uses made of rock conventions by individual performers lead us to the question of form: how are the conventions of sexuality we've been discussing embodied in rock?

This is a complex question and all we can do here is point to some of the work that needs to be done before we can answer it adequately. First, then, we need to look at the *history* of rock. We need to investigate how rock 'n' roll

originally affected youthful presentations of sexuality and how these presentations have changed in rock's subsequent development. Most rock analysts look
at the emergence of rock 'n' roll as the only event needing explanation. Rock
'n' roll's subsequent corruption and 'emasculation' (note the word) are understood as a straightforward effect of the rock business's attempt to control its
market or as an aspect of American institutional racism—and so Pat Boone got
to make money out of his insipid versions of black tracks. But, from our perspective, the process of 'decline'—the successful creation of teenybop idols like
Fabian, the sales shift from crude dance music to well-crafted romantic ballads,
the late fifties popularity of sweet black music and girl groups like the
Shirelles—must be analysed in equal detail. The decline of rock 'n' roll rested
on a process of 'feminization'.

The most interesting sexual aspect of the emergence of British beat in the
mid-sixties was its blurring of the by then conventional teenage distinction
between girls' music—soft ballads—and boys' music—hard-line rock 'n' roll.
There was still a contrast between, say, the Beatles and the Stones—the one a
girls' band, the other a boys' band—but it was a contrast not easily maintained.
The British sound in general, the Beatles in particular, fused a rough R & B beat
with yearning vocal harmonies derived from black and white romantic pop.
The resulting music articulated simultaneously the conventions of feminine
and masculine sexuality, and the Beatles' own image was ambiguous, neither
boys-together aggression nor boy-next-door pathos. This ambiguity was
symbolized in Lennon and McCartney's unusual lyrical use of the third
person— 'I saw *her* standing there', '*She* loves *you*'. In performance, the Beatles
did not make an issue of their own sexual status, did not, despite the screaming girls, treat the audience as their sexual object. The mods from this period
turned out to be the most interesting of Britain's post-war youth groups—
offering girls a more visible, active, and collective role (particularly on the
dance floor) than in previous or subsequent groups and allowing boys the
vanity, the petulance, the soft sharpness that are usually regarded as sissy.
Given this, the most important thing about late sixties rock was not its well-
discussed, counter-cultural origins, but the way in which it was consolidated
as the central form of mass youth music in its cock rock form, as a male form
of expression. The 'progressive' music of which everyone expected so much
in 1967–8 became, in its popular form, the heavy metal macho style of Led
Zeppelin, on the one hand, and the technically facile hi-fi formula of Yes, on
the other. If the commercialization of rock 'n' roll in the 1950s was a process of
'feminization', the commercialization of rock in the 1960s was a process
of 'masculinization'.

In the seventies, rock's sexual moments have been more particular in their
effects but no less difficult to account for. Where did glam and glitter rock come
from? Why did youth music suddenly become a means for the expression of
sexual ambiguity? Rock was used this way not only by obviously arty performers like Lou Reed and David Bowie, but also by mainstream teenybop packages
like the Sweet and by mainstream rockers like Rod Stewart. The most recent
issue for debate has been punk's sexual meaning. Punk involved an attack on
both romantic and permissive conventions and in their refusal to let their

sexuality be constructed as a commodity some punks went as far as to deny their sexuality any significance at all. 'My love lies limp', boasted Mark Perry of Alternative TV. 'What is sex anyway?' asked Johnny Rotten, 'Just thirty seconds of squelching noises.' Punk was the first form of rock not to rest on love songs, and one of its effects has been to allow female voices to be heard that are not often allowed expression on record, stage, or radio—shrill, assertive, impure individual voices, the sounds of singers like Poly Styrene, Siouxsie, Fay Fife of the Rezillos, Pauline of Penetration. Punk's female musicians have a strident insistency that is far removed from the appeal of most post-war glamour girls. The historical problem is to explain their commercial success, to account for the punks' interruption of the long-standing rock equation of sex and pleasure.

These questions can only be answered by placing rock in its cultural and ideological context as a form of entertainment, but a second major task for rock analysts is to study the sexual language of its musical roots—rhythm and blues, soul, country, folk, and the rest. The difficulty is to work out the relationship of form and content. Compare, for example, Bob Dylan's and Bob Marley's current use of their supporting women singers. Dylan is a sophisticated rock star, the most significant voice of the music's cultural claims, including its claim to be sexually liberating. His most recent lyrics, at least, reflect a critical self-understanding that isn't obviously sexist. But musically and visually his back-up trio are used only as a source of glamour, their traditional pop use. Marley is an orthodox Rastafarian, subscribes to a belief, an institution, a way of life in which women have as subordinate a place as in any other sexually repressive religion. And yet Marley's I-Threes sing and present themselves with grace and dignity, with independence and power. In general, it seems that soul and country musics, blatantly sexist in their organization and presentation, in their lyrical themes and concerns, allow their female performers an autonomous musical power that is rarely achieved by women in rock. We have already mentioned the paradoxes of a comparison of Tammy Wynette's 'Stand by Your Man' and Helen Reddy's 'I Am Woman'. The lyrics of 'Stand by Your Man' celebrate women's duty to men, implore women to enjoy subordinating themselves to men's needs—lyrically the song is a ballad of sexual submissiveness. But the female authority of Tammy Wynette's voice involves a knowledge of the world that is in clear contrast to the gooey idealism of Helen Reddy's sound. 'Sometimes it's hard to be a woman,' Tammy Wynette begins, and you can hear that it's hard and you can hear that Tammy Wynette knows why—her voice is a collective one. 'I am woman,' sings Helen Reddy, and what you hear is the voice of an idealized consumer, even if the commodity for consumption in this instance is a packaged version of women's liberation.

On the Representation of Sexuality

JENNY TAYLOR AND DAVE LAING

> Woman . . . stands in patriarchal culture as signifier to the male other,
> bound by a symbolic order in which man can live out his fantasies and
> obsessions through linguistic command by imposing them on the silent image
> still tied to her place as bearer of meaning and not maker of meaning.
> (Mulvey 1975: 7)

As Mulvey states, this perspective refers to cultural practice in general and so
would provide a useful alternative starting point for Frith and McRobbie's
examination of the place of female singers in rock. For film in particular,
Mulvey argues, the basis of an implicitly erotic pleasure lies in 'scopophilia',
that pleasure in looking which involves objectifying the other through the gaze.
She distinguishes three types of interacting 'look'—the gaze of the audience,
the gaze of the camera and the gaze of the subject within the film itself. Film
provides pleasure-in-looking both through voyeurism—creating the illusion
for the audience that they are looking in on a private world as privileged
peeping toms—and through narcissism, where the self is (mis)-perceived as
the idealized other. There is a tension between these two forms of looking—
where the (male) self remains detached in objectifying the female image but
also identifies with the male subject of the film. Hollywood cinema resolves this
tension by interlocking the story with the look, when the synchronic moment
only signifies in a diachronic framework and, conversely, where the moment
justifies and makes the story possible.

If this model is applied to *Saturday Night Fever*, these structures seem to be
reproduced but in an inverted form, and in a way that realigns the relationship
between voyeurism and narcissism for the male viewer. It also refers to, and
implicitly parodies, the 'showgirl' musical genre. As Frith and McRobbie imply,
Travolta is both subject and object in the film and the outcome is ambivalent,
implying not a single 'statement' of sexuality, but a multiplicity of discourses
around sexuality. Early in the film, Travolta is displayed reclining in his
bedroom (dressing room), where the camera glides up his thigh and over his
torso. He is shown in underpants posing before the mirror. The auidence witnesses this private scene. But the result, although apparently comparable, is
totally different from the Hollywood representation of a showgirl getting ready
for the performance. Here, the camera's gaze is ironic, tongue-in-cheek,

'Disco-Pleasure-Discourse', *Screen Education*, 31 (1979), 44–8.

self-referring, and the audience both participates in the process of narcissism and at the same time sees it as a *display* of narcissism, to *itself.* Travolta doesn't simply connote 'looked-atness': he is both the gaze and its object. The music and the disco scenes in particular consolidate this process, while also reconciling displayed image and narrative sequence. The songs are both assertive and narrative, while in the dances, Travolta sets up a relationship with his audience as participants as well as spectators, in a structure to which women are marginal. They are literally 'hangers-on', both within the film itself and in their positioning as spectators of it.

This kind of analysis can be extended beyond the musical film, to rock music as live performance and even perhaps to radio and records, where looking does not accompany listening. A pertinent example is what Frith and McRobbie call 'cock rock' with its 'aggressive expression of male sexuality'. They account for the small proportion of girls in a 'cock rock' audience by the fact that girls' notion of sexuality is soft and gentle, while here they are confronted with the iconography of 'male sexual performance' (Frith and McRobbie 1979: 5–6). In the alternative perspective we have sketched in, this situation can be explained in terms of the narcissistic celebration of male power which *structurally* excludes the female spectator and produces the ecstatic male response to Thin Lizzy and other bands. It is surprising, here, that the authors do not remark on the masturbatory imagery of such performances. Like Travolta, Thin Lizzy's Phil Lynott is both objectified and identified with, in the male gaze.

We don't have the space to develop this line of argument further, but one or two more general points need to be made about Frith and McRobbie's account of the rock/sexuality relationship. The first point is that, for them, the linkage is essentially a sociological one. Through music (among other agencies) teenagers 'learn' adult sexual behaviour and are socialized into the already constructed sex (or more precisely, gender) roles provided by a patriarchal, capitalist society. (Frith and McRobbie 1979: 9–10). The connection is made, we take the authors to be saying, through the *content* (lyrics, images) of rock music which glamorizes the stereotypical attributes. One consequence of this argument, with its implication that the music *reflects* the elements of the stereotype in its own content, is that the authors are led to conclude that 'cock rock' and 'teenybop' are the pure forms of the realization of the dominant ideology within rock music. Other genres then have to be seen as either mixtures of the two or variations on one or the other, so that Leonard Cohen or Jackson Browne become big girls' versions of David Cassidy. Such oversimplification tends to ignore the specificity of the musical; this might be more clearly demonstrated through a list of 'exceptions' to the cock rock/teenybop polarity.

Secondly, without denying the social relationships which the concept 'sex-role stereotype' refers to, we regard its static character as a barrier to understanding the constant generation of subject-positions for the spectator/listener within music. *Repetition* (of songs and within them), that widely recognized feature of rock music, is a crucial means by which individuals are constantly interpellated into gender-specific subject-positions.

The final general point arises from Frith and McRobbie's statements, at several points in their article, that rock music is in some sense more sexual than other popular cultural forms. The implication is that sexuality is more or less repressed or suppressed in cultural practices, an implication which assumes sexuality to have an essential or 'natural' form. This seems to us problematic: what is at issue is not how much is revealed or expressed by a Frank Sinatra or a Thin Lizzy, but the radically different codes and conventions of representation involved in different genres.

Auditory Pleasures

So far, we have discussed the sexuality in rock primarily in terms of gesture and image, the visual. But what of the musical contexts in which listening predominates? What is required here is an account of the auditory (invocating drive) and its forms of pleasure to match the analyses of Mulvey and others on the work of the visual (scopic drive, scopophilia). This might well be the starting point for an attempt to specify the effects of music as organized sound. The difficulties caused by not identifying such a specificity can be seen in Frith and McRobbie's comparison of two records by women singers, Tammy Wynette and Helen Reddy. The comparison focuses on the relation between linguistic meaning (the lyrics) and musical connotation (sound of the voice) in each record. But the attempt to specify why Wynette's voice is 'more valuable' collapses almost immediately into a list of cultural equivalents to musical genres. Thus Wynette's voice is authentic because it is stylistically related to a folk-like idiom (country music), and its authenticity is not affected by the reactionary message of the lyrics in the song. Helen Reddy is the polar opposite: not even the progressive message of her song can rescue the voice from its consumerist lack of authenticity (its stylistic features belong to a popular music without folk roots). This kind of aesthetic approach leads the article into its most unsatisfactory section, where the most banal concepts of 'facts of life' and 'fantasy' are quoted from Hayakawa's reactionary article on pop lyrics and Lloyd's sentimental socialist-realist view of folksongs. On the following page, the (Lukácsian) concepts of 'realism' and 'naturalism' pop up to complete the confusion. We cannot here enter into the general argument about realist views of art, but can only reiterate the position that cultural production occurs always in relation to ideology and not to the 'real world'.

What, then, would a different approach to these two recordings be like? Recalling our emphasis on the need to understand the character of listening-pleasure, Roland Barthes's article 'The Grain of the Voice' offers a preliminary attempt to draw distinctions. It presents a distinction between 'pheno-song' and 'geno-song'. The former describes' everything in the performance which is in the service of communication, representation, expression . . . '. The geno-song (the grain) is:

> The volume of the singing and speaking voice, the space where significations germinate 'from within language and in its very materiality' . . . It is that apex (or that depth) of production where the melody really works at the language— not at what is says, but the voluptuousness of its sound—the language works and identifies with that work. (Barthes 1977: 182)

This is, writes Barthes, 'the impossible account of an individual thrill that I constantly experience in listening to singing'; and 'grain of the voice' is undoubtedly a difficult concept to employ. Yet its primary distinction, between the working of the voice as communicator of the message and its emotional implications, and this something else of the geno-song, is surely important, especially since Barthes also writes of the different effects on the listening subject of each. While the pheno-song works to reassure, to reconstitute the subject in its precarious unity, the geno-song offers access to '*jouissance*, to loss . . .' (179).

A further point raised by Frith and McRobbie's discussion of the Wynette/Reddy comparison is that the effect of a record cannot simply be read off from the structure of the music itself. The play of discourses within a record may prescribe a preferred subject-position for the listener by foregrounding certain elements (lyric message, vocal style or rhythm); but the listening subject has his or her own *idiolect* based on a historical (class and gender position, conscious ideology) as well as a psychic structure. When the authors seem to be offering the *real* meaning of these two records, it is their own reading as listeners among other listeners which is being presented. In that reading, Reddy's voice is 'cute, show-biz self-consciousness', 'gooey idealism', and that of 'an idealized consumer'. Wynette has 'country strength and confidence' and 'her voice is a collective one' which 'involves a knowledge of the world'. But how are these judgements arrived at? What musical features of each voice produce these meanings for these particular listeners?

At the level of the performance as a whole, a similarity is apparent in the *bravura* character of the singing, where both singers operate 'at the top of their voices', rising to crescendos. The contrast is with the *confidential style* of other women singers like Joni Mitchell and Joan Armatrading, to name artists mentioned with approval by Frith and McRobbie. In Barthes's terminology, both Reddy and Wynette are firmly on the side of the pheno-type, with the dramatic and the expressive predominant. The differences between the two voices appear at the level of the details of singing style, the phrasing. Wynette's singing is full of embellishment, of the twangy melisma of the white Southern accent. Reddy sings 'straight', as befits the anthemic nature of her song ('I Am Woman'). The distinction for Frith and McRobbie is one of genre, where the two genres in question have associated moral as well as stylistic qualities.

As we have already indicated, these moral qualities, which allow Wynette to be more highly valued, derive from the different relationship to commercial entertainment each genre is seen as having, at least in its origins. How a record by Tammy Wynette, a media star of greater magnitude than Helen Reddy, can retain the authenticity of a non-commercialized folk art is not explained by the authors. Presumably, some tenacity of tradition is at work here, or perhaps a tautologous process whereby the primary ideological connotation of country music for its devotees is 'truth to life', so that the recognition of a voice as 'country' immediately defines it as authentic. In this *culturalist* account, the response of someone for whom country music connoted the sentimentality of unsophisticated rednecks would we assume be diametrically different.

If, as we are arguing, Frith and McRobbie's aesthetic here is rejoining a well-worn critical onslaught on 'commercialism' in popular culture, it does so in a novel way. Most critics of pop music have, like Hayakawa, attacked it at the level of lyrics. Frith and McRobbie shift the ground to the sound of the voice, but in doing so they assume a necessary dominance in these two records of that sound over the sense of the lyrics and indeed, from a progressive political viewpoint, a contradiction between the two. Without a very detailed examination of the records this analysis cannot be fully tested, yet doubts arise. If both records are examples of Barthes's 'pheno-type', where vocal delivery is precisely that, a delivery of a verbal message and its attendant emotion (in contrast to, say the old Beatles song 'Misery', where the vocal exuberance has no relation to the self-pitying lyrics), perhaps the effect of Wynette's 'strength and confidence' is to confirm the submissive message of the words.

Rock Genres

Our final comment on *Rock and Sexuality* concern the authors' attempts to define rock music as a continent within the world of popular music, and to define the 'sub-genres' of cock rock and teenybop. In our view, they are more successful in founding the latter as the type of products which

> ... foreground convention and stereotypicality in order to gain instant recognition of its type ... and to institute a type of aesthetic play among the conventions in order to pose the audience with a question that would keep them coming back—not 'what is going to happen next?', to which they would already have the answer, but 'how?'   (Gledhill 1978: 11)

In this sense, rock in general does not seem to be a genre. Frith and McRobbie note that the term is beset with confusion in its general use and for their own definition fall back on its social effects and relations: 'its function as a youth cultural form'. Whether or not this is empirically verifiable in terms of audience numbers, it is uncertain that this 'youthfulness' remains at the heart of the conventions and stereotypes which structure the wide variety of music grouped by the authors under the head of 'rock'. Perhaps the term no longer has any analytical value and it should be left to the discourse of the culture industry where it distinguishes one type of product to be marketed differently from others.

We mentioned earlier our belief that Frith and McRobbie's comment that 'the cock rock/teenybop contrast is clearly something general in rock, applicable to other genres' was mistaken and reductionist in the form in which it was presented. What this contrast does perhaps represent is not two paradigmatic forms of music, but two different discourses of sexuality (in Foucault's sense of the term). One is defiantly 'speaking out': self-assertive, self-regarding, redefining or reaffirming the boundaries of 'normal' sexuality. The other is confidential, private, 'confessional', setting up a relationship between singer and listener which implies a 'hidden truth' of sexuality to be revealed. But this is only one level of the play of discourses that constitute a musical product and this distinction can be found as much *within* the work of an artist or genre as between different performers. Another, to return to Laura Mulvey, is the specific form taken by the symbolic order of patriarchal culture in popular music, where the listening equivalent of the male 'voyeuristic gaze' is all per-vasive; even when Tammy Wynette sings 'to' other women, she is also singing *at* men. That's why an analysis is needed not only of rock music's genres and signifying practices, but also of their relations to the proliferating discourses around sexuality.

On Music and Masculinity

CHARLES FORD

Giovanni's claim, in the first recitative of the second act of *Don Giovanni*, that women, 'per me son necessarie più del pan che mangio, pi dell'aria che spiro!' (are more necessary to me than the bread I eat and the air I breathe), identifies him unequivocally with the discourse of Enlightened libertinage. . . . [S]uch materialist determinism always implied its own contradiction, in the form of a natural amoral absolute. Giovanni expresses this metaphysic in an ironic euphemism. 'Il che in me sento sì esteso sentimento, vo' bene a tutte quante: le donne poi che calcolar non sanno, il mio buon natural chiamano inganno' (I feel such an extensive sentiment within myself that I want to please all women: but because women do not understand such things, they call my natural goodness deceit). But whatever the explicit reason, all his intentions— the deceits, the attempted rapes, and the murder of the Commendatore—are governed by what Sade referred to as the perpetual destructive agitation of a *malfaisant* nature.

This aggressive negativity is musically articulated through the libertarian denial of pre-established, regular rhythmic conventions. Such disruptions arise in the basic 8-bar arpeggiation of 'Fin ch'han dal vino' (1–16) when Mozart begins to repeat its 2-bar sub-groups, thereby breaking down any sense of rhythmic hierarchy (25–32). In the next period, this repetitiveness combines with an off-beat woodwind twitch, resulting in an accumulating dissonant energy that bursts through the limits of the 8-bar model (37–44). This combination of repetition and extension becomes critical in the two passages with *fp* marks on every bar, which fragment the autonomy of the 2-bar sub-groups, to give a series of dissonant shocks (86–92, 105–15). Listening is subordinated to the tyranny of the moment, transforming the psychological structure of the libertine's victim into the most intense musical excitement, reaching a climax of breathless dissonance in the final 16-bar vocal group that flows over into the frenzied abandon of the orchestral playout.

We hear similar techniques of acceleration and disruption in the opening to the Act 2 finale, and in Giovanni's third aria, 'Metà di voi quà vadano', the surface of which is saturated with syncopation and extended upbeats in both the vocal and orchestral parts. But these same rhythmic devices are just as fascinating in Giovanni's slower, more lyrical music. In Giovanni's second attempt to seduce Zerlina at the beginning of the first finale, his libertine rhythmic pushiness takes the form of extended upbeats, the success of which is

Così? Sexual Politics in Mozart's Operas (Manchester: Manchester University Press, 1991), 116–23.

Ex. 7

Ex. 1. *Don Giovanni*, no. 13

registered when Zerlina takes them over in 113: Ex. 7. But in the recitative before 'La ci darem la mano', Giovanni reverses these dynamic rhythmic strategies by slowing down the musical process. He sings three well-prepared high d²s across (17–19), the last of which is retained for half a bar in order to excite Zerlina's expectations for the next flattering conceit in the series, 'quegli occhi briconcelli, quei labbretti sì belli, quelle dituccie candide e odorose' (those roguish eyes, those lips so sweet, those pale and fragrant fingers).

Giovanni is at the centre of a structure of dramatic relationships, but he is none the less isolated, opposed to all the others (Dent 1960: 158). At the end of Act 1 Giovanni displays his debt to the Classical Stoicism that proved so influential for both Kant and Sade. Compare his proud expression of fearlessness in the face of death with the words of Seneca:

> *Ma non manco in me coraggio* (But my courage does not fail me)
> *No mi perdo o mio confondo* (I'm not lost or confused)
> *Se cadesse ancora i mondo* (Even if the world collapses)
> *Nulla mai timor mi fa.* (Nothing can daunt me.)
>
> There in the midst of the storm is tranquillity,
> There is a mind worthy of immortality.
>
> (Quotation from Gay 1969: 86)

We only really approach Giovanni through his servant Leporello, who mediates, like an Arlecchino figure (Dent 1960: 156), between his master's *ataraxia* and the audience. Leporello also provides musical mediation, for he is identified with the F major harmony that serves as a pivot between D minor and B♭ major in the opening scena (in which his melody for 'Voglio far il gentil uomo' generates most of the material), and in the second finale's reworking of the same harmonic process.

Leporello, though disgusted by his master's behaviour, needs his wage, and it is this, the fundamentally economic basis of their relationship, that thematizes the incipient bourgeois moral dilemma concerning what one might or might not do for money (similar problems emerge for Rocco in Act 1 of *Fidelio*). Leporello's servitude, combined with his appeals to the audience to 'just look at what the libertine is doing now!', define the essentially aristocratic nature of his master's sexual power, as *other* to the ideological profile of the audience. Leporello's inane repetitions of Giovanni's words quoted above, and even his final death rattle, inject comical doubt into his master's posturing as an autonomous (a)moral Stoic hero. The group only joins in with Giovanni's cries of *Viva la libertà!* in the first finale after Leporello steps forward to repeat his master's words. Only then do they become truly revolutionary, for Leporello is the Arlecchino of the ascendant bourgeoisie. His 'Catalogue' aria, whilst celebrating Giovanni's sexual catholicism, demonstrates its archaic political basis by way of a potentially enormous ternary *da capo* form, with a slow central section, and the final limb omitted, to taunt Elvira: 'voi sapete quel che fa' (you know what he does). This political critique of Giovanni is also articulated by harmonic means. The large-scale harmonic function of Giovanni's cries of *Viva la libertà!* underline the hypocrisy of his supposed libertarianism, since they comprise a *false* resolution of the overall opposition between the C major tonic, and the extreme subdominant of E♭ major. The real harmonic development comes later, with Giovanni's attempted rape of Zerlina, whose screams interrupt the contrived chaos of dances.

By the time that Mozart set *Don Giovanni*, it was generally thought of as a decidedly un-Enlightened, hack theatre piece. Rather than attempting to retrieve its suitably disenchanted mythological aspects, Mozart thematized them, so as to question again, through the medium of music, the relationship between these old-fashioned values and the contemporary audience. *Don Giovanni* is a dynamically retrospective opera. The two events that motivate the narrative both happen in the first scene, and the harmonic processes, and the thematic and textural details that accompany them, recur throughout the opera. The first half of the first finale constantly recollects both this first scene and its own, more recent melodic and harmonic past, as the harmony is allowed to drift steadily flatwards through the cycle of fifths, from C to E♭ major—the point at which we enter the libidinal *sanctum sanctorium* of Giovanni's home. The combined effect is comparable to that of the psychoanalytic project, in which the patient returns, through recollection, to their own inner, desiring nature.

As da Ponte remarked, Mozart treated the idea of the stone guest with the utmost seriousness (Dent 1960: 145 f.). The cemetery scene is built around an experimental thirds-related harmony, and Giovanni's final confrontation with the statue contains some of the most dissonant music that Mozart ever composed. Between these two terrible manifestations of the supernatural (after another of Anna and Ottavio's rejection cameos) lies the mundane humour of the supper scene, which is complicated by the reversal of dramatic roles between master and servant, as Giovanni directs our attention to Leporello's clandestine sharing of his dinner. Because Leporello is thereby rendered objective, we begin for the first time to approach the truth of Giovanni as a 'free' subject, who sees, knows and controls all, including our own way into the drama. But what gives this scene its chilling intensity is the contradiction between this new sense of direct contact with Giovanni's subjective freedom, which is supported by the super-realist technique of using known, up-to-the minute, popular music on stage, and the heavily marked, 'external' modulations between each dance tune that grind inexorably through the familiar series, D major—F major—B♭ major (112–17, 157–61). The pair carry on the comedy in a weird hermetic realm, poised within the pre-established, mythical and harmonic destiny, that moves so relentlessly towards its terrible conclusion. Elvira's attempted intercession was also a well-established function of the myth, a last attempt to redeem Giovanni from the devil. Everything is in the hands of a known, but only dimly understood, fate—the mythological heritage of the past.

The stone guest appears at the moment when a familiar large-scale harmonic process arrives at its goal of D minor. This highly determined structural function is further intensified by the recollection of the first bars of the Overture—a music like nothing that has been heard since then, and which, because it comes from beyond the frame of the drama, seems to point back to our own psychological past, rather than to that of the drama. The effect is still chilling, but in its day, the sound of three trombones, which were only ever heard in church or to announce similar supernatural phenomena in *opera seria*, swelling the *ff tutti* diminished seventh chord, must have been terrifying (Dent 1960: 169). Their sound connotes a more general cultural past, a world of religious and mythical speculation that Enlightenment materialist *opera buffa* stood to reject.

Giovanni's proud acceptance of the stone man's invitation to partake of *cibo celeste*—'Ho fermo il cor in petto, non ho timor; verrò' (a celestial snack—The heart holds firm in my breast, I have no fear; I'll come) (512–16) is set by contextually aberrant, dotted rhythm, Baroque-style counterpoint, reminscent of that used to express the outmoded reaction of Elvira's 'Ah fuggi il traditor'. The archaic quality of this gesture is commensurate with the archaic structural function of Giovanni's G minor cadence, which marks the (real-time) centre of a ternary harmonic form in D minor (473–602). The fundamentally aristocratic basis of Giovanni's stoic pride identifies him with the absolute moral power of this mythological authority figure of the *ancien régime*. The statue's decisive cadence—'Ah tempo più non vè!' (Ah there is no more time)—rewrites Giovanni's attack on the Commendatore in the first scene, and the violent gestures in the lower strings that lead up to this moment suggest that the duel is being fought again, with reversed roles. The potential confusion of identities becomes explicit in Giovanni's last moments, when who is singing *Sì!* and who is singing *No!* becomes almost impossible to distinguish. Giovanni's libertine refusal of all empathy or compassion meets the magnified image of itself in the confrontation with the stone guest. The two men are no longer different characters, but negative and positive personifications of the same fundamental stoic rationalism that refuses all compassion for the sake of preserving an (a)moral autonomy. This is the meaning of the epilogue's equation: 'de perfidi la morte alla vita è sempre ugual' (the death of the wicked is always like their lives). Neither the deus ex machina nor his extraordinarily dissonant music has anything to do with the rest of the opera, and, from the miraculous way in which Giovanni escapes at the end of Act 1, he also would seem to transcend the dramatic structure of relationships, in which he is at once so essential.

We can trace a three-way identification between Giovanni, Leporello, and the Commendatore in the various relationships between the 'Catalogue' aria, Giovanni's 'Metà di voi quà vadano' (no. 17), and the cemetery *terzetto* (no. 22), all of which enjoy a similar melodic anonymity, and lively interplay between voice and orchestra. In the last of these, Giovanni's earlier gestures to Masetto are identified with the statue's nods: Ex. 8. We might consider Leporello, Giovanni, and the statue as three aspects of the same man: his objective *persona* that we relate to, the remote, insistent subjectivity of Giovanni himself, and his conscience, or super-ego (Donnington 1981: 448). Leporello demonstrates his privileged insight when he accuses Giovanni of having a *core di sasso* (heart of stone), during the scene with Elvira, just before announcing the arrival of *l'uom di sasso* (the man of stone).

Giovanni is damned by those same external forces that were heard as the dreadful modulations grinding away between the dance tunes of the supper scene. This damnation, by virtue of the extraordinary nature of its musical presentation, seems to belong to the past, and to have no bearing on the charismatic impression of Giovanni, that we are given by both the lyrical beauty of Elvira's yearnings and the dynamic excitement of his own music. The brutality of Giovanni's libertinage is celebrated musically throughout the opera, as a series of thrilling moments, as an insistence on the *now*, but always under the shadow of its transcendent damnation from the past, which is as perfect and convincing but as irrelevant as the *categorical imperative*. Giovanni must be destroyed by the flames that the equally self-determining stoic—Masonic Tamino is allowed to pass through, for whilst Giovanni refused Elvira's Marian intercession, Tamino is guided through nature by his idealized love for its appointed feminine intermediary.

In dealing with the past so seriously, the opera questions the relationship between aristocratic particularism—Giovanni's sexuality in the sphere of the political—and the introspective subjectivism of the German-speaking, Viennese middle classes, which was equally concerned with inner, systematic

Ex. 8

Don Giovanni, no. 17

Noi___ far dob-biamo il   res-to,   e già ve-drai co - s'è   co-s'è   co - s'è

no. 22

Col - la mar-mo - rea tes - ta   ci fa   co - sì,   co - sì, autonomy. But this latter group's obsession with the 'inner life' above all else, affirmed their political helplessness in the face of material oppression from despotic aristocratic figures such as Giovanni. The sexual problem of the opera is, in this sense, as one with what at that time was a more general, unspeakable, *unpredicatable*, political problem. Because an individualist morality (like Kant's) cannot account for the *effects* of actions, this culture was as unable to deal with the nobility's personal habits, as it was with its political institutions. Werther's defence of the rapist was grounded in the notion that no one can be blamed, for we are all in the hands of a nature that is one moment benign, and the next malevolent. Because sexual violence is justifiable, or at least, not culpable, within the terms of such 'progressive' radical individualism, Giovanni had to be damned 'externally'. The ascendant bourgeoisie sought shelter from the rational—Stoic particularism of the nobility, in a figure from the same class, but one who was imbued with a transcendent moral authority. Many progressive, liberal minds found such a figure in Joseph II, in his battle against the feudal nobility. In this sense then, the opera was culturally affirmative.

The antagonism between the material, musical celebration of Giovanni's libidinal energies, and his ideal damnation by his moral *alter ego*, generates the same guilt-ridden tension as that between the material determinism and the a priori absolutism of libertinage. Instead of blasphemy—the traditional reason for Giovanni's damnation—it is the first manifestations of the erotic that lurk in these darkened scenes, this static twilight realm. The erotic was by definition damned, but unable to be legislated against, unable to be contained by Giovanni's avengers, since it was the dark side of the absolute, *noumenal* realm of nature, unavailable, a priori, to the juridical concepts of reason. In the same logical moment that it shifted the essentiality of the Christian soul over on to the individual libido (Foucault 1979: 3), the Enlightenment rewrote blasphemy as sexual transgression against the inwardly intuited voice of the individual secular conscience, demanding that the other be treated as an end in itself.

The bourgeoisie inherited this conception of the erotic as transgression (see Battailk 1962), but only in opposition to the Enlightenment's more sensitive, subjectivist discourse of love. The two terms are defined in terms of their mutual otherness; each is what the other is not. Whereas the discourse of love concerns eternal unity and passive feeling, that of eroticism concerns the moment of difference and active desire. It is the same tension between alienation and guilt that constituted Sade's complex, Enlightened sexuality, which is known today as pornography. Like Giovanni's libertinage, this discourse and imagery is damned by definition, but is none the less contained and exploited. *Il dissoluto punito o sia il Don Giovanni* (The Profligate Punished, or the Don Giovanni) is couched in the same self-consciously 'sinful' terms that define the pornographic today, but whilst the damnation is dramatically explicit, the eroticism, or implicit violence against women, is only (!) musical (see Brownmilter 1975: 289).

On the Sapphonic Voice

ELIZABETH WOOD

Si tu veux que je reste auprès de toi
Disperse moins ta voix,
Prends le diapason
De l'intime durée.

(If you want me to stay with you,
Do not disperse your voice,
Pitch it
To the intimate moments.)

(Natalie Barney, 'Un panier de
framboises')

My preface is an anecdote from the lesbian life of Natalie Barney (1877–1972). In Paris-Lesbos in the early 1900s, Barney lost her lover, writer Renée Vivien, to the Baroness Hélène van Zylen de Nyevelt. In an attempt to win Vivien back, the Amazon of Letters sent a vocal emissary to avenue du Bois, where the baroness lived, to serenade Vivien. The Leporello who voiced Giovanni-Barney's desire was her friend the opera diva and reigning 'Carmen', Emma Calvé (1858–1942). Calvé's serenade began with the celebrated lament 'J'ai perdu mon Euridice' from Gluck's opera *Orfeo ed Euridice*.

Gluck's Orfeo was originally sung in 1764 (in Italian) by a castrato, a decade later (in French) by a tenor. For the opera's revival at the Théâtre Lyrique in 1859, Berlioz transposed Orfeo's tenor part down from F major to C for the voice of Pauline Viardot-Garcia (1821–1910). Berlioz's description then of Viardot's performance in 'virile antique costume', weeping by the side of her dead lover, conveys messages a Barney *abbandonata* meant her unseen lover to hear:

> Madame Viardot makes of [the lament] one of the prodigies of expressions . . . delivered in three different ways: firstly, with a contained grief and in slow movement; then in sotto voce, pianissimo, and with a trembling voice choked by a flood of tears; finally, after the second adagio . . . with a more animated movement . . . throwing herself, mad with despair . . . with bitter cries and sobs of a distracted grief. (Berlioz 1973: 19–20)

Initially, it seems, Barney's Orphic emissary failed her. Only when Calvé sang Carmen again did windows open and Vivien appear to a waiting Barney on the street below (Chalon 1979: 76–7, 89). In the opera, Orfeo's lament serves as

'Sapphonics', in P. Brett, E. Wood, and G. C. Thomas (eds.), *Queering the Pitch: The New Gay and Lesbian Musicology* (London: Routledge, 1994), 28–33.

epilogue to a reunion and rescue that also failed. It inscribes Orfeo's suffering and loss. But given the private context of Calvé's performance the lament succeeded: as epilogue to a contested, but only temporarily interrupted, love affair; prelude to renewed seduction; and ironic warning to every woman involved. In the opera, Orfeo had been prohibited both from looking at the beloved and from explaining to her why he was required to exert such 'unnatural' control over what he so 'naturally' desired. Orfeo may not see the thing he wants or he will lose it. As metaphor, as myth, the opera's conventional meaning is both emphasized and subverted by the lesbian context, a travesty Orfeo represents: her embodiment of a desire between women that society and culture prohibit and silence, her longing for what women may not have, makes visible the experience of lesbian invisibility as it gives voice to forbidden desire.

Both the female Orpheus and her lesbian listener divine difference. Pauline Viardot's daughter, the composer Louise Héritte-Viardot, recalls: 'My mother had been much worried about the opera, for she did not know how to treat the part. She had thought out all the details most carefully, had studied the classic sources and had sketched her whole costume herself. But Orpheus *the man* had been as a sealed book to her until [during the dress rehearsal] her hour of inspiration came.' Because the singer's daughter finds Orpheus *the woman* 'difficult to speak of', she produces two unnamed listeners as evidence and mute witnesses to its Sapphonic effect. One, 'a young girl, fell in love with Orpheus. She grew thin and pale, and her mother in despair resolved to ask my mother's help' to 'cure' her. The two mothers conspired to disillusion the girl. 'Trembling with excitement at the prospect of seeing her beloved', she met instead a monstrous reversal, a fake: Viardot's siren Orpheus disguised as harpy 'in dressing-gown, unkempt hair, cross, irritable, thoroughly disagreeable'. The other, a widowed goldworker who lived with her sister, had anonymously left flowers in Viardot's dressing room during every performance, having 'spent most of her earnings on flowers and theatre tickets, as to see and hear Orpheus was her idea of bliss'. When Viardot discovered this admirer's identity, she embraced and visited her: the diva and her fan became lifelong friends (Héritte-Viardot 1978: 102–5).

While in modern opera practice the substitution of female mezzo or contralto for castrato voice is well established, some men still find the female Orpheus unsettling and inauthentic. John Eliot Gardiner deplores the habit as 'alien, fudged, distorted'. For Tom Hammond, 'the deep maternal contralto . . . cannot approach dramatic conviction. A woman's voice inevitably deploys entirely extraneous and disturbing sexual overtones which are not only inappropriate to the personality of Orfeo but . . . do little to conjure up the elegiac and other-worldly character of the castrato voice' (Howard 1981: 112–18, 105–11). Their reactions suggest it is the sound as much as spectacle of desire in the body of the female Orpheus that disturbs because it sends the wrong message. How did Viardot or Calvé sound?

Contemporary reports suggest a big, strong voice with an exceptional 3-to 3½-octave range from G below C to the high F of the Queen of the Night (Pleasants 1967: 85). Whether defined as dramatic soprano or coloratura mezzo, I call Sapphonic this type of voice that refuses standard categories and is today considered a rare phenomenon. Its flexibility, versatility, and power cross over and integrate the physical (and psychological?) boundaries of sites that produce vocal pitch and tone and are commonly distinguished in the female voice as head (soprano), middle (mezzo), and chest (contralto) registers.

In the contralto register, Viardot's lower octave and Calvé's 'voix de poitrine' could produce a powerful 'masculine' sound, or what Paul Robinson calls in Verdi's mezzo roles a 'baritonal fierceness': 'It would be a mistake to call them mannish, but they are indelicate in the extreme' (Robinson 1986: 174–7). In defiant political roles such as Lady Macbeth, Verdi exploits in the female chest voice its paradoxical effects of sexual ambiguity, overpowering vocal authority, and potential for violence.

As this voice makes its sudden ascent from chest to head register, its break through sonic and anatomical boundaries is technically hazardous. 'The peculiar quality of Madame Viardot's voice—its unevenness, its occasional harshness and feebleness, consistent with tones of the gentlest sweetness', suggested to Henry Chorley 'that nature had given her a rebel to subdue, not a vassal to command. From the first she chose to possess certain upper notes which must needs be fabricated, and which never could be produced without the appearance of effort' (Christiansen 1984: 79, 81). Calvé's octave ascent to a high pianissimo D flat, which reached and sustained a floating tessitura for an extraordinary duration, produced what Desmond Shawe-Taylor describes as 'certain curious notes—strange, sexless, superhuman, uncanny' (Rosenthal 1965: 63–8). Calvé called this her 'fourth' voice and claimed that a castrato singer in Rome's Sistine Chapel choir, Domenico Mustafa (1829–1912), taught her how to produce it—a fascinating historical moment of transvestic vocal exchange between differently sexed and gendered bodies: a literally unsexed 'fourth' voice for a 'third' sex.

The high head or fourth voice 'fabricated' by Viardot and Calvé is 'false' (falsetto): an artificial or 'unnatural' sound, signifying to some the uncannily queer lost sound of a castrato or male falsetto, to others a 'sexless' boy chorister. Where the castrato had a comparable three-octave range to Viardot and Calvé (an octave higher than the baritone), the falsettist must extend the upper register to take on boy alto or soprano roles. Both male and female falsetto, using Viardot's technique of 'covered tone' or *sotto voce* (literally 'under the voice'), suppress head and chest resonance to produce a clear, light, high sound. This fourth voice, says Isaac Nathan, a nineteenth-century music theorist and composer, is a 'species of ventriloquism', 'an inward and suppressed quality of tone, that conveys the illusion of being heard at a distance' (1823: 63).

Castrato and falsetto have been theorized mostly in terms of male voice and male desire. Wayne Koestenbaum, who cites Nathan, proceeds brilliantly to connect theories of production in voice manuals with the discourse of homosexuality (1991). He suggests the so-called 'unnatural' male falsetto (especially in its ornamental trill, vibrato, and tremolo), which sounds outside a 'normal' range and requires long discipline, work, and training to produce, is 'part of the history of effeminacy', a fourth voice 'for a fourth sex, not properly housed in the body'.

Is singing itself 'natural'? asks Koestenbaum. Are vocal registers 'a fact of nature', or constructed categories of gender and sexuality? Whether 'register represents a zone of opportunity or of prohibition, register-theory expresses two central dualities: true versus false, and male versus female. It is only loosely accurate to say that manuals privilege chest production as male and true, and dismiss head production as female and false', but register-theory 'gives most weight to the difference between natural and unnatural', a duality that reflects, even foreshadows, he thinks, distinctions between hetero- and homosexuality.

Voice theories of the falsetto as a defective and degenerate 'break' with 'natural' singing are linked to medical theories of sexual perversion. As Sander Gilman remarks on 'vocal stigmata': 'The change of voice signalled the mas-culinization of the male; its absence signalled the breaking of the voice, the male's inability to assume any but a 'perverted' sexual identity' (1988: 322–3). Gilman notes that clinical case studies of men in the 1890s by sexologist Richard Krafft-Ebing, among others, that 'regularly record the nature of the patient's voice', considered the high breaking voice a standard sign of homo-sexuality. More recently another medical expert, John Money, finds in the fab-ricated voice a defining characteristic of transsexualism: the female-to-male transsexual modulates intonation and pitch in the voice 'to be more baritonal and mannish'; the male-to-female transsexual 'to a feminine-sounding husky falsetto' (Garber 1992: 106).

Koestenbaum suggests the 'break' between registers '(called Il Ponticello, the little bridge) is the place *within* one voice where the split between male and female occurs, and that failure to disguise this gendered break is, like falsetto, fatal to the art of "natural" voice production' (1991: 220). Calvé and Viardot valued the break—a place of risk, of breakdown, which training usually seeks to disguise or erase—as an asset. So did admirers: Turgenev prized Viardot's 'defective' voice for its mental as well as technical risks over 'a beautiful but stupid one, a voice in which beauty is only superficial' (Vechten 1920: preface). The extreme range in one female voice from richly dark deep chest tones to piercingly clear high falsetto, and its defective break at crossing register borders, produces an effect I call sonic cross-dressing: a merging rather than splitting of 'butch' authority and 'femme' ambiguity, an acceptance and inte-gration of male and female.

This border-crossing voice I call Sapphonic is a transvestic enigma, belong-ing to neither male nor female as constructed—a synthesis, not a split. Having this voice entails risk, but not a necessary loss: it can be *both* butch and femme, *both* male and female. Its challenge is to the polarities of both gender and sex-uality as these have been socially constructed and as stable, unchallengeable binary symmetry, for it suggests that both gender and sexuality are transfer-able. In acoustic effect, its combination of different registers refuses vocal cat-egories and natural/unnatural polarities, and confounds simplistic messages about female desire (and relationships among female desire, class, age, sexual status, and identity) in music's texts and opera's roles conventionally assigned to specific female voice-types. For listeners, the Sapphonic voice is a destabilizing agent of fantasy and desire. The woman with this voice, this capacity to embody and traverse a range of sonic possibilities and overflow sonic boundaries, may vocalize inadmissible sexualities and a thrilling readiness to go beyond so-called natural limits, an erotics of risk and defiance, a desire for desire itself.

On Black Music and Authenticity

DAVID HATCH AND STEPHEN MILLWARD

The concept of black music has become something of a shibboleth, to the extent that even to question its pre-eminence amounts to heresy. This state of affairs is typified by the fact that white contributions to blues and even rock & roll are often ignored or grossly undervalued. For instance, in the standard discographies of blues—Dixon and Godrich (1982) and Leadbitter and Slaven (1968)—white musicians are only included either by mistake or as incidentals. In Dixon and Godrich, many of the talented white blues artists are omitted, for example, Jimmie Rodgers, Frank Hutchison, and Dick Justice. Furthermore, Jimmy Davis, the eventual Governor of Louisiana, is included only on the grounds that he accompanied the black guitarist Oscar Woods in certain recording sessions. Similarly, Leadbitter and Slaven, in their introduction, imply that blues records made by white artists would be of no interest to collectors and scholars. The white one-man band, Harmonica Frank Floyd, achieved his listing in error, owing principally to his authentic 'black sound'. Leadbitter and Slaven had, however, planned to produce a rock & roll discography which, we may be sure, would have included at least the major white performers.

In some measure these attitudes were reinforced in the first instance by all of us who collected blues records and wrote on the subject in the early 1960s. However, few of those individuals would have either anticipated or remained sanguine about the present position.

We are still of the opinion, of course, that those designated as black have made the major contributions to the development of pop music from its earliest origins. Nevertheless this view does not necessarily support the rejection of all white achievements nor the reification of all black performances. Inverted racism is no less patronizing than other forms of discrimination.

As any student of American history will know, delineation of people in terms of black and white has always been enormously complex in both theoretical and practical terms. The traditional dichotomous distinction in fact belies these complexities. In dividing persons into those who are black and those who are white we are merely distinguishing between those who are completely white and those who are not. Any such rigid distinction ignores not only the legal but the social realities in the United States.

The whole basis of racial segregation is undermined in terms of fact, if not in terms of consequence, by the phenomenon of 'passing for white'. Though

From Blues to Rock: An Analytical History of Pop Music (Manchester: Manchester University Press, 1987), 116–20.

official figures cannot, by definition, be available, Stetson Kennedy (1959) reported at that time an estimate of between five to eight million persons as having successfully passed for white in the USA (52). Obviously many of these people will have had both children and grandchildren by now. Ortiz Walton (1972) refers to an assessment made by Robert Stuckert that in 1960 21 per cent of 'white Americans' were of partially black descent (47).

Legally speaking, the definition as to what constituted a black person varied from state to state under the 'Jim Crow' laws. In Alabama, Arkansas, and Mississippi, anyone with a 'visible' and/or 'appreciable' degree of 'Negro blood' was subject to segregational laws as a black person whereas in Indiana and Louisiana the colour line was drawn at one-eighth and one-sixteenth Negro blood respectively. Clearly, then, it was possible to change one's status—and therefore legal rights—by moving from one state to another.

Such factors render particularly nonsensical any equation of race with musical (or any other) ability. The logic of this kind of racial distinction would lead us to expect that all of the greatest musicians in the blues, soul, and rhythm & blues fields would be those most obviously black in appearance. In fact this is demonstrably not the case: many of the most eminent artists in 'black music' would not correspond to this classification, for example Charley Patton, Robert Johnson, Chuck Berry, Little Richard, and Sam Cooke.

The rigid distinction between 'black' and 'white' is, however, despite its illogicality, a fact of life and has led, throughout the history of the United States, to degradation and suffering for those classed as black. In the pop business, until very recently, it has always been the white musicians and entrepreneurs who have most clearly profited. Jimmie Rodgers, as we have already noted, became extremely wealthy whereas artists such as Charley Patton, Willie Johnson, and Willie McTell died in relative poverty and obscurity. A comparison between the earnings and acclaim achieved by, on the one hand, Elvis Presley and, on the other, Chuck Berry further demonstrates the continuing discrepancy in financial reward and popular acceptance. This disparity is typified by what is perhaps an apocryphal story of how the Rolling Stones arrived for a recording session at Chess to find Muddy Waters painting the studio.

These inequalities were not, however, always a matter of racial division, for not only were middle-class blacks generally contemptuous of rural Southern music but at the same time there had also been a tradition—from W. C. Handy to Berry Gordy—of successfully exploiting that 'commodity'.

In recent times it has often been the case that the fact of racial segregation has blurred other divisions in American society. At least as important, from a strictly musical point of view, have been regional and class distinctions. The promotion of the concept of black music which has been motivated largely by non-musical factors might be described as the marketing of a heritage.

Perhaps the greatest musical asset for this exercise was what came to be known as soul music. For many of those to whom blues represented the degradation of Southern rural life, soul was an acceptable metamorphosis. Many soul recordings were overtly political in terms of their rejection of the notion of Blacks as second-class citizens. Many writers associated with the 'black consciousness' movement of the 1960s, particularly Eldridge Cleaver, objected to country blues on the grounds that it was insufficiently outspoken against the 'black condition'. Whereas much early soul music was produced and recorded in the South, it is nevertheless true that the music did not reflect specifically regional concerns. On the contrary, soul was accepted as an expression of black solidarity, cutting across geographical and class boundaries.

The term 'soul' both delineated a music and constituted the realization of a new-found pride in a racial identity. It was originally used as a label for a jazz style of the late 1950s which incorporated gospel music and blues, thus acknowledging the roots of 'contemporary black music'. A distinct political character was evident in the work of leading artists operating in this field, culminating in the work of Oscar Brown Jr. whose 1961 album *Sin and Soul* included explicit comments on the oppression of Blacks such as 'Work Song' and 'Bid 'em in'. Established modern jazz musicians were influenced by the new climate: Charles Mingus issued such items as 'Fables of Faubus'—Orval Faubus was a segregationist Governor of Arkansas—on his album *Mingus Ah Um* (1959), while Max Roach recorded a political statement of LP length, *We Insist! Freedom Now Suite* (1960).

By the early 1960s there was a general sense of disillusionment with the strategy of the Civil Rights movement. Many felt that the death of Martin Luther King in 1968 symbolized the impotence of that philosophy. As far as many young Blacks were concerned the modest, even subservient, requests for what were already their constitutional rights were viewed as indicative of an 'Uncle Tom' approach. Following the adoption of Sam Cooke's 'A Change is Gonna Come' (1965) as a black anthem, soul music was increasingly used as a vehicle for a more forceful expression of political statements and demands. Instances included 'Say it Loud—I'm Black and I'm Proud' (James Brown, 1968), 'Give More Power to the People' (the Chi-Lites, 1971), and 'Young, Gifted and Black', a Nina Simone song dating from 1968, which seemed to amount to a statement of triumph by 1972 when Aretha Franklin's version was released.

. . . [E]arly soul singers such as Solomon Burke and Arthur Alexander employed aspects of country music in their work. While we may regard such experiments as resulting from conscious decisions on the part of the artists, we must recognize that—given the fact that the power-base of the pop music industry, especially in the South, was still under white control—involvement by white songwriters, musicians, producers, and entrepreneurs in the development of soul was almost inevitable. Though there was an apparent increase in the participation by Blacks in the music that they now regarded as their own property, the relationship between soul (and its successors) and white pop music was to continue.

This may be illustrated by the importance to soul of essentially white guitar styles. Steve Cropper, who appeared on innumerable soul recordings made in the city of Memphis, played in a style much closer to that of other white musicians such as Chet Atkins and Scotty Moore than to the leading blues and R & B guitarists of the period. Cropper became so influential that for a time his was *the* guitar sound in soul music, avoiding almost entirely the use of vibrato so common amongst his black counterparts. The use of the wah-wah pedal was crucial to the success of the records of Isaac Hayes, commencing with 'Shaft' in 1971; by then this technique was well established in rock music, having been originally introduced by such players as Frank Zappa and Eric Clapton. It remained a feature of soul recordings for many years, most obviously in the work of the Isley Brothers, as on the album *3 + 3* (1973) and many others.

On Africanisms

PORTIA MAULTSBY

The conceptualization of music-making as a participatory group activity is evident in the processes by which black Americans prepare for a performance. Since the 1950s, for example, black music promoters have advertised concerts as social gatherings where active audience involvement is expected. Promotional materials encourage potential concertgoers to 'Come and be moved by' a gospel music concert or to 'Come and jam with', 'Come and get down with', or 'Come and party with' a secular music concert. As Nketia notes, regardless of context—church, club, dance hall, or concert hall—public performance of black music serves

> a multiple role in relation to the community: it provides at once an opportunity for sharing in creative experience, for participating in music as a form of community experience, and for using music as an avenue for the expression of group sentiments.   (1974: 22)

This communal approach to music-making is further demonstrated in the way contemporary performers adapt recorded versions of their songs for performance on the concert stage. Many begin their songs with ad lib 'rapping' (secular) or 'sermonettes' (sacred) to establish rapport with the audience. When the singing actually begins, the style of the performance complements the 'we are here to jam' or 'we are here to be moved' attitude of the audience/congregation. The audience/congregation is encouraged to participate in any way, sometimes even to join performers on stage. Soul singer Sam Moore of the duo Sam and Dave recalls how he 'would stop the band and get hand-clapping going in the audience [and] make them stand up' (1983). Many black performers use this technique to ensure the active participation of audience members in the music event.

Music-making in Africa requires the active involvement of all present at the musical event. This approach to performance generates many of the cultural and aesthetic components that uniquely characterize music-making throughout the African diaspora. In a study of gospel music, ethnomusicologist Mellonee Burnim defines three areas of aesthetic significance in the black music tradition: delivery style, sound quality, and mechanics of delivery (1985: 154). These categories are useful in examining qualities common to both African and African-derived music.

'Africanisms in African-American Music', in Joseph E. Holloway (ed.), *Africanisms in American Culture* (Bloomington: Indiana University Press, 1990), 188–92.

Style of Delivery

Style of delivery refers to the physical mode of presentation—how performers employ body movements, facial expressions, and clothing within the performance context. Burnim accurately asserts that music-making 'in Black culture symbolizes vitality, a sense of aliveness' (1985: 159). This 'aliveness' is expressed through visual, physical, and musical modes, all of which are interrelated in African musical performances. Olly Wilson defines the African musical experience as a

> multi-media one in which many kinds of collective human output are inextricably linked. Hence, a typical traditional [African] ceremony will include music, dance, the plastic arts (in the form of elaborate masks and/or costumes) and perhaps ritualistic drama. (1981: 99)

In African-American culture, the element of dress in musical performance is as important as the musical sound itself. When performers appear on stage, even before a musical sound is heard, audience members verbally and physically respond if costumes meet their aesthetic expectations. Performers establish an image, communicate a philosophy, and create an atmosphere of 'aliveness' through the colourful and flamboyant costumes they wear. In the gospel tradition, Burnim observed that performers dress in 'robes of bold, vivid colours and design'. She also noted:

> At the 1979 James Cleveland Gospel Music Workshop of America in New Orleans, Louisiana, one evening's activities included a competition to select the best dressed male and female in gospel choir attire. The fashions ranged from brightly colored gowns and tuxedos to matching hooded capes lined in red. (1988: 115)

Ethnomusicologist Joyce Jackson, in her study of black gospel quartets, also observed that costumes are judged as part of the overall performance in gospel quartet competitions (1988: 161–90).

The importance of dress in black music performances is demonstrated further in the popular tradition. In the film *That Rhythm . . . Those Blues*, vocalist Ruth Brown recalled how audiences expected performers to dress in the latest fashions. Responding to this expectation, Brown labelled herself as one of the first female singers

> that became known for the crinoline and multi-petticoats and the shoes that matched the dresses. All of the singing groups [of the 1950s and 1960s] were impeccably dressed [in co-ordinated outfits] when they went on stage. If they wore white shoes . . . they were *white* shoes. Griffin shoe polish made all the money in the world.

The array of colours and fashions seen in concert halls, black churches, and other black performance sites is a vital part of the total visual experience. It is such a fundamental part of black cultural expression that these same principles of dress are observed by the audience. For example, audiences at Harlem's Apollo theatre always wore the latest fashions. During the 1930s the men 'appeared in tight-belted, high-waisted coats' and the women 'gracefully glided through the lobby in tight slinky dresses, high heels, and veils' (Fox 1983: 69).

The visual dimension of performance, according to Burnim's model, extends beyond dress to the physical behaviour of musicians and their audiences. In communicating with their audiences, musicians display an intensity of emotion and total physical involvement through use of the entire body. Nketia points out that physical expression is part and parcel of music-making in African cultures:

> The values of African societies do not inhibit this. . . . it is encouraged, for through it, individuals relate to musical events or performing groups, and interact socially with others in a musical situation. Moreover, motor response intensifies one's enjoyment of music through the feelings of increased involvement and the propulsion that articulating the beat by physical movement generates.   (1974: 206–7)

Accounts of religious services conducted by slaves illustrate the retention of these cultural values and attitudes in the New World. During the worship, slaves became active participants, freely responding verbally and physically to the sermon, the prayer, the music, and each other. This behaviour prompted missionary Charles Colcock Jones to describe a revival meeting of slaves as a 'confusion of sights and sounds'!

> Some were standing, others sitting, others moving from one seat to another, several exhorting along the aisles. The whole congregation kept up one loud monotonous strain, interrupted by various sounds: groans and screams and clapping hands. One woman specially under the influence of the excitement went across the church in a quick succession of leaps; now down on her knees with a sharp crack that smote upon my ear the full length of the church, then up again; now with her arms about some brother or sister, and again tossing them wildly in the air and clapping her hands together and accompanying the whole by a series of short, sharp shrieks. . . . Considering the mere excitement manifested in these disorderly ways, I could but ask: What religion is there in this? (Myers 1972: 483)

Observers of other religious gatherings of slaves noted that 'there is much melody in their voices; and when they enjoy a hymn, there is a raised expression of the face . . . '. And 'they sang so that it was a pleasure to hear, with all their souls and with all their bodies in unison; for their bodies wagged, their heads nodded, their feet stamped, their knees shook, their elbows and their hands beat time to the tunes and the words which they sing . . .' (Reed and Matheson 1835: 219; Bremer 1854: 393).

The style of delivery that characterized musical performance during the seventeenth, eighteenth, and nineteenth centuries continues to be operative in both sacred and secular spheres of contemporary black America: black people consciously use their entire bodies in musical expression, and music and movement are conceived as a single unit. These concepts clearly are demonstrated in the presentation style of performers of popular music. Soul singer Al Braggs, for example, concluded his shows by pulling out all the vocal and choreographic stops . . . in the general manner of James Brown or Little Richard. He screams; he groans; he crawls rhythmically across the stage on his stomach dragging the microphone behind him; he leaps over, under, and around the microphone behind him; he lies on his back and kicks his feet in the air; he does some syncopated push-ups; he falls halfway over the edge of the stage and grabs the nearest hands; initiating a few unfinished dance steps, he does the limbo; he bumps and grinds; and gradually maneuvers himself off stage with a flying split or two, still twitching and shouting.   (Keil 1966: 122)

This 'unification of song and dance', as Burnim describes it, characterizes contemporary performances of black music. In the gospel tradition, choirs 'march' in synchronized movements through the church during the processional and 'step', 'clap', and 'shout' (religious dance) to the music performed during the worship (1985: 160). This intrinsic relationship between music and movement is also seen during performances by popular music groups. Sam Moore commented that he and his partner, Dave Prater, 'danced and moved around so much' during their performances that they lost 'at least four or five pounds a night in sweat' (1983). The accompanying musicians also danced in synchronized steps while playing their instruments, a concept patterned after black marching bands.

Sound Quality

The participatory dimension of music performance is only one aspect of the conceptual approach to music-making. Descriptions of black music performances over several centuries reveal that timbre is a primary feature that distinguishes this tradition from all others. The concept of sound that governs African-American music is unmistakably grounded in the African past. As Francis Bebey suggests.

The objective of African music is not necessarily to produce sounds agreeable to the ear, but to translate everyday experiences into living sound. In a musical environment whose constant purpose is to depict life, nature, or the supernatural, the musician wisely avoids using beauty as his criterion because no criterion could be more arbitrary.

Consequently, African voices adapt themselves to their musical contexts—a mellow tone to welcome a new bride; a husky voice to recount an indiscreet adventure; a satirical inflection for a teasing tone, with laughter bubbling up to compensate for the mockery—they may be soft or harsh as circumstances demand.   (1975: 115)

In Africa and throughout the diaspora, black musicians produce an array of unique sounds, many of which imitate those of nature, animals, spirits, and speech. They reproduce these sounds using a variety of techniques, including striking the chest and manoeuvring the tongue, mouth, cheek, and throat. When arranged in an order and bound together by continuity of time, these sounds form the basis for musical composition.

The unique sound associated with black music results from the manipulation of timbre, texture, and shading in ways uncommon to Western practice.

Musicians bring intensity to their performance by alternating lyrical, percussive, and raspy timbres; juxtaposing vocal and instrumental textures; changing pitch and dynamic levels; alternating straight with vibrato tones; and weaving moans, shouts, grunts, hollers, and screams into the melody. The arbitrary notion of beauty has resulted in descriptions of black music as 'weird', 'strange', 'noise', 'yelling', 'hollering', 'hooting', 'screaming'. The use of these words clearly indicates that the black music tradition does not adhere to European-American aesthetic values.

Instrumental sounds in African and African-derived music imitate timbres produced by the voice. Bebey observes that

> Western distinctions between instrumental and vocal music are evidently unthinkable in Africa where the human voice and musical instruments 'speak' the same language, express the same feelings, and unanimously recreate the universe each time that thought is transformed into sound.   (1975: 122)

Black instrumentalists produce a wide range of vocally derived sounds— 'hollers', 'cries', 'grunts', 'screams', 'moans', and 'whines', among others—by varying timbre, range, texture, and shading. They create these sounds by altering traditional embouchures, playing techniques, and fingerings and by adding distorting devices. The vocal dimension of instrumental sounds is reflected in such phrases as 'make it talk', 'talk to me', and 'I hear ya talkin'' used by black people to communicate that their aesthetic expectations have been met.

On Musical Behaviour

JOHN BLACKING

The importance of creative listening is too often ignored in discussions of musical ability, and yet it is as fundamental to music as it is to language. The interesting thing about child prodigies is not so much that some children are born with apparently exceptional gifts, but that a child can respond to the organized sounds of music before he has been taught to recognize them. We know, too, that children who are not prodigies may be equally responsive, though they may not relate to music in a positive way and seek to reproduce their experience.

In societies where music is not written down, informed and accurate listening is as important and as much a measure of musical ability as is performance, because it is the only means of ensuring continuity of the musical tradition. Music is a product of the behaviour of human groups, whether formal or informal: it is humanly organized sound. And, although different societies tend to have different ideas about what they regard as music, all definitions are based on some consensus of opinion about the principles on which the sounds of music should be organized. No such consensus can exist until there is some common ground of experience, and unless different people are able to hear and recognize patterns in the sounds that reach their ears.

In so far as music is a cultural tradition that can be shared and transmitted, it cannot exist unless at least some human beings possess, or have developed, a capacity for structured listening. Musical performance, as distinct from the production of noise, is inconceivable without the perception of order in sound.

If my emphasis on the primacy of listening may seem too far-fetched, consider what would happen even to a tradition of written music if mere performance were regarded as the criterion of musical ability. Musicians know that it is possible to get away with a bad or inaccurate performance with an audience that looks but does not listen; and even listening audiences can be trained to accept gross deviations from familiar scores of Chopin or Beethoven, which were at first currently fashionable but later became part of a pianistic tradition. The continuity of music depends as much on the demands of critical listeners as on a supply of performers.

When I say that music cannot exist without the perception of order in the realm of sound, I am not arguing that some kind of theory of music must precede musical composition and performance: this would obviously be

How Musical is Man? (London: Faber, 1976), 10–12, 25–6.

untrue of most great classical compositions and of the work of so-called 'folk' musicians. I am suggesting that a perception of sonic order, whether it be innate or learned, or both, must be in the mind before it emerges as music.

I deliberately use the term 'sonic order' and stress experiences of external listening because I want to emphasize that any assessment of man's musicality must be based on descriptions of a distinctive and limited field of human behaviour which we will provisionally call 'musical'. Sonic order may be created incidentally as a result of principles of organization that are non-musical or extramusical, such as the selection of equidistantly spaced holes on a flute or frets on a stringed instrument. Similarly, an apparent lack of sonic order may express ordered arrangements of numbers, people, mathematical formulae, or any elements that can be transformed into sound, such as the application of a sine curve to an electronic machine.

If a composer tells me that I must not expect to hear any order 'in the notes', but that I may observe it in patterns of circles and cones that are given to performers, or in numbers that are fed into a machine, I may prefer to call the noise reactionary magic rather than avant-garde music; but I cannot exclude it from any estimation of human musicality, even though it probably does not belong to the area of behaviour that includes the music of the Bushmen, the Bemba, the Balinese, Bach, Beethoven, and Bartók. It is humanly organized sound, intended for other human ears and possibly enjoyed by the composer's friends, and thus concerned with communication and relationships between people.

[. . .]

The study of music in culture is what Alan Merriam advocated in his important book, *The Anthropology of Music* (Evanston, Ill.: Northwestern University Press, 1964), but ethnomusicologists have yet to produce systematic cultural analyses of music that explain how a musical system is part of other systems of relationships within a culture. It is not enough to identify a characteristic musical style in its own terms and view it in relation to its society (to paraphrase a definition of one of the aims of ethnomusicology by Mantle Hood, who has done more for the subject than almost any other living ethnomusicologist). We must recognize that no musical style has 'its own terms': its terms are the terms of its society and culture, and of the bodies of the human beings who listen to it, and create and perform it.

We can no longer study music as a thing in itself when research in ethnomusicology makes it clear that musical things are not always strictly musical, and that the expression of tonal relationships in patterns of sound may be secondary to extramusical relationships which the tones represent. We may agree that music is sound that is organized into socially accepted patterns, that music-making is to be regarded as a form of learned behaviour, and that musical styles are based on what man has chosen to select from nature as a part of his cultural expression rather than on what nature has imposed on him. But the nature from which man has selected his musical styles is not only external to him; it includes his own nature—his psychophysical capacities and the ways in which these have been structured by his experiences of interaction with people and things, which are part of the adaptive process of maturation in culture. We do not know which of these psychophysical capacities, apart from hearing, are essential for music-making, or whether any of them are specific to music. It seems that musical activities are associated with specific parts of the brain, and that these are not the same as the language centres. But we shall never know what to look for until we study the creative processes that are present even in a learned performance of music, much as they are present in the sentences of a learned language.

Ethnomusicology's claim to be a new method of analysing music and music history must rest on an assumption not yet generally accepted, namely, that because music is humanly organized sound, there ought to be a relationship between patterns of human organization and the patterns of sound produced as a result of human interaction. I am chiefly interested in the analysis of musical structures because this is the first step toward understanding musical processes and hence assessing musicality. We may never be able to understand exactly how another person feels about a piece of music, but we can perhaps understand the structural factors that generate the feelings. Attention to music's function in society is necessary only in so far as it may help us to explain the structures.

On Music and Dance

RICHARD LEPPERT

In all their popularity, country dances, whether English or French-inspired, demanded the imposition of mechanisms to control their meaning in ways that supported the sociocultural ideologies of the upper classes. This was notably achieved in contemporaneous dance treatises which consistently attempted to preserve in all social dancing the aristocratic air of the minuet via the careful articulation of body carriage and gesture. Kellom Tomlinson in his *The Art of Dancing* (1735, though written in 1724) thus provided minute directions to achieve proper standing, walking, and bowing (eleven pages to the last)—all prior to one's setting foot on a dance floor; and he described the body, part by intricate part, as regards the function of each in dancing, from the nose (which 'points out the graceful Twists or Turns the Head makes') down to the joints of the toes (Tomlinson 1735: 22). Pierre Rameau's treatise devoted nearly fifty pages to the proper movements of the arms and wrists in various dances, and likewise provided an acutely detailed account of the proper manner to doff one's hat, replete with engraved illustration (Rameau 1728). Only men of leisure could hope to have sufficient time available to learn such skills of self-definition as given in John Essex's amended 1710 English translation of a famous treatise by Raoul Auger Feuillet, where no less than six pages of notational signs were required to account for the requisite hand gestures and foot movements proper to social dancing (Feuillet 1710: 7–12). Ironically, the precision of decorum demanded by these treatises could hardly be maintained in a country dance, but this in fact undoubtedly only heightened concern therewith. In any event, there can be no question that dance and dance gesture, as well as body carriage not strictly part of but appropriate to the dance (standing, etc.), were self-consciously perceived as a principal means of establishing a class hierarchy of the human body. As Giovanni-Andrea Gallini, one of the most famous dance-masters of his time, put it:

> When once an habit of easy dignity, with an unaffected air of portliness, has been sufficiently familiarised, it will constantly shew itself in every even the most indifferent gesture or action of the possessor ... Does he come into a room? His air immediately strikes the company in his favor, and gives a pre-possessing idea to his advantage.

Music and Image: Domesticity, Ideology and Socio-Cultural Formation in Eighteenth-Century England (Cambridge: Cambridge University Press, 1988), 101–3.

Gallini was specific as to what he meant by contrast to this portrait, as when he described a young woman lacking in all such skills. Failing to execute a correct 'curtesy', she 'hangs her head, and makes her obeisance with her eyes fixed on the ground, or pokes out her head, sticking back her arms, *like one of the figures in Hogarth's dance* [my italics]'. In a word, such a lady gave the appearance of an urban peasant (Gallini n.d.: 126, 128–9).

It is significant that Gallini would refer to a printed image by which to make his point. He did so precisely because the memorable/memory image is what his prescribed gestures were intended to create, the failure to do so threatening instead to result in a grotesquerie from the Hogarthian pantheon. It is important to point out that the convention of gesture as outlined for the social dancing carried over into imagery, in particular—for my concerns—to portraiture, by which the same class-specific, class-defining meanings were commonly achieved by artists and described by artist-theoreticians.

John Weaver in his *Anatomical and Mechanical Lectures upon Dancing* (1721) explicitly outlined the class distinctions delineated by body carriage and physical motion. In his politics of motion, the upper classes moved with seamless smoothness, at once natural-(ized) and ordered. The lower classes by contrast moved haltingly, without grace. Without question Weaver's paradigm is true as regards a peasant's execution of the minuet, but it is patently false with respect to the rhythms labouring people establish in the routines of their work. Conversely, persons unused to working with their hands immediately display clumsiness when required to take up an unfamiliar tool. This says something quite obvious: as long as one group defines the rules (in this case, ones outlining the means by which bodily grace is measured) only they can win the game:

> From the Regular or Irregular Position, and Motion of the Body, we distinguish the handsome Presence, and Deportment of the fine Gentleman, from the awkward Behaviour of the unpolish'd Peasant; we discover the graceful Mien of a young Lady, from the ungainly Carriage of her Maid; and this Regulation even stamps Impressions on the Mind, which we receive from the outward Figure of the Body; for as the Soul is inform'd from the external Objects of Sensation, how careful ought we to be, to give the most agreeable Impressions, which cannot be affected without this Regularity; and how commendable, how advantageous is it, for a Gentleman, or Lady, to be *Adroit* at every Step, and, that every Motion, and Action of the Body, be consonant to Symmetry and Grace. (Weaver 1721: p. viii–ix)

It is tempting to explain these gestural intricacies to French influences of the early eighteenth century and to the minuet in particular: all very un-English. But such an explanation fails when we examine a book by Thomas Wilson on English country dancing published at the end of my period in 1820. What is striking about this treatise is evident in its title, *The Complete System of English Country Dancing*. That is, country dancing was here *rationalized*. What this text established was an order, a scheme of classification, one presuming its opposite, disorder. What I suggest here is not a false accusation; to be sure, from Playford onwards country dances were passed on through instructions, either verbally or with choreographic notation—but in Playford, as in dance fans, these instructions were normally very cursory. By contrast, what Wilson had in mind was something very different. He opened his lengthy book (over 300 pages) with the following:

> A COUNTRY DANCE, As it is named, is almost universally known as the national Dance of the English, and as correctly known, is constructed on mathematical and other scientific principles, clearly displayed in its operative effect, when properly and well performed.   (Wilson 1820: 1)

Wilson thus established at the outset two significant premisses: first, that country dances were national in character, and second (in fact as corollary to the first) that they were constituted on rational grounds ('mathematical and other scientific principles'). That is to say that country dances were quintessentially English precisely because they were highly rationalized. I am suggesting that by the early years of the nineteenth century in England the *contredanse*, represented in Mozart as revolutionary, had been completely subsumed by the dominant culture (though to be sure that was a culture reformulating itself within boundaries that now also encompassed the wealthy sectors of the middle class).

Toward the end of the book Wilson appended a previously published chapter on ballroom etiquette as it related particularly to country dances, and to more recently introduced species such as quadrilles and waltzes. With respect to country dancing, Wilson outlined a code of behaviour dependent on (self-) policing, all in an effort to control spontaneity:

> No person during a Country Dance, should hiss, clap, or make any other noise, to interrupt the good order of the company.
>
> No Lady or Gentleman must, during a Country Dance, attempt at Reels, or any other Figures, in the same room.
>
> Snapping the fingers, in Country Dancing and Reels, and the sudden howl or yell too frequently practised, ought particularly to be avoided, as partaking too much of the customs of barbarous nations [in part he makes reference here to the Scots, whom the English essentially considered ungovernable].   (267)

And if disputes arose they must be referred to the Master of Ceremonies 'and his decision abided by'. The Master of Ceremonies, playing the twin role of king and chief justice, was himself to wear a sash 'or some conspicuous ensignia' to distinguish him from the rest. And in this metaphorical nation, whose citizens ideally moved only to prescribed order, there was even to be a written constitution: 'To preserve greater order, and to prevent disputes, it is advisable, that the proprietors, or the conductors of Public Balls and Assemblies, should have the foregoing Etiquette, particularly so much of it as relates to the company, written and hung up in some conspicuous part of the room, during such evenings as the Balls or Assemblies may be held' (268–9).

On Music and Orientalism

RALPH P. LOCKE

Opera is rich in works that construct visions of the non-Western world and its inhabitants: Rameau's *Les indes galantes*, Mozart's *Die Entführung aus dem Serail* (The Abduction from the Harem), Bizet's *Les pêcheurs de perles* (The Pearl Fishers), Verdi's *Aida*, Strauss's *Salome*, Puccini's *Turandot*. In these operas the representation of what recent critical theory calls 'the Other' is most clearly announced in the basic plot, in characters' names, and in costumes, sets and props. But to what extent do the libretto and the music also participate in this project?

This question, at least as regards music, easily lends itself to a narrower formulation: to what extent do these operas signal Otherness—Turkishness, Indianness, Chineseness, and so on—through musical materials that depart from Western stylistic norms or even reflect specific musical practices of the region in question (drones and ostinato rhythms, distinctive modes and melodic patterns, even whole borrowed tunes)? Scholars and critics have repeatedly posed the problem in these terms, only to find themselves frustrated by three limitations: general stylistic aberrations are often applied indiscriminately by composers to vastly different geographical settings; borrowed tunes and the like tend to lose distinctive features by being uprooted and transplanted; and whole stretches of these operas are written in an entirely Western idiom. There is, to be sure, more to be said about such styles and 'borrowings', some of which prove to be more distinctive—and even more characteristic of the region in question—than a first hearing would suggest (as we shall see in regard to the Bacchanale).

Here, though, I would like primarily to emphasize a broader and possibly more fruitful approach: treating these operas as works inscribed with an ideologically driven view of the East, a view now generally known as 'Orientalism'. By focusing on the larger attitude towards the East in an 'Oriental'—indeed, one might say 'Orientalist'—opera, rather than restricting our focus only to its most striking or anomalous passages, we free ourselves to consider a wide range of operatic techniques, including how individual figures are characterized: by means of basic structural manipulations (such as a love duet in which one of the characters dominates), revealing contrasts of musical style, distinctive orchestrational combinations, and so on.

Contemporary with the mature works of Verdi and Wagner, *Samson et Dalila*

'Constructing the Oriental "Other": Saint-Saëns's *Samson et Dalila*', *Cambridge Opera Journal*, 3:3 (1991), excerpted and adapted from 261–3, 266–8, 285–8 by the author.

(first performed in 1877, and in Saint-Saëns's manuscript called simply *Dalila*) is an intriguingly atypical example of Orientalism. The paradigmatic plot for Orientalist operas, seen in close to pure form in Meyerbeer's *L'africaine*, Félicien David's *La perle du Brésil*, Verdi's *Aida*, Delibes's *Lakmé*, and Puccini's *Madama Butterfly*, could be summarized as follows (in words that, I hope, also capture certain attitudes of the time):

> young, tolerant, brave, possibly naive, white-European tenor-hero intrudes, at risk of disloyalty to his own people and colonialist ethic, into mysterious, dark-skinned colonized territory represented by sexy dancing girls and deeply affectionate, sensitive lyric soprano, incurring wrath of brutal, intransigent tribal chieftain (bass or bass-baritone) and blindly obedient chorus of male savages.

Samson, in contrast, is set in the biblical world; its heroine is a ripe mezzo (*L'africaine* set the precedent), indeed a vile seductress, rather than a delicate soprano, and the natives are an imperial power holding the West (the Hebrews) captive, an inverted power relationship that is set right by Samson's God-ordained act of destruction, which would also have been understood as an act of national liberation. The mixture of plots enriches rather than confuses, largely because the added elements (national liberation, Western piety, *femme fatale*) reinforce rather than contradict the opera's underlying binary opposition between a morally superior 'us' (or 'collective Self') and an appealing but dangerous 'them' ('collective Other') who come close to causing 'our' downfall. At certain points, though, Saint-Saëns subverts the very binarism that he and his librettist have established in the opera's plot. [. . .]

Most obviously exotic in style are the two ballets. The 'Dance of the Priestesses of Dagon' (Act 1) gives the fullest glimpse of the Philistine maidens, who wave their garlands invitingly in front of the Hebrew warriors but with no apparent ill intent; Delilah, joining in their 'voluptuous gestures', provokes Samson in a more calculating manner, despite his efforts to avert his eyes from 'the enchantress'. Part of the demure yet intriguing effect in this dance comes from the elusive modal language of the music: the opening phrase (see Ex. 9) uses a minor third degree but a major sixth, in addition to a lowered seventh, that single most distinctive sign of temporal or geographical displacement in Western music of recent centuries. Certain orchestrational touches reinforce the sense of Easternness or perhaps 'ancientness' (e.g. the fourth beat of Ex. 9,

Ex. 9. Act 1, Dance of the Priestesses

lightly graced by a tap on the tambourine and flicked notes in the harp). Though it would be hard to claim anything specifically Middle Eastern or bib-lical here, the music characterizes for us the pagan priestesses who dance to it as voluptuous yet innocently so.

The music of the even more famous Bacchanale (Act 3) gestures more plainly toward local colour, in a quasi-ethnographic sense. In this ballet, the Philistine princes and maidens prolong their debauched revels beyond daybreak, urged on by hypnotic rhythms in the castanets, timpani, and low strings (notably an asymmetrical ostinato: 3 + 3 + 2), and by florid melodies and garish harmonies based on the Arab Hijāz mode, which Saint-Saëns chose no doubt for its strik-ingly 'foreign' augmented second between degrees 2 and 3. (See Ex. 10a and, for comparison, Ex. 10b: a North African muezzin call, likewise in Hijāz.) The rhapsodic oboe solo that opens the number (Ex. 11) captures something of the improvisatory freedom that Westerners find so remarkable in much Middle Eastern music, and its opening bears an uncanny resemblance to Ex. 10b and other related versions of the muezzin's call to prayer available in transcription and on disc. But the evocation of Hijāz here amounts almost to caricature, in that Saint-Saëns presents the augmented second at not one but two places in the scale: between degrees 2 and 3 but also between 6 and 7. This is, to be sure, an option in traditional Arab music (it is called 'Hijāz Kār'), but one is at least as likely to pair a lower tetrachord in Hijāz with an upper tetrachord from a dif-ferent mode. Saint-Saëns's repeated privileging of the augmented second

Ex. 10a. Act 3, Bacchanale: melody resembling Hijaz mode

Ex. 10b. *Adhan* (muezzin call) in Hijaz mode, transcribed by Joseph Rouanet in Algeria in the early twentieth century; La Musique arabe, in *Encyclopédie de la musique et dictionnaire du Conservatoir* , ed. Albert Lavignac and Lionel de La Laurencie (Paris, 1920–31), pt. l, vol. v (1922), 2818–19

Ex. 11. Act 3, Bacchanale: opening oboe solo

degree in the Bacchanale can be seen as an instance of the standard Oriental-ist practice of emphasizing what differs most from Western practice; such an emphasis reifies the Easterner's difference, thereby widening rather than bridg-ing the dichotomous gap between Self and Other.

Like the 'Dance of the Priestesses', the Bacchanale is sensuously (and, at its close, powerfully) orchestrated, and features many other surprising touches that, however fantastic their origin, add further strangeness—clear instances of the 'Other' as at once monstrous/frightful and attractive. [. . .]

The problem of how to 'read' the Philistines—whether as the 'Other' or as an aspect of 'us'—arises most insistently in Act 3, where we finally encounter the Philistine customs and religion in full dress. As in the Abimelech scene in Act 1, much of the music here is given a mocking edge. The chorus of Philistines taunts the blinded strongman, in a manner reminiscent of the Bach Passions, though Saint-Saëns denies his crowd any dignity. We seem, indeed, to have been thrown into a comic opera: 'Prends garde à tes pas! Samson! Samson! Sa colère est plaisante! Ah! ah! ah! ah! ah!' (Watch your step, Samson! His anger is ludicrous! Ha, ha, ha, ha, ha!) Delilah adds her own insults, in music that is largely a brittle, sarcastic rewriting of her supposedly sincere love music in Act 2, a blast of abusiveness that stirs Samson's vengeful wrath and that, no less important, may cause operagoers—trained to trust words and music of love—to feel disgust for this subversive harridan. The High Priest now has his one and only confrontation with Samson and proves how shallow he is by calling on Samson to 'amuse us by singing again to your lover the sweet offers' that brought his downfall ('Divertis-nous, | En redisant à ton amante | Les doux propos'), and by ridiculing the impotent 'anger' of Samson's God.

Just what the Philistines as a whole are worth is revealed in the big triumphal hymn ('Gloire à Dagon vainqueur'), a fascinating mix of Bach and Offenbach. This number, the last in the opera except for Samson's brief prayer for strength and the act of destruction itself, begins with a hearty, major-mode turn-plus-scalar-descent figure presented in unison by the strings and suggesting festive music of the Baroque; any sacred implications, though, are immediately dis-tanced when the High Priest and Delilah enter singing, against the orchestra's Baroque figure, an overly simple cantus firmus in exact canon (Ex. 12), sug-gesting archaic rigidity and perhaps also, precisely by contrast to the grand outward gestures and lavish orchestration, banality or lack of ethical substance. The instrumental forces become more shrill as the hymn proceeds (extensive

Ex. 12. Act 3, Hymn to Dagon (from the opening section)

melodic passages for glockenspiel!), and—at the singers' words 'Dagon se révèle' (Dagon reveals himself), when the sacred fire flares up—the music changes into a *con brio* dance, something between a quick polka and a cancan, above which Delilah eventually adds some coloratura swoops (Ex. 13) and (with the High Priest) fifteen measures of chromatic vocalizing that Collet reads as ecstatic, though the swoops at least might be read as vulgarly theatrical—or perhaps simply as Italian-operatic. The choice of a trite hopping dance—music that is utterly philistine (with a small 'p')—for a moment of supposed religious exaltation seems, on one level, clearly conscious, a final castigation of the degenerate Philistines and the ungodliness of their religion. A second, 'endotic' reading, though, is also possible: that Saint-Saëns, under the guise of castigating some safely distant other time and place, was in fact reproaching his European contemporaries, including autocratic governmental leaders and narrow-minded churchly authorities. Indeed, Saint-Saëns was throughout his life an outspoken republican and anticlericalist.

I would suggest a third possible reading of the Hymn to Dagon, more positive than those just discussed, but not incompatible with them. Perhaps Saint-Saëns felt free here to give expression to a more joyful, populist view of religious celebration than was considered strictly acceptable in the official, often sanctimonious high culture of the day. Realms of joyful feeling, even dancelike impulses—major elements in certain sacred works of Bach, Handel, or Haydn—had in nineteenth-century sacred music largely been repressed as unseemly. (We regularly encounter them again in our own century, e.g. in choral works of Mahler, Stravinsky, Honegger, Orff, Poulenc, Bernstein.) If Saint-Saëns—a confirmed atheist—did at times feel hemmed in by the proprieties of bourgeois religiosity, represented for example by the choral festivals of England (for which he composed several now forgotten works, including a major one that explicitly contrasts paganism and Christianity: *La Lyre et la harpe*), he may have welcomed, or at least unconsciously responded to, the possibility of giving voice to a more sensual and unbuttoned strain of religious feeling.

Ex. 13. Act 3, Hymn to Dagon (dance-like section)

Such straightforward appreciation of the hymn leads us to a fourth and final interpretive possibility that reads the number as at once positive *and* negative: perhaps Saint-Saëns intended the very grandeur and spunk of this music to form an ironic contrast to the cruelty of the Philistines' behaviour and the barbarity of their religion. Operagoers may have inferred the double message in the Dagon scene as targeting not just the Philistines themselves but also the current-day inheritors of the Philistines' territory (and, etymologically, of their name): the Palestinians. Westerners have often emphasized the achievements of ancient Middle Eastern peoples, precisely in order to set in relief what they see as the near-total lack of present-day achievement and culture in the region. Émile Baumann seems to be pointing in this direction when he argues that the musical richness of Saint-Saëns's hymn scene 'will turn to the profit of the drama': Samson calling out to God his 'invocation of vengeance' amid something that, to Baumann, sounds like 'the passing sword of the exterminating angel' ('a hissing scale' in the violins, 'followed by the descending fracas of the trombones'), at which point the heathen temple collapses (Baumann 1905: 409). We are presumably all the more impressed and edified by the Philistines' sudden downfall, and their demotion from imperial rulers to uncivilized tribesmen wandering among ruins, because their religious music so successfully combined 'the grandeur of a page of Handel with something more lively and colorful' (Tiersot 1924: 96). But such an interpretation does not foreclose the possibility that the cause of their downfall, namely the hollowness of their souls, is audible in the hymn to Dagon that preceded and perhaps motivated it.

References

Bataille, Georges (1962), *Death and Sensuality* (New York: Walker).

Barthes, Roland (1977), 'The Grain of the Voice' (originally published as 'Le Grain de la voix', *Musique en jeu* 9), in Stephen Heath (ed. and trans.), *Image-Music-Text* (London: Fontana), 179–89.

Bauman, Émile (1905), *Les Grandes Formes de la musique: L'Œuvre de C. Saint-Saëns* (Paris).

Bebey, Francis (1975), *African Music: A People's Art*, trans. Josephine Bennett (New York: Lawrence Hill).

Berlioz, Hector (1973), *Gluck and His Operas*, trans. Edwin Evans (1915) (Westport, Conn.: Greenwood Press).

Blacking, John (1976), *How Musical Is Man?* (London: Faber; 1st pub. 1973).

Bohlman, Philip V. (1993), 'Musicology as a Political Act', *Journal of Musicology* 11:4, 411–36.

Bremer, Frederika (1854), *Homes of the New World*, 1, trans. Mary Howitt (New York: Harper).

Brownmiller, Susan (1975), *Against Our Wills: Men, Women and Rape* (Harmondsworth: Penguin).

Burnim, Mellonee (1985), 'The Black Gospel Music Tradition: A Complex of Ideology, Aesthetic, and Behaviour', in Irene V. Jackson (ed.), *More Than Dancing* (Westport, Conn.: Greenwood Press).

——(1988), 'Functional Dimensions of Gospel Music Performance', *Western Journal of Black Studies* 12.

Chalon, Jean (1979), *Portrait of a Seductress: The World of Natalie Barney*, trans. Carol Burko (New York: Crown).

Christiansen, Rupert (1984), *Prima Donna: A History* (New York: Viking).

Dellamora, Richard, and Fischlin, Daniel (1997) (eds.), *The Work of Opera: Genre Nationhood, and Sexual Difference* (New York: Columbia University Press).

Dent, Edward J. (1960), *Mozart's Operas* (1913) (London: Oxford University Press).

Dixon, R. M. W., and Godrich, J. (1982), *Blues and Gospel Records: 1902–1943* (Essex: Storyville).

Donnington, Robert (1981), 'Don Giovanni Goes to Hell', *Musical Times*, June.

Feuillet, Raoul Auger (1710), *For the Further Improvement of Dancing*, trans. John Essex (London).

Ford, Charles (1991), *Così? Sexual Politics in Mozart's Operas* (Manchester: Manchester University Press).

Foucault, Michel (1979), *The History of Sexuality*, vol. i, trans. R. Hurley (Harmondsworth: Penguin).

Fox, Ted (1983), *Showtime at the Apollo* (New York: Holt, Rinehart & Winston).

Frith, Simon (1996), *Performing Rites* (Oxford: Oxford University Press).

——and McRobbie, Angela (1979), 'Rock and Sexuality', *Screen Education* 29, 3–19.

Gallini, Giovanni-Andrea (n.d.), *Critical Observations on the Art of Dancing* (London).

Garber, Marjorie (1992), *Vested Interests: Cross Dressing & Cultural Anxiety* (New York: Routledge).

Gay, Peter (1969), *The Enlightenment: An Interpretation*, vol. i: *The Rise of Modern Paganism* (London: Wildwood House).

Gilman, Sander L. (1988), 'Strauss and the Pervert', in Arthur Groos and Roger Parker (eds.), *Reading Opera* (Princeton: Princeton University Press), 306–27.

Gledhill, Christine (1978), '*Klute*: A Contemporary *film noir* and Feminist Criticism', in E. Ann Kaplan (ed.), *Women in Film* (London: BFI).

Hatch, David, and Millward, Stephen (1987), *From Blues to Rock: An Analytical History of Pop Music* (Manchester: Manchester University Press).

Héritte-Viardot, Louise (1978), *Memories and Adventures*, trans. E. S. Buchheim (1913) (New York: Da Capo Press).

Howard, Patricia (1981) (ed.), *C. W. von Gluck: Orfeo* (Cambridge: Cambridge University Press).

Jackson, Joyce (1988), 'The Performing Black Sacred Quartet: An Expression of Cultural Values and Aesthetics', Ph.D. dissertation, Indiana University.

Keil, Charles (1966), *Urban Blues* (Chicago: University of Chicago Press).

Kennedy, Stetson (1959), *Jim Crow Guide to the U.S.A.* (Westport, Conn.: Greenwood Press).

Koestenbaum, Wayne (1991), 'The Queen's Throat: (Homo)sexuality and the Art of Singing', in Diana Fuss (ed.), *Inside/Out: Lesbian Theories, Gay Theories* (New York: Routledge), 205–34.

Leadbitter, Mike, and Slaven, Neil (1968), *Blues Records: 1943–1966* (London: Oak Publications).

Leppert, Richard (1988), *Music and Image: Domesticity, Ideology and Socio-Cultural Formation in Eighteenth-Century England* (Cambridge: Cambridge University Press).

——(1993), *The Sight of Sound: Music, Representation, and the History of the Body* (Berkeley: University of California Press).

Locke, Ralph P. (1991), 'Constructing the Oriental "Other": Saint-Saëns's *Samson et Dalila*', *Cambridge Opera Journal* 3:3, 261–302.

——(1998), 'Cutthroats and Casbah Dancers, Muezzins and Timeless Sands: Images of the Middle East', in Jonathan Bellman (ed.), *The Exotic in Western Music* (Boston: Northeastern University Press), 104–36, 326–33. A fuller version but with less ample footnotes is in *Nineteenth-Century Music* 22 (1998–99) 20–53.

McClary, Susan (1991), 'Getting Down off the Beanstalk', in *Feminine Endings: Music, Gender, and Sexuality* (Minneapolis: University of Minnesota Press), 112–31.

Maultsby, Portia (1990), 'Africanisms in African-American Music', in Joseph E. Holloway (ed.), *Africanisms in Amerian Culture* (Bloomington: Indiana University Press).

Merriam, Alan P. (1964), *The Anthropology of Music* (Evanston, Ill.: Northwestern University Press).

Meyer, Leonard B. (1960), 'Universalism and Relativism in the Study of Ethnic Music', *Ethnomusicology* 4:2, 49–54.

Moore, Sam (1983), interview with Portia Maultsby, 25 Feb.

Mulvey, Laura (1975), 'Visual Pleasure and Narrative Cinema', *Screen* 16:3, 6–18.

Myers, Robert Manson (1972) (ed.), *The Children of Pride* (New Haven: Yale University Press).

Nathan, Isaac (1823), *An Essay on the History and Theory of Music* (London: Whittaker).

Nattiez, Jean-Jacques (1990), *Music and Discourse: Toward a Semiology of Music*, trans. Carolyn Abbate (Princeton: Princeton University Press).

Nketia, J. H. Kwabena (1974), *The Music of Africa* (New York: Norton).

Pleasants, Henry (1967), *The Great Singers from the Dawn of Opera to Our Own Time* (London: Gollancz).

Rameau, Pierre (1728), *The Dancing-Master*, trans. J. Essex (London).

Reed, Andrew, and Matheson, James (1835), *A Narrative of the Visit to the American Churches* (London: Jackson & Walford).

Robinson, Paul (1986), *Opera and Ideas: From Mozart to Strauss* (Ithaca, NY: Cornell University Press).

Rosenthal, Harold (1965) (ed.), *The Opera Bedside Book* (London: Gollancz).

Rouanet, Joseph (1922), 'La Musique arabe', in Albert Lavignac and Lionel de La Laurencie (eds.), *Encyclopédie de la musique et dictionnaire du Conservatoire* (Paris, 1920–31), pt. 1, vol. v.

Said, Edward, W. (1995), *Orientalism* (1st pub. 1978) (Harmondsworth: Penguin, new edn. with afterword).

Solie, Ruth A. (1993), *Musicology and Difference* (Berkeley: University of California Press).

Taylor, Jenny, and Laing, Dave (1979), 'Disco-Pleasure-Discourse', *Screen Education* 31, 43–8.

Tiersot, Julien (1924), *Un demi-siècle de musique française (1870–1919)* (Paris, 2nd edn.).

Tomlinson, Kellom (1735), *The Art of Dancing Explained by Reading and Figures* (London).

Vechten, Carl Van (1920), *Interpretations* (New York: Alfred A. Knopf).

Walton, Ortiz (1972), *Music Black, White & Blue: A Sociological Survey of the Use and Misuse of Afro-American Music* (New York: Morrow).

Weaver, John (1721), *Anatomical and Mechanical Lectures upon Dancing* (London).

Wilson, Olly (1981), 'The Association of Movement and Music as a Manifestation of a Black Conceptual Approach to Music', in Report of the 12th Congress, London, American Musicological Society, 98–105.

Wilson, Thomas (1820), *The Complete System of English Country Dancing* (London).

Wood, Elizabeth (1994), 'Sapphonics', in P. Brett, E. Wood, and G. C. Thomas (eds.), *Queering the Pitch: The New Gay and Lesbian Musicology* (London: Routledge), 27–66.

Part III
Music and Class

Introduction

Much work on music and class has focused on the role culture plays in a society's power relationships. The sociocultural formation has consequently been examined so as to tease out the dominant ideology embedded within it, and to show how this has been evaded or resisted by subordinate social groups. Among the more fruitful critical methods that have been used are those that study subcultural style (often borrowing anthropological tools such as homology and *bricolage*), those that seek out implied subject positions (the particular social group a cultural artefact is addressing), and those that adopt either Louis Althusser's idea of interpellation, or Antonio Gramsci's idea of hegemony. Althusser's theory of interpellation, put simply, is that ideology works by 'calling out' to you in a manner that produces self-recognition: for example, if I recognize myself as 'stiff upper lipped', I know I am typically English. Gramsci's theory of hegemony concerns the means by which a ruling group exercises moral and intellectual leadership. Hegemony works by persuasion, and a culture offers various arenas for hegemonic negotiation (popular music is one such). If hegemony fails then coercion becomes necessary.

Theodor Adorno's writings did not become known to many Anglo-American musicologists until the late 1970s, at which time they began to set the agenda for debates about musical modernism and the social and aesthetic values of popular music. He railed against what he saw as the passivity of the masses, the standardization of successes, and the manipulative strategies of the culture industry with such a fiercesome intellect that he had to be tackled head on before a new theoretical framework could develop. His insights, however, still cannot be simply dismissed or ignored (see Subotnik 1991: 15–83 and Paddison 1993). Adorno insists that if music is experienced by people as ideology, a term which for him means something that 'befuddles their perception of social reality' (1976: 55), then the relation of music to social class is of pressing concern. In discussing questions of musical preferences, he is at pains to distinguish strata ('subjectively characterized units' such as 'urban housewives between the ages of 35 and 40') from class as a 'theoretical-objective concept' (56). Empirical results showing the listening habits of different social strata are, Adorno claims, 'more reflective of the supply planned according to strata and offered for sale by the culture industry than they are indicative of any class significance of musical phenomena' (60). He is also keen to dismiss matters pertaining to the social background of composers and, in an argument not entirely free from economic determinism, concludes: 'Society controlled music by holding its composers on a tight and not so very golden leash; potential petitioner status never favors social opposition' (58).

For Adorno, music possesses a 'truth content' that differs from the ideological role music plays, and this is located in its formal constitution. Here we may find 'the problematics, however sublimated, of realities which [a] stratum prefers to dodge' (60). Nevertheless, music's social function may 'diverge from the social meaning it embodies' (62), an assertion Adorno illustrates with reference to Hollywood's treatment of Chopin. Adorno's concerns with ideology as 'false consciousness' and with the manipulations of a 'culture industry' are typical of the Frankfurt School (of which he was a prominent member).

Dave Harker discusses A. L. Lloyd's theory of 'industrial folksong'. Lloyd was inclined towards dogma in deciding what were to be considered genuine examples of the genre, and was not beyond a certain amount of tampering with their texts. In this, the influence of the British Communist Party's cultural policy was, Harker suggests, a significant factor. A major figure in the folksong Second Revival, Lloyd presents a challenge to the ideas of forerunners like Cecil Sharp while succumbing to a similar tendency to create mythical figures. Harker finds Lloyd's 'typical' worker no more convincing than Sharp's 'peasant', and accuses Lloyd of ignoring historical evidence where it fails to support his definition of folksong.

I have included an excerpt from my study of song in the Victorian middle-class home to illustrate some of the hegemonic negotiations that occur when songs pass from a working-class to middle-class milieu and vice versa. For this cross-class interaction, there had to be places available as arenas of negotiation, such as music halls, pleasure gardens, and parks. The excerpt deals with questions of intention and reception, and considers ways in which the Victorian working class responded to bourgeois song.

Paul Willis makes use of homological analysis to understand what he terms 'subordinate cultures'—later, to be labelled 'subcultures'; the classic text being Hebdige (1979). The idea of homology is indebted to Claude Lévi-Strauss's structural anthropology, and is used to draw attention to parallels between the structure of social groups and the structure of their cultural activities and artefacts. The first extract is part of an extended critical analysis of the links between rock 'n' roll and bikers in the late 1960s and early 1970s. It can easily be argued that the case is overstated, especially regarding the 'eclipse of tonality' and the suppression of the 'discontinuities of the bar structure' in rock 'n' roll, but the homology presented is a credible one.

In the theoretical appendix to his book, Willis emphasizes the interpretative nature of homological analysis, which requires identification of a social group and that group's cultural preferences. These preferences are not 'randomly proximate' to the group, but 'differentially sought out' (191). It is active social engagement with cultural items that produces meaning. Here, Willis makes the important qualification that there is 'not a limited scope for the production of meanings', and argues for 'a more structural analysis of the "objective possibilities" of particular items in an assessment of their role in cultural relationships' (193). What he means by 'objective possibilities' is outlined in the second excerpt from his book.

Semioticians often attack homology theory on the grounds that signs are conventional and arbitrary (although, whether or not the musical sign is as arbitrary as the linguistic sign may be debated). Some of the problems with homologies may be suggested by noting that, in the period prior to Paul Willis's study, Marlon Brando and his gang of bikers in the film *The Wild One* were depicted as modern jazz fans (the rebel music of 1954 when the film was made), and that, by 1975, the heavy beat of British and American large-capacity twin-engine motorbikes had largely given way to the high-pitched whir of Japanese two-strokes.

Moving further along the path opened up by Paul Willis's 'objective possibilities', Richard Middleton shows how a concept of 'articulation' can explain the appropriation of musical forms and practices by different classes, and make possible a Marxist limit position (the importance of the economy *in the last instance*) which avoids collapsing into economic determinism: 'The argument is that while elements of culture are not directly, eternally or exclusively tied to specific economically determined factors such as class position, they *are* determined in the final instance by such factors, through the operation of articulating principles which *are* tied to class position. These operate by combining existing elements into new patterns or by attaching new connotations to them' (8). Once acquired, these connotations can be very resistant to change, and so Middleton would accept a qualified notion of homology: 'For it seems likely that some signifying structures are more *easily* articulated to the interests of one group than are some others; similarly, that they are more easily articulated to the interests of one group than to those of another' (10). The given extract considers how articulations of musical materials work in practice, and is especially insightful regarding the changes that occur in Presley's songs.

This section concludes with a satirical piece by Dai Griffiths taken from a *Critical Musicology* newsletter. The mixture of social commitment, humour, and critique is characteristic of his work, as it was of the Critical Musicology meetings held in the UK in the early 1990s. Griffiths seeks to couch his erudition in a deceptively simple and direct style of writing, in contrast to those who apply theoretical obfuscation to jejune ideas.

On Classes and Strata

THEODOR W. ADORNO

Inquiries into the social distributions and preferences of musical con-sumption tell us little about the class aspect. The musical sociologist is faced with a choice between flat statements that apply the class concept to music—without any justification other than the current political aims of the powers that be—and a body of research that equates pure science with knowing whether middle-income urban housewives between the ages of 35 and 40 would rather hear Mozart or Tchaikovsky, and how they differ in this point from a statistically comparable group of peasant women. If anything at all has been surveyed here it is strata defined as subjectively characterized units. They must not be confused with the class as a theoretical-objective concept.

Nor would the origin, the social background of composers let us infer anything cogent about the class import of music. Such elements may play a part in music—can anyone perceive the sort of beery cosiness which Richard Strauss exudes at the wrong moments, in Mycenae or in eighteenth-century nobility, without thinking of rich philistines?—but their definition tends to evaporate and to grow vague. In attempting a social interpretation of Strauss's effect in the era of his fame one would surely have a better right to associate him with words like *heavy industry, imperialism,* grande bourgeoisie. Con-versely, there is not much modern music with more of a *haut monde* habitus than Ravel's, and he came out of the most cramped lower-middle-class cir-cumstances. A differential analysis of family backgrounds is unproductive. Those of Mozart and Beethoven were similar; so, probably, were their milieus once Beethoven had moved to Vienna, rather better off than the materially insecure Austrian native; the age difference between them was no more than fourteen years. And yet Beethoven's social climate with its touch of Rousseau, Kant, Fichte, Hegel, is altogether incompatible with Mozart's.

We might cite cases that work better, but the chances are that the idea itself, the search for correspondences between class membership and a composer's social origin, involves an error in principle. The strongest argument against it is not even that in music the so-called social standpoint which an individual occupies is not directly translated into the tone language. To be considered first of all is whether, from the viewpoint of the producers' class membership, there has ever been anything other than bourgeois music—a problem, by the way, which affects the sociology of art far beyond music. In feudal and absolutist times mental labour was not too highly esteemed, and the ruling classes

Introduction to the Sociology of Music, trans. E. B. Ashton (New York: Seabury Press, 1976), 56–7, 60–2, 68–9.

generally used to delegate such labour rather than perform it themselves. Even the products of medieval courts and chivalry would have to be further investigated to establish in what measure those poets and musicians really were representative of the classes to which, as knights, they formally belonged. On the other hand, the social status of the proletariat within bourgeois society served largely to impede artistic production by workers and workers' children. The realism taught by want is not as one with the free unfoldment of consciousness.

[. . .]

The very simplest of these reflections shows how little an inventory of the stratification of consuming habits would contribute to insights into the context of music, ideology, and classes. Any assumption of a special affinity for ideologically kindred music in the conservatively class-conscious upper stratum, for instance, would in all likelihood be contradicted by the findings. Actually great music is apt to be preferred there, and that, as Hegel said, implies a sense of needs; what that music receives into its own formal constitution is the problematics, however sublimated, of realities which that stratum prefers to dodge. In this sense the music they appreciate upstairs is less ideological, not more, than the one they like downstairs. The ideological role which that music plays in privileged households is the role of their privilege and altogether different from its own truth content.

Empirical sociology has projected another, equally crude dichotomy: that today's upper stratum likes to interpret itself as idealistic while the lower boasts of its realism. Yet the purely hedonistic music consumed below stairs is surely not more realistic than the one valid above; it does even more to veil reality. If it occurred to an East German sociologist to speak of the extra-aesthetic leaning which the uneducated feel to music as to something unintellectual, a mere sensual stimulus, and to describe this leaning as materialistic in nature and therefore compatible with Marxism, such a description would be a demagogic swindle. Even if we accepted the philistine hypothesis, it would remain true that such stimuli, even in entertainment music, are more apt to occur in the expensive product of skilled arrangers than in the cheap domain of mouth organ and zither clubs. Above all, music is indelibly a matter of the mind since even on its lowest level the sensual element cannot be literally savoured like a leg of veal. It is precisely where the way of serving it is culinary that its preparation has been ideological from the start.

We can infer from this why a recourse to listening habits remains so fruitless for the relation of music and classes. The reception of music can turn it into something altogether different; indeed, it will presumably and regularly become different from what is currently believed to be its inalienable content. The musical effect comes to diverge from, if not to conflict with, the character of what has been consumed: this is what makes the analysis of effects so unfit to yield insights into the specific social sense of music.

An instructive model is Chopin. If a social bearing can without arbitrariness be attributed to any music at all, Chopin's music is aristocratic—in a pathos disdaining all prosaic sobriety, in a kind of luxury in suffering, also in the self-evident assumption of a homogeneous audience committed to good manners. Chopin's differentiated eroticism is conceivable only in turning one's back upon material practice, and so is his eclectic dread of banality amidst a traditionalism he does not sensationally violate anywhere. Seignorial, finally, is the habitus of an exuberance squandered. Corresponding to all this in Chopin's day was the social locus of his effect, and indeed, even as a pianist he would not so much appear on public concert stages as at the soirées of high society.

Yet this music, exclusive in both origin and attitude, has within a hundred years become exceedingly popular and ultimately, by way of one or two Hollywood hits, a mass item. Chopin's aristocratic side was the very one to invite socialization. Countless millions hum the melody of the Polonaise in A flat major, and when they strike that pose of a chosen one at the piano to tinkle out some of the less demanding Préludes or Nocturnes, we may assume that they are vaguely counting themselves with the elite. The role which Chopin, an important composer of great originality and an unmistakable tone, came to play in the musical household of the masses resembled the role Van Dyck or Gainsborough played in their visual household—if indeed his ill-suited function was not that of a writer who acquaints his millions of customers with the alleged morals and mores of countesses. This is how much, and with respect to class relations in particular, a music's social function may diverge from the social meaning it embodies, even when the embodiment is as obvious as Chopin.

[. . .]

If music can harangue, it is none the less doubtful what for, and what against. Kurt Weill's music made him seem a leftist social critic in the pre-fascist years; in the Third Reich he found apocryphal successors who would at least rearrange his musical dramaturgy and much of Brecht's epic theatre so as to fit the collectivism of Hitler's dictatorship. As a matter of principle, instead of searching for the musical expression of class standpoints one will do better so to conceive the relation of music to the classes that any music will present the picture of antagonistic society as a whole—and will do it less in the language it speaks than in its inner structural composition. One criterion of the truth of music is whether greasepaint is found to cover up the antagonism that extends to its relations with the audience—thus involving it in the more hopeless aesthetic contradictions—or whether the antagonistic experience is faced in the music's own structure.

Intramusical tensions are the unconscious phenomena of social tensions. Ever since the Industrial Revolution all of music has been suffering from the unreconciled state of the universal and the particular, from the chasm between their traditional, encompassing forms and the specific musical occurrences within those forms. It was this that eventually compelled the cancellation of the schemata—in other words, the new music. In that music the social tendency itself turns into sound. The divergence of general and individual interests is musically admitted, whereas the official ideology teaches the harmony of both. Authentic music, like probably any authentic art, is as much a cryptogram of the unreconciled antithesis between individual fate and human destiny as it is a presentation of the bonds, however questionable, that tie the antagonistic individual interests into a whole, and as it is finally a presentation of the hope for real reconcilement. The elements of stratification touching the several musics are secondary in comparison.

Music has something to do with classes in so far as it reflects the class relationship *in toto*. The standpoints which the musical idiom occupies in the process remain epiphenomena as opposed to that phenomenon of the essence. The purer and more unalloyed its grasp of the antagonism and the more profound its representation, the less ideological the music and the more correct its posture as objective consciousness. An objection to the effect that representation itself is reconcilement already, and is thus ideological, would touch upon the wound of art in general. Yet representation does justice to reality in so far as the organized and differentiated totality, the totality from which representation derives its idea, attests that through all sacrifice and all distress the life of mankind goes on.

In the exuberance of the nascent bourgeois era this was expressed in the humour of Haydn, who smiled at the world's course as an estranged bustle while affirming it with that same smile. It is by the anti-ideological resolution of conflicts, by a cognitive behaviour without an inkling of the object of its cognition, that great music takes a stand in social struggles: by enlightenment, not by aligning itself, as one likes to call that, with an ideology. The very content of its manifest ideological positions is historically vulnerable; Beethoven's pathos of humanity, meant critically on the spot, can be debased into a ritual celebration of the status quo. This change of functions gave Beethoven his position as a classic, from which he ought to be rescued.

On Industrial Folksong

DAVE HARKER

What was novel (and to some people, disturbing) about Lloyd's account of *Folk Song in England*, was not so much the megalomaniac breadth promised by the book's title, as the development of his theory about 'industrial folksong', which was, evidently, nothing less than 'the musical and poetic expression of the fantasy of the lower classes—and by no means exclusively the country workers'. Given the logical extension of this argument, which hinted that once the 'lower classes' became the working class, then 'folksong' had to be understood as working-class song, the outrage of the Cold Warriors in the English Folk Dance and Song Society was as inevitable as it was anti-intellectualist. But as it happens Lloyd's assertions remained very little different to Sharp's, in that, after the 'Fall',

> when the mainly unwritten culture of the peasantry was reduced to rubble, the field was by no means left free to 'bourgeois' culture, that is to the fine arts and popular entertainments licensed and provided by the established order . . . As the old lyric of the countryside crumbled away, a new lyric of the industrial towns arose, frail at first but getting stronger, reflecting the life and aspirations of a raw class in the making, of men handling new-fashioned tools, thinking new thoughts, standing in a novel relationship to each other and to their masters.   (Lloyd 1967: 316)

There then follows a sentimental glorification of what Lloyd pronounced to be the 'typical creator of industrial ballads', who

> made his song under a hedge perhaps, sheltering from the rain after a fruitless trudge round the mills for work, or who sat up all night by candlelight with a stub of pencil in his fist, writing an elegy on his neighbours killed in yesterday's pit-explosion.   (1967: 330)

Not only that, but Lloyd seems to have been specially gifted to read such people's mind. 'He'

> had a narrow political horizon as a rule, but he understood solidarity with his work-mates, could tell when he was hurt, and more and more in the nineteenth century he realized the need for fighting and said so in his songs.   (1967: 330)

Leaving aside the masculinist attitudes, what was happening here was another kind of homogenizing process, similar to that carried through by Sharp on

Fakesong: The Manufacture of British 'Folksong' 1700 to the Present Day (Milton Keynes: Open University Press, 1985), 248–53.

his 'peasants'. True, Lloyd feels keenly that workers had their own dignity, and some of them had developed class-consciousness; but the Worker as Hero (rarely Heroine) had still to be spoken *for* by the sympathetic mediator, and have even 'his' songs interpreted for the benefit of twentieth-century counterparts. There is little sense, in Lloyd's writings, of the working class being conscious of its own making, of a body of widely different women and men feeling and acting together, first at an economic and then at a political level, struggling to wrest control over their own lives from the ruling class. There is little sense, either, of the *positive* achievements of that formative working-class culture, of the institutions they built and maintained, their appropriation of aspects of the products of other class's culture, of their victories, creativity, and self-reliance.

Unfortunately, as with Sharp, Lloyd may have allowed his theoretical assumptions to work their way through into his collecting and publishing activity. It is not simply that he seems not to have known that a working-class family would not have been able to afford candles: rush-lights would have had to suffice. His understanding of the complexity and materiality of working-class culture remains superficial, and distorts his analysis. For example, during the great pitmen's strike in the north-east of England in 1844, we know that the Ranter Methodist preachers who controlled the union bureaucracy and its paper used religiose verse to bolster morale, and almost certainly sought to censor the songs which went into broadsides for the collection money. They could not control what rank-and-file pitmen and women sang, of course. When you compare the original manuscript of the pessimistic song which Lloyd decided to retitle as 'The Coal Owner and the Pitman's Wife' with his own collected versions of the fiercely militant 'Blackleg Miner', it is easy to understand what the Marxist conception of combined and uneven development can really mean! The problem is, however, that Lloyd thought fit to change the broadside text of the former piece, at times significantly, in his published work; and he confuses the reader by issuing varying versions of the latter, orally transmitted piece. And while he might have pleaded singability as a key criterion in the first edition of 'Come All Ye Bold Miners', no such excuse can exist for the 1978 edition of that work, after the issue had been brought to his attention. Similarly, we are entitled to ask why the brutal class-hatred of the chorus of Tommy Armstrong's 'Durham Strike', which Lloyd rechristened 'The Durham Lock-out', was silently edited out in 1952, and returned only as another verse in 1978. Further detailed study might well reveal other anomalies elsewhere.

The problem was, and is, that very little sustained and detailed research has yet been done on the culture of the majority of English people. This is hardly Lloyd's fault; but it does mean that his generalizations need careful scrutiny. For example, one study has shown that Lloyd had mistaken ideas about the differences between the early English concert hall and what became the music hall, stemming from the same undialectical puritanism which characterizes many CP attitudes towards commercial institutions used by workers, and paralleling Sharp's own fervent anti-commercialism. Yet it ill behoves a person unable to offer a scientific and non-contradictory definition of what he likes, and calls 'folksong', to castigate and smear the music and songs taken up and used by contemporary working-class people:

> Donkey and horse both have four legs and may pull carts but they are not the same beast; nor are the compositions of a Dylan or a Donovan folk songs by any workable definition. (Lloyd 1967: 409)

That the search for a 'workable definition' of 'folksong' is fundamentally incompatible with the materialist analysis of workers' culture and history seems never to have occurred to Lloyd. He, like Sharp, knew an elephant when he saw one; and if we choose to demur, then he seems content to rest on his authority. Any serious examination of this theoretical contradiction, of course, also represented a threat to Lloyd's hard-won position within the Second Folksong Revival.

Lloyd claimed the the Second Revival was not only based on the work of Sharp and other 'splendid pioneers', but was also in some mysterious way 'coming from below now'. This is disingenuous, at best. In fact, the history of the Second Folksong Revival as we have seen was closely involved with the cultural policy of the CPGB. The strategy was to popularize selected and modified elements of the musical culture of British workers in order to counterbalance the records from US industry, which were understood to be having deleterious effects on the culture of contemporary working-class youths. In order to side-step the worst problems posed by McCarthyism, CP intellectuals chose to emulate Fabian tactics and to permeate the clubs, at the same time as supporting institutions such as the Workers' Music Association and Topic Records. It is ironic that Lloyd should still be claiming in 1967 that 'folksong' had appealed 'for the most part' to 'young people searching for something more sustaining than the mumbled withdrawals or frantic despair of the pops', given the commercial success the Revival was currently enjoying. Lloyd, MacColl, and others won a share of the 'financial reward' accruing from the 'folk' boom: after all, they had done much of the spadework, and questions of professionalism, commercialism, and the role of capital in workers' culture always have been much more problematical than Lloyd was prepared to concede.

Such minor contradictions give us a hint of more fundamental problems with what has to be seen as Lloyd's mechanistic conception of the relationship between cultural practice and capitalist social relations, whether in history or today. According to him, 'folksong' in England constituted a recognizable body of songs,

> evolved by labouring people to suit their ways and conditions of life, and they reflect the aspirations that rise from those ways and conditions. In the process of creating this fund of song, economic conditions are more decisive than any relative distance from formal culture, book education and the like, for our experience shows that, as elsewhere, the most inventive bearers of English folk song are likely to be the liveliest-minded, best-informed of their community, but among the poorest. (1967: 22–3)

It is pointless to blame Lloyd for not producing answers to questions which still trouble contemporary cultural theorists; but this does not mean that we have to be taken in by sweeping and unsubstantiated generalizations about 'the true laconically dramatic style' of the broadside balladeer, who, according to Lloyd, was 'not poet, but a craftsman of sorts, a humble journalist in verse'. This is Sharp-ing with a vengeance, as is Lloyd's use of the comparison of 'folksong' to a pebble, an inanimate object being worked over by unconscious natural forces, rather than a product of workers' conscious cultural practice. Time and time again Lloyd wrenches us back in his description from the brink of a materialist history, trailing a liberal-populist rhetoric. Thus, while admitting that song-origins and factors of song-development were 'as mixed as Psyche's seeds', he lapses into banalities in order to rationalize what are, fundamentally, assertions based on subjective value-judgements:

> It is a poor folklorist who is not also in part sociologist, and the sociologist in us must ask why should we be interested in folk poems of a certain quality (to our way of thinking), and not in other versions that may (to us) seem short of beauty but nevertheless reach a vast public and are accepted with pleasure, and even passion. (1967: 31)

Why could not the production of a Dylan (or even a Donovan), which also gave pleasure to working-class people, be included? For all the habit of self-deprecation, Lloyd knew his 'good-style folk singer' when he listened to one.

How did Lloyd argue that songs come to represent community, let alone class interests?

> The idividual creation, or creation-by-variation if you will, is only effective if the song-maker is expressing the thought and feelings of his community, for only then is his song taken up by his neighbours and passed into general currency. (1967: 69)

Thus far 'folksong' is no different from any other kind of song, so Lloyd has to continue his prescription:

> Among creators of folk song the desire to explore the obscure margins of private experience is always less than the wish to impose individual order on common experience. So before he starts composing the maker is affected by the outlook and aspirations of his community; in short, each folk song at its inception is at least partly a product of social determinism. (1967: 69)

Did not Brecht and many other artists do this? Which songs have *not* been subject to constraints imposed by material factors? Where is the evidence to support Lloyd's factitious generalization about the psychology of the largely anonymous authors of the songs he publishes? And it is of note that, while he does attempt to reinsert some materialist analysis into the flabby idealist ideology of the Second Revival, he does so not only in a vulgar Marxist fashion, but as though in support of bourgeois pluralism. Surely, in composing a photofit picture of the 'typical' worker-songwriter, Lloyd was paralleling the production by the contemporary songwriter MacColl, and various associated lefties, of that bizarre working-class myth, *The Big Hewer* (Harker 1980: 180–5). The individual will to impose order on common experience is not that of any putative songwriter in history, but Lloyd's and MacColl's, just as Sharp constructed his mythical 'peasant'. Lloyd's appropriation of a selective version of workers' culture is just as culturally imperialist as Sharp's, and just as authoritarian, however well it fitted into the anachronistic attempt to foist a deformed version of 'socialist realism' onto English history.

Apart from the great respect in which Lloyd was (and is) held, not only on the left, but also amongst liberal intellectuals in Britain and elsewhere, one reason why he does not usually get tarred with Sharpism is his habitual self-effacement. *Folk Song in England*, the most important single book on English workers' songs ever written, is introduced by its author as 'a book for beginners and not specialists'. In spite of anything like adequate references to sources and suchlike scholarly apparatus, Lloyd nevertheless feels confident in making enormous claims and pronouncements:

> The folk songs are lower-class songs specifically in so far as they arise from the common experience of labouring people and express the identity of interest of those people, very often in opposition to the interests of the master. (Lloyd 1967: 179)

This paraphrase of a key passage from Edward Thompson's *The Making of the English Working Class* (1968: 9–10) is alright so far as it goes, but unlike the historian's account of political organization, Lloyd fails to show how (or even if) the 'common experience' of an entire class is articulated through the songs he cites. The key theoretical issue is sidestepped by mere prescription, the appeal to authority, and suchlike disreputable manoeuvres; and thus the most difficult part of the emerging historical materialist theory of culture is short-circuited. 'Industrial folksong' *had* to be

> the kind of vernacular songs made by workers themselves directly out of their own experiences, expressing their own interests and aspirations, and incidentally passed on among themselves mainly by oral means, though this is no *sine qua non*. The kind of songs created from outside by learned writers, on behalf of the working class, is not our concern here. (1967: 317–18)

But what of that enormous body of songs written by non-learned writers, whose names are known to us, for use on broadsides bought by workers, and in concert halls, whose audience were overwhelmingly working class? What of the hymns, poems, and anthems made and used by working women and men in chapels, pubs, clubs, and union halls? To Lloyd, the matter is cut and dried: concert hall songs, for example, and other 'Productions of this stamp cannot be considered folk songs by any workable definition'. But, yet again, isn't that the point? Is the 'refining definition' by example and fiat offered by Lloyd workable at all? The historical fact is that many concert hall artists, like George Ridley and Ned Corvan in the north-east, were working class, and worked and wrote for the working class (Harker 1981); but instead of trying to make his definition fit the historical evidence, Lloyd adopts the reverse policy. What doesn't fit is left out or downgraded.

On Music and Hegemony

DEREK B. SCOTT

For an outlaw to be acceptable to the bourgeoisie, he had to be, in political terms, a reformer not a revolutionary. Robin Hood emerges from his assimilation as a true patriot; he has no wish to abolish the monarchy and is ready to swear allegiance to a just king. In some ways, the enthusiasm shown for Garibaldi (albeit a republican) in the 1860s is related to the enthusiasm for the outlaw patriot. A million people turned out to welcome him in London on his visit in 1864. There were Garibaldi blouses, Garibaldi Staffordshire figures, Garibaldi biscuits, and Garibaldi songs. Besides Olivieri's Italian 'National Hymn' which had become well known in J. Oxenford's translation as 'Garibaldi's Hymn' (1861), the latter included a 'Garibaldi' of 1860 and a 'Garibaldi' of 1864; moreover, after Italian unity in 1870 interest continued for some time yet, as is shown by 'Garibaldi the True' of 1874.

Another type of outlaw ballad (for example, 'The Wolf') worked in a different way. Here the protagonist boasts of his villainy but keeps his identity anonymous; thus, an important distinction is drawn between this kind of song and unacceptable 'low' ballads such as 'Sam Hall'. In 'A Bandit's Life is the Life for Me!' of 1872, the singer adopts the persona of a roguish brigand who dwells in the mountains with his brave comrades. The appeal of the song would appear to lie in its offering the singer opportunity for a melodramatic performance calculated to inspire just the right degree of fear to stimulate excitement but not alarm on the part of listeners. The drawing-room audience is shielded from anxiety by two distancing devices: the musical accompaniment is based on a typical guitar-strumming pattern, and the bandit sings only of robbing monks and pilgrims. A clear hint is therefore given in both words and music that this is not Britain. Finally, the century which gave the world Frankenstein's monster and Count Dracula also produced the drawing-room ballad for a demonic outcast. 'Will-o'-the-Wisp' of 1860 comes complete with ghoulish laughter and a delight in evil:

> To mark their shriek as they sink and die,
> Is merry sport for me,
> I dance, I dance, I'm here, I'm there,
> Who tries to catch me catches but air;
> The mortal who follows me follows in vain,

The Singing Bourgeois: Songs of the Victorian Drawing Room and Parlour (Milton Keynes: Open University Press, 1989), 182–7.

For I laugh, ha! ha! I laugh, ho! ho!
I laugh at their folly and pain.

Where songs of outcasts were concerned, a working-class vernacular culture existed which rejected the ethics and morality of the bourgeois drawing room. A mid-century writer, commenting on the public house 'free-and-easy' entertainment, notes 'how alien the costermonger race is in sympathy and life from the respectable and well-to-do. Their songs are not ours, nor their aims nor conventional observances' (Ritchie 1858: 205). This cultural activity flourished in the pub, which was so markedly working class as to be unavailable as an arena for hegemonic negotiation. The music hall, on the other hand, frequently functioned as such. In a previous chapter it was seen how the music hall played a part in winning over a large portion of the working class to imperialist sentiment; but the music hall also provided a vehicle for bourgeois morality and values in the songs of 'respectable' entertainers like Harry Clifton in its early years, and Felix McGlennon in the later century. Clifton specialized in motto songs (for example, 'Bear it Like a Man', 'Work, Boys, Work', and 'Paddle Your Own Canoe'), though the only song of his well known today is 'Pretty Polly Perkins of Paddington Green' (parodied as 'Cushie Butterfield'). Felix McGlennon's [most familiar song now,] and one which follows an equally elevated plane of thought [to 'That, Is Love'], is 'Comrades' (1890). Some music halls, like Wilton's in London's East End, went in for regular doses of uplifting culture; there, 'an entirely local audience of sailors, tradesmen and worse' were regularly treated to a half-hour's 'drawing-room entertainment' given by 'a small troupe in evening dress, with a piano, who recited and sang operatic and ballad numbers' (Bratton 1975: 30).

Blackface minstrel troupes, who often appeared at music halls as well as more 'respectable' establishments, also included ballads (and parodies of ballads) in their entertainments. Minstrels, perhaps more than any other group of performers, helped to disseminate bourgeois song among the working class, since they performed in a wide variety of venues—large public halls, theatres, and pleasure gardens. Harry Hunter, the interlocutor of Moore's minstrels, shared Clifton's passion for earnest motto songs (for example, 'Keep a Good Heart', and 'There's Danger in Delay'). The influence of the minstrels was spread far and wide by their being imitated in villages and by urban street performers.

Street singers of all kinds—glee singers, ballad singers, blackface 'Ethiopians'—who had bourgeois songs in their repertoire, provided another source of access to this material for the working class. The street singers themselves, according to one of their number, picked up tunes 'mostly . . . from the street bands, and sometimes from the cheap concerts, or from the gallery of the theatre, where the street ballad-singers very often go, for the express purpose of learning the airs' (Mayhew 1861–2: 196). Some of these singers, of course, learned songs to earn money in middle-class neighbourhoods rather than their own. Nevertheless, the printing of drawing-room ballads as broadsides shows that an interest existed in working-class environs. Other street entertainment was provided by the variety of mechanical instruments which had begun to appear at the end of the eighteenth century. On a recent recording of nineteenth-century mechanical instruments (Saydisc 1983), a *Cabinetto* paper-roll organ can be heard playing blackface minstrel songs, a *Celestine* paper-roll organ playing Nonconformist hymns, and a street piano (commonly known as a 'barrel organ') playing music-hall songs. These instruments, particularly the street pianos (which were developed in the 1870s from the cylinder piano), were mostly made by Italian immigrants living in London. They were pushed around by itinerant street 'musicians' who often had no knowledge of music and cared little for their maintenance and tuning. Legislation was introduced in 1864 to combat what was being declared a public nuisance. However, care is needed in defining the class nature of the public to whom they had supposedly become such a nuisance. Consider, for example, the following contemporary words of caution:

> Let not those who write abusive letters to the newspapers, and bring in bills to
> abolish street music, think they will be able to loosen the firm hold which the
> barrel-organist has over the British public. Your cook is his friend, your house-
> maid is his admirer; the policeman and the baker's young man look on him in
> the light of a formidable rival.   (Haweis 1871: 535)

The 'players' of mechanical instruments did take pains, all the same, to appeal to both a middle-class and a working-class audience, for obvious economic reasons. As one of them explains to Mayhew, 'You must have some opera tunes for the gentlemen, and some for the poor people, and they like the dancing tune' (1861–2: 175). In concluding this brief survey of street music, a mention must be given to the German Bands; these other groups of immigrant musicians constituted '*the second great fact* of street music' according to Haweis (he gave priority to the barrel-organists). They, too, had a varied repertoire which included Italian arias, occasional movements of symphonies, ballads, music-hall songs, and dances.

The working class found further access to performances of bourgeois music in parks (military bandstands), spas (spa orchestras), and fairgrounds (especially after the perfection of the steam organ in the 1870s). There were also the cheap concerts, already briefly mentioned, such as those begun in the Crystal Palace by August Manns in 1855, which took place in a hall holding so many people that 'only a small charge was made for admission' (Raynor 1980: 205). The pleasure gardens are usually referred to as being in decline in the nineteenth century. Part of this decline has been attributed to the need for land for housing and industry, but that fails to account for the opening of new pleasure gardens like the Eagle Tavern in 1822 and Cremorne in 1836; the latter replaced Ranelagh (closed 1803) as Chelsea's pleasure garden. It would seem reasonable to suppose that the meaning of the word 'decline' is in no small measure related to the hostile bourgeois reaction to the pleasure gardens being increasingly invaded by the petite bourgeoisie and wealthier working class (together with what they saw as a consequent increase in vulgarity and rowdiness). The bourgeoisie were beginning to feel alarmed at the 'thousands of idle pleasure-seekers' (Ritchie 1858: 198) in the gardens in the 1850s. The wages boom of the 1860s and expansion of leisure time encouraged further working-class interest in pleasure gardens. During this decade the wealthy residents of Chelsea complained that the value of their property was falling on account of its propinquity to Cremorne. When the garden closed in 1877, its 'open air dissipation' was compared to the 'indoor dissipation of the music hall' (Lee 1970: 92).

Having seen how the working class found access to bourgeois song, the next thing to consider is the question of intention and reception involving this cultural material; for, if a relative autonomy exists, allowing meaning to be made in the process of consumption, then the meaning constructed by the working class during the consumption of bourgeois art may differ from that intended by its bourgeois creator. Tennyson, for example, might write of 'Airy Fairy Lilian', but the working class might make a new meaning of this epithet. The dialectic between intention and reception emerges in examinations made by the Select Committee on Dramatic Literature in 1832. Thomas Morton, answering questions, remarks that there is 'a tendency in the audience to force passages never meant by the author into political meanings'. As an illustration, he recalls that when the king commanded a performance of *Massaniello* during the time of the revolution in France,

> handbills were printed about the town to induce the public to assemble in the theatre, not to partake with His Majesty in the social enjoyment of the drama, but to teach him, through the story of Massaniello the Fisherman, the danger to his throne if he disobeyed the wish of his people, and the King was advised to change the play in consequence of that.

The author of the play, James Kenney, was later brought before the Committee, and he explained with bewildered irritation,

> there is no question, if I may be allowed the expression, that it has a Tory moral. The revolutionary fisherman is humiliated, and a lesson is taught very opposite to a revolutionary one.

Some of the songs of Tom Moore provide a musical parallel to the above. 'The Minstrel Boy', for example, as performed by a celebrated singer in the Crystal Palace, may have been considered a purely uplifting aesthetic experience for the huge audience, and an occasion for winning wider appreciation of bourgeois art:

> I shall never forget Grisi's rendering of 'The Minstrel Boy' at the Crystal Palace. She refused to sing again after three encores. The audience who had listened to her singing spellbound, rose in a mass, and the applause was like thunder. (Pearsall 1972: 74)

Yet 'The Minstrel Boy' also came to be appropriated as an Irish rebel song. The Anglo-Irish bourgeoisie, too, in struggling to shake off English political and economic restraints, lighted upon Moore's songs: 'The Shan Van Vocht', a rewritten 'Love's Young Dream', was published in the *Nation*, 29 October 1842, Dublin. The 'Shan Van Vocht' is the 'Poor Old Woman' who had come to symbolize a distressed Ireland. It is doubtful, however, that any Moore song held the same popularity as the songs born out of the people's own struggles, like Caroll

Malone's ballad of 1798, 'The Croppy Boy' (cropped hair was the style of French revolutionaries). The *Westminster Review* in 1855 notes that this song 'has even now, in that unhappy isle, a fatal attraction and dread significance' (37). 'The Croppy Boy' was not absorbed by bourgeois culture until the present century, when it was recorded by the concert tenor John McCormack and also featured prominently in the 'sirens' chapter of James Joyce's landmark of literary modernism, *Ulysses*.

There were a variety of ways in which the working class could respond to bourgeois song. It could be accepted without conscious alteration, any changes to words and tune being attributable to oral transmission. Thus the present-day 'Jingle Bells' is a simplified version of James Pierpont's 'The One Horse Open Sleigh' of 1857, published by Oliver Ditson & Co., Boston. The bourgeois song becomes, in cases like this, a sort of 'folksong', although one to be weeded out by mediators who have felt able to define what true folksong is (see Harker 1985: 193). Fred Jordan, for example, a Shropshire farmer 'discovered' by Peter Kennedy in 1952 whilst on a field trip recording for the BBC Folksong Archive, had bourgeois songs like Henry Clay Work's 'Grandfather's Clock' in his repertoire which earlier collectors would have rejected. A common method of working-class appropriation of bourgeois song was deliberately to change the words, but to model the new text around the original text. A nineteenth-century broadside ballad published by Pitts, 'The Chartist Song', uses Burns's 'For A' That, an' A' That' as its basis. The first stanza runs,

> Art thou poor but honest man
> Sorely oppressed and a' that.
> Attention give to Chartist plan
> 'Twill cheer they heart for a' that.
> For a' that and a' that,
> Though landlords gripe and a' that,
> I'll show thee friend before we part
> The rights of men and a' that.

The Burns original begins,

> Is there, for honest poverty,
> That hangs his head, an' a' that?
> The coward slave, we pass him by,
> We dare be puir for a' that!

Throughout 'The Chartist Song', Burns's emphasis on moral victory is transformed into the desire for political victory.

Sometimes the new text, while loosely based on the original, is changed in order to make the song more relevant to the social circumstances of the singer. Henry Clay Work's 'The Ship That Never Return'd' (1865) was transformed into the railroad song 'The Wreck of the Old '97', in which appropriated form it has survived today while the original has been forgotten. Sometimes the new text parodies the original in an attempt to ridicule its sentiments, a technique Joe Hill uses in 'The Preacher and the Slave', a parody of 'Sweet By and By'. A new text may show the influence of the bourgeois original but depart from it so radically as to require a new tune. 'The Spinner's Ship', a union song of the Preston strike of 1854, shows the influence of Charles Mackay's text to Henry Russell's song 'Cheer, Boys! Cheer!' (1852) but has dispensed with the latter's tune. Conversely, the tune may be retained but the original text completely ignored. This was, of course, common practice when the tune was a traditional air but also happened when the tune was of recent bourgeois origin: 'Strike for Better Wages', a song of the London Dock Strike of 1889, used the tune of Root's 'Tramp! Tramp! Tramp!' of 1864. It most often occurred with blackface minstrel songs, a well-known example being Joe Wilson's 'Keep Yor Feet Still!' which used the tune of Handby's 'Darling Nelly Gray'. Occasionally the tune survived more or less intact as a dance and the words disappeared altogether, as happened with 'The Dashing White Sergeant' in Britain and 'Turkey in the Straw' in the United States.

What also must be considered is the collision between bourgeois and working-class musical practice. It should not be assumed that bourgeois song was automatically simplified when adopted by a working-class singer. The author recollects hearing an archive recording of a 'folksinger' performing 'The Mistletoe Bough' with decorations not in the original. Here, for example, is one of his concluding phrases, followed by Bishop's melody.

Embellishments found in vernacular musical practice (for example, slides and decorative two-note runs up or down to a main melody note) often derive from traditional methods of enhancing an unaccompanied tune, whereas the ornamentation in bourgeois music is frequently designed to exploit the tensions of a harmonic background. Another difference between bourgeois and working-class song performance is that of *timbre*, the colour of the sound. The timbre of the 'untrained' voice lends a more natural emphasis to words, since the tone is produced as in speech, forward in the mouth, with a considerable volume of air passing down the nose; the classical singer employs artifices like the chest register and consciously avoids a nasal tone. The appropriation of bourgeois song had its effects on working-class song, however, most noticeably in the increasing fondness shown for the major key rather than the old modes. Furthermore, there was a growing assumption of accompanying harmony to tunes, and a tendency for them to imply the characteristic chord progressions of bourgeois songs.

On Subculture and Homology

PAUL WILLIS

The classical European tradition has steadily forced the body and dancing out of music, and made it progressively unavailable to the masses, and progressively harder to dance to. The absolute ascendancy of the beat in rock 'n' roll firmly establishes the ascendancy of the body over the mind— it reflects the motorbike boys' culture very closely. The eclipse of tonality and melody in the music is also the eclipse of abstraction in the bike culture.

Second, and in a related way, the suppression of structured time in the music, its ability to stop, start, and be faded, matches the motorbike boys' restless concrete lifestyle. As we have seen, it is no accident that the boys preferred singles, nor is it an accident that the rock 'n' roll form is the most suited to singles and its modern technology (fading, etc.). Both the music and its 'singles' form are supremely relevant to the style of the bike culture. For the boys, music has to accompany not determine, it has to respond in the realm of their immediate activity, not in a separate realm with its own timing and logic which require acts of entering into.

In one way, and concentrating on its oppositional aspects, the whole motorbike culture was an attempt to stop or subvert bourgeois, industrial, capitalist notions of time—the basic, experiential discipline its members faced in the work they still took so seriously. The culture did not attempt to impute causalities or logical progression to things. It was about living and experiencing in a concrete, essentially timeless, world—certainly timeless in the sense of refusing to accept ordered, rational sequences. Hearing the steady strum of the motorbike exhaust (reminiscent of the 'pulse' of their music) riding nowhere in particular (as in Joe's dream) is a steady state of being, not a purposive, time-bound action towards a functional end. In a curious way, death on the motorbike stopped time altogether: it fixed and secured this symbolic state for ever. In sum, they were exploring a state, a space, rather than a linear logic. The stream-like quality of rock 'n' roll matched, reflected, and fitted in with this concern. It could be stopped, or broken off or easily changed (as with the single) and did not intrude, with its own discipline, into concrete and spontaneous activity. As the music suppressed the discontinuities of the bar structure, it also suppressed ordered, rational time. The stream 'pulse' quality of the music could be taken and used as timelessness—or certainly as an escape from bourgeois time. In this sense, there was a profound inner connection with a

Profane Culture (London: Routledge, 1978), 77–9, 198–201.

lifestyle that was so utterly concerned with concrete action in the present and the immediate secure experiencing of the world.

[. . .]

The 'Objective Possibilities' of Cultural Items

Broadly there seem to be three possibilities in the analysis of a cultural item. It could be argued that its value and meaning is totally socially given. That is: the item itself is a cypher, without inherent structure or meaning, so that it is the social group and its expectations which supply a content. There is extreme difficulty, of course, in explaining why it should be one item and not another, one whole *genre* and not another, which is taken as the receptacle for particular kinds of socially created meanings and values. One could only explain this most basically in terms of historical accident. It could be, for instance, that a certain group is naturally exposed to certain music, so that proximity breeds a relationship which is, in the beginning, accidental in the sense that there is nothing intrinsic in the art-form which makes it, and no other form, suitable for a certain group. Once this original point of contact is made, then the process might become more continuous and directional. Because the original group value the art-form, later groups take over what they imagine to be established ways of appreciating it. Accumulation and substantiation through time could develop into what looks like a fully-blown 'aesthetic' so that people assume values and meanings to be located within the art-form rather than in their perceptions of it. Other art-forms may be rejected on the apparent basis of their intrinsic inferiority. Values held to be within the art-form may be defended as having a substantial and autonomous existence. In fact, those values, and those imagined superiorities, would be nothing more than the accumulated, located reflections of a particular way of life 'read' into the music. In this sense, a cultural item is like a mirror linked to a memory bank, holding, but without an intrinsic or transformative grasp, valued and significant images derived in the first place from society. The vantage-point of the social actors totally determines the cultural item.

Such a theory has many advantages, of course. It gets over the problem of having to analyse anything that might amount to an internal aesthetic. There would be no reason to attempt an analysis of the internal structure and quality of, for instance, pop music. The analysis would be completely social and proceed totally in terms of the qualities ascribed to the artefacts from the outside.

A polar opposite form of analysis would view the meaning and value of a cultural item as totally intrinsic and autonomous. The cultural item would consist, always, of the same immanent qualities. It would keep an essential integrity no matter what social group was responding to it. The first approach suggests, of course, that different social groups could see totally different things within the same cultural item—at least in so far as they had no knowledge of, or no influence upon, one another's tastes. The cultural item derives its meaning from outside itself and is, therefore, different for different groups.

The analysis in the second case must proceed through two stages. First, is the evaluation of the internal structure of the cultural item in its own terms: we might see this as a universal aesthetic. The cultural item would *be* the same, although the profile may alter (as the angle of vision altered), no matter from what vantage-point it was seen. Second, is the analysis of how this structure is interpreted by social groups. There can be no simple elision of codes here, though, and this makes a properly social analysis difficult. The cultural item itself would not simply mirror the social and cultural interests of any social group. It would stand its ground against the contingencies of social interpretation with a universal and unchangeable internal relation of parts and feelings. What particular groups make of it need not intrinsically connect with this.

In some senses, it is easier to imagine cultural items as having an independent objective existence separate from one another and quite apart from their social location. This is an aspect of the common-sense and powerful ideological view of social atomization and random causality which is based on the obvious physical separability of things. It saves us from the work of charting relativism and interdependency. However, this view is basically untenable. The divergence of critical opinion and social response over time, and even within the same period, demonstrates that immanent qualities are less autonomous and 'there' in cultural items than we might suppose. Furthermore, the notion of a radical epistemological disjunction between the social group and the items of its cultural field rules out the possibility of a proper social analysis, of any understanding of dialectical change and development.

My position lies somewhere between those sketched above. I argue that the importance, value, and meaning of a cultural item is given socially, but within objective limitations imposed by its own internal structure: by its 'objective possibilities'. It is the 'objective possibilities' which are taken up into homological social relationships with the social group. They should be thought of not so much in terms of content, but in terms of structure. Content is really only supplied in the last analysis by the social act and the social relationship. The same set of possibilities can encourage or hold different meanings in different ways. They can simply reflect certain preferred meanings and structures of attitude and feeling. On the other hand, because they relate to something material in the cultural item, something specific, unique and not given from the outside, the 'objective possibilities' can also suggest new meanings, or certainly influence and develop given meanings in unexpected directions. This uncertain process is at the heart of the flux from which the generation of culture flows. The scope for the interpretation or influence of the 'objective possibilities' of an item is not, however, infinite. They constitute a limiting as well as an enabling structure. It is also true that what has been made of these possibilities historically is a powerful and limiting influence on what is taken from them currently.

However, since the 'objective possibilities' are literally *possibilities*—without being quite open they are polyvalent—particular social groups can always find their distinctive form of relation to previously unseen aspects of traditional items. In fact, this is one of the classic constituting mechanisms of minority and dominated cultures. Since the obvious potential for a meaningful relation with important cultural items will already have been exploited by the dominant culture, subordinate cultures have to explore the neglected or unseen possibilities to generate their own meanings. The other important process in the development of subordinate cultures is the creative exploitation of the 'objective possibilities' of new objects and artefacts—provided by the dominant system but not fully culturally utilized by it. Often subordinate groups will seize upon the possibilities of functional artless or narrowly applied items which have been ignored by the dominant culture except for their obvious uses.

On Articulating the Popular

RICHARD MIDDLETON

The apparent coherence of most musical styles, and of the relationship they have with the societies in which they exist, is not 'natural' but contrived; it is the product of cultural work. Particularly in complex, internally differentiated societies, musical styles are assemblages of elements from a variety of sources, each with a variety of histories and connotations, and these assemblages can, in appropriate circumstances, be prised open and the elements rearticulated in different contexts. Sometimes this is obvious, as when parody (in the widest sense of the term) is used. At other times it is relatively hidden, smoothed over by extensive cultivation, familiarity, and the techniques of what Bourdieu calls 'legitimation', only to be revealed when constituent elements are wrenched away and placed in a new setting. This happens, for instance, when the *volkstümlich* tunes so popular in early nineteenth-century bourgeois domestic song (where they signify according to romantic conceptions of nation and community) are used by working-class singers for disaster ballads; when sentimental Tin Pan Alley ballad melody is 'gospelized' by Ray Charles or Otis Redding; or when the heavy four-four of the quick march (goose step?) is appropriated by the early punk bands as a mode of critique.

The strength with which particular potentially contradictory relationships are held together depends not only on the amount of objective 'fit' between the components but also on the strength of the articulating principle involved, which is in turn connected with objective social factors. John Lennon's 'Imagine', so powerful when one is listening to it, may afterwards be quite easily broken down into fairly disparate elements: radical text; rock-ballad melody, harmony, and orchestration; singer-songwriter ('confessional') piano; soul/gospel-tinged singing. What is tying these together is an ideal, or to put it more concretely, a certain position associated with some alienated intellectuals in late capitalist society. This hard-fought-for (and affecting) 'coherence' lacks sufficient material support (in terms of defined social interests) and ideological legitimacy (or threat) to sustain itself as more than a personal, transitory, hence ultimately sentimental reorientation of the musical traditions concerned. The dominant sectors of society found no difficulty in tolerating or even nodding approval of its message, a development which reached its apogee when the 1988 Conference of the British Conservative Party bellowed out the song with no hint of embarrassment.

Studying Popular Music (Milton Keynes: Open University Press, 1990), 16–21.

Ex. 14

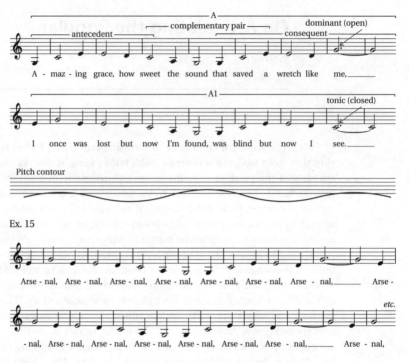

Ex. 15

Compare this case with a more collective process of rearticulation. The American revivalist hymn 'Amazing Grace' (*c.*1800) is an excellent example of the symmetries Maróthy ascribes to bourgeois song (Maróthy 1974). The words are organized around symmetrical pairs (grace/wretch; lost/found; blind/see) and the tune, at least in its best known version, not only divides into an open/closed parallelism, through its cadence structure, but within this, the subsidiary phrases form complementary pairs; moreover, the overall pitch contour follows the arch shape typical of this song type (see Ex. 14). There are many 'folk' variants of this tune which adapt it to rather different musical traditions. But the more recent adoption of the tune by British football crowds probably follows the Judy Collins 1971 hit, which retains all the features of the 'bourgeois' version. Now, however, the words become repetitive (just the name of the team). And a simple change to the tune has radical results. It is shortened to just the second and third phrases, both of which are cadentially 'open', and so what had been a self-sufficient arch shape is turned into continuous, open-ended variative repetition (see Ex. 15). 'Spiritual lyricism' is transformed into an unending, circling chant of collective support for the team. It is easy to see how the two versions 'fit' typical articulating principles traditionally associated with the bourgeoisie ('individualism') and the working class ('collectivism'). The football chant articulates its tradition to the specific interests of team supporters and soccer gangs. When, within the wider discursive context, it can be related to 'typical (mindless) working-class collectivism', it is tolerated; transmuted into the beery conviviality of a pop group like Slade, the culture represented by such chants can be patronized. But the latent threat deriving from the social power behind such chanting can often be felt, and of course erupts in the panic over 'football hooliganism'.

It is instructive to apply this analytical perspective to early rock 'n' roll—to Elvis Presley, let us say. At first rock 'n' roll was generally seen in terms of *rebellion*: this was viewed positively, by fans and fellow-travellers, or negatively, by outraged defenders of established cultural interests; in any case, it was a new music, set against existing popular types. Subsequently a more sophisticated interpretation historicized this account, describing what happened to popular music in the late 1950s and early 1960s in terms of the *incorporation* or *co-option* of rock 'n' roll into the repertoire of the hegemonic bloc. But still, the vital point is missing—that rock 'n' roll was internally contradictory from the start: not just boogie rhythms, rough sound, blues shouts, and physical involvement but also sentimental ballad melodies and forms, 'angelic' backing vocal effects and 'novelty' gimmicks.

In the case of Elvis, this problem is particularly striking because within the rock discourse he has been widely seen as both the music's first hero and its most prominent backslider. Most rock critics take this line, seeing Elvis's career as a progressive sell-out to the music industry, a transition from 'folk' authenticity (the Sun singles of 1954–5) to a sophisticated professionalism (epitomized by the ballads and movies of the 1960s) in which the dollars multiplied but musical values went by the board. But in post-war America a pure 'folk' role, untouched by commercial influences, had become impossible. The dissemination of music by radio and gramophone record permeated the whole country and every social stratum. The performers whom the young Elvis heard and learned from—gospel singers, bluesmen like Arthur Crudup, Bill Broonzy, Junior Parker, and Howlin' Wolf, country and western stars such as Bob Wills, Hank Williams, and Roy Acuff—were *commercial* artists; they, like Elvis himself, did not separate themselves from the whole wash of music that was available. When Sam Phillips, founder of Sun Records and 'creator' of Elvis Presley, said, 'If I could find a white man who had the Negro sound and the Negro feel, I could make a billion dollars' (quoted in Hopkins 1971: 66), the twin motivations, artistic and commercial, were not separated or separable. If we look at the music Elvis produced throughout his career, we find confirmation that the 'decline-and-fall' view will not stand up.

Elvis's two most notable contributions to the language of rock 'n' roll are first, the assimilation of 'romantic lyricism' and second, what I call 'boogification'. Both techniques can be found in classic form in his first national hit, 'Heartbreak Hotel' (1956). This was by origin a country and western song but its vocal has the shape of a typical blues shout. Nevertheless the rough tone, irregular rhythms and 'dirty' intonation that most blues singers would have used are for the most part conspicuously absent in Elvis's performance; his tone is full, rich and well produced, his intonation is precise, stable and 'correct', the notes are sustained and held right through, and the phrasing is legato. At the same time this lyrical continuity is subverted by 'boogification'. As in boogie-woogie, the basic vocal rhythms are triplets (♪♪♪ ♪ ♪)) and, again as in

boogie-woogie, the *off*-beat quaver is often given an unexpected accent (e.g.
♩ ♪)), producing syncopation and cross-rhythm. The effect is physical,
demanding movement, jerking the body into activity. Elvis, however, extends
the technique. He adds extra off-beat notes not demanded by words or vocal
line, often splitting up syllables or even consonants, slurring words together,
disguising the verbal sense (see Ex. 16). Occasionally, a 'sustained' note has
something like a rhythm vibrato (in triplet rhythm): listen for instance to
'Although' at the start of the second and last choruses, 'Now' at the start of the
third, and 'Well' at the start of the fourth.

The overall effect of the boogification technique is, of course, sexy, but it is
also a bit jittery and absurd; the sensuality seems almost out of control. The
combination of boogification with romantic lyricism in 'Heartbreak Hotel'—
one element deriving from established Tin Pan Alley technique, the other from
the black American subculture—produces a style already, at this early stage in
Elvis's career, teetering on the edge of that melodrama into which he was so
often to fall. The articulation of the two together, in terms and in a context set
by the values of the new youth culture, epitomizes the overall problematic proposed by this music-historical moment; broadly speaking, we can think of
romantic fantasy 'made young', 'given flesh', made to 'move' physically, while
conversely an increased corporeal freedom is presented, in line with the experience of adolescent sexuality in Protestant bourgeois society, in a guarded,
personalized, even ironic manner.

The same fusion of techniques can be found even earlier, while Elvis was still
recording for Sun. 'Milkcow Blues Boogie' (1955) is perhaps the best example
since the techniques are so well integrated, though Elvis's treatment of the song
is at such a quick tempo that the operation of the techniques themselves is less
clear than in 'Heartbreak Hotel'. The lyrical approach—the rich tone, the
singing *through* the note, the sustained legato, the controlled phrase-endings—
is most apparent for the last line of each chorus. Boogification pervades the
entire vocal, though the quick tempo means there is less scope for accenting
off-beat notes, and often the effect is so fast as to be a rhythm vibrato. The
tempo also makes accurate notation harder. However, Ex. 17 gives some typical
manifestations.

Ex. 16

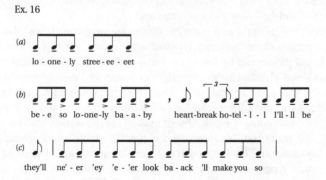

Both romantic lyricism and boogification not only date back to the beginnings of Elvis's career but also continue to be used throughout its development. There is no watershed, or 'fall from grace'. What we do see, however, is a kind of stylistic specialization. Songs which integrate the techniques like 'Milkcow Blues Boogie' (or 'Mystery Train') in the Sun period or 'Heartbreak Hotel' in the early Victor period, become less common. The techniques tend to diverge, romantic lyricism being channelled into ballads, boogification into a particular kind of rock 'n' roll song which I shall call 'mannerist'.

Elvis's huge ballad repertoire needs little commentary here, save to stress that it began not with the move to RCA but at Sun, 'Love Me Tender' (1956) and 'That's When Your Heartaches Begin' (1957) being preceded by equally sentimental ballads cut for Sam Phillips; indeed, it began earlier—when, as a boy, Elvis was entered for a talent contest at the Mississippi-Alabama Fair, it was the sentimental country and western number 'Old Shep' that he sang.

'Mannerist rock' is associated most clearly with songs, many written for Elvis by Otis Blackwell, like 'Don't Be Cruel' (1956), 'All Shook Up' (1957) and 'Please Don't Drag That String Around' (1963). The techniques of boogification are exaggerated, overplayed, even parodied. By pushing them into mannerism, Elvis distances himself from their demands, physical, and psychological. In 'All Shook Up', for example, the old techniques are still there (Ex. 18), but the triviality of the lyrics and Elvis's light, amused vocal tone tell us that this is not serious. Mannerism is usually seen as an RCA development; but once again we find that it was already developing during the Sun period, notably in 'Baby Let's Play House' (1955). Clearly, it is the certain amount of 'slack' within the articulative relationships, the fact that the combination of techniques does not fix any constituent 100 per cent to the others, that explains the possibility of differential development of elements in the mixture—rather than 'changes in style'.

Ex. 17

Ex. 18

Elvis's importance, then, lies not so much in the mix of elements (blues/country/Tin Pan Alley) which he helped to bring into being in rock 'n' roll, but in what he did with it. He transformed them—articulated them—into particular patterns. The only workable categorization of Elvis's music, as we have seen, is not by historical period but by song-type—or more precisely, by apparently self-contradictory assemblages of musical elements as they are mediated by the differential demands of varied songs at various moments. What *does* happen historically is that integrated songs become gradually less common through the course of Elvis's career, while the song-types tend to diverge, as the relatively small, well-defined audience of the Sun days gives way to a large, heterogeneous market demanding different types for different subsections. Elvis is all things to his audience *throughout* his career, but the nature of the audience changes, and with it the nature and range of the articulations of the musical materials. The unifying factor is Elvis himself—or rather, Elvis constructed in particular categories, acting as embodiments of particular articulating principles, tied to particular sets of social needs and interests.

Without this kind of analytical framework, respecting the complex levels of mediation involved and their relative autonomy, Elvis becomes simply the plaything of naked political forces (rebellious/manipulative); and the fact that the young rock 'n' roller sang ballads from the start, that the older Hollywood star could still sing rock 'n' roll songs and was still respected by rock 'n' roll fans, that his 'blues' were 'romantic' (a kind of fantasy), his ballads often 'realistic' (given flesh), or that he could make boogification ironic—all this is inexplicable.

On Grammar Schoolboy Music

DAI GRIFFITHS

1. The school I went to had just gone comprehensive when I arrived, but the policy in its early days was to preserve the appearance and procedure of the grammar, while entertaining lots of people from the secondary modern previously regarded as talentless. The teachers who arrived from the secondary modern were regarded as being hilariously down on their subject areas. Although the grammar had always been mixed—the school was good in treating boys and girls with fairness—I did glimpse the last throes of grammar schoolboys, a unique presence in all walks of life in post-war Britain, music included.

2. Grammar schoolboys were driven by academic achievement: getting eleven O-levels was quite usual in our school. But you could already tell that they'd end up emotional wrecks. At the age when most kids got on with families and work, grammar schoolboys turned to books for kicks.

3. Grammar schoolboy music is tough and gritty. The classic exponents of grammar schoolboy music were the New Manchester School and its acolytes. Grammar schoolboy music is scored for orchestras, not studios. Grammar schoolboy music is uncompromising: it doesn't compromise with pop music, in particular.

4. The trouble with grammar schoolboy music is that it gets interesting only when it stops being grammar schoolboy music: when it 'discovers' tonality, when it 'celebrates' some unusual instrument, when it risks some electricity. Otherwise grammar schoolboy music is one long procession of tough sound. You never know when grammar schoolboy music is going to end, or why it started.

5. Grammar schoolboy music has no sense of camp, no time for aestheticism. This is why grammar schoolboy operas are the dullest things. Grammar schoolboys like myths and legends, and love Greek and Latin myths because Latin and Greek were taught in grammar school. When grammar schoolboys try to appear up-to-date the results are embarrassing: that's because they're grammar schoolboys.

6. The key attitude of grammar schoolboys is petulance. If you don't follow their tortuous complexities and share in their generous self-laceration, then you're either thick, like someone from the secondary modern, or you're just not radical enough. The political stance of the grammar schoolboy is a

'Genre: Grammar Schoolboy Music', *Critical Musicology Newsletter*, 3 (July 1995) (Oxford: Oxford Brookes University).

right laugh: men of the left, they'll go miles to avoid pandering to ordinary people.

7. Grammar schoolboy music finds its legitimation in music history, continuing a deep obsession in British musical thinking, crucially mediated through post-war America, with the music of middle Europe. The key figure, grammar schoolboy music's best friend (even if he's no longer recognized as such), is Schoenberg. Here's music you can talk about and admire without ever really having to say why it's any good or why you like it. Schoenberg has a sad old story about someone in a lift telling him that he'd heard *Pierrot Lunaire* and couldn't understand what all the bother was about. That's a big grammar schoolboy thing: one day, the masses are going to catch up, and everyone'll see that they were right all along. Schoenberg's writings are the manifesto of grammar schoolboy music: regulating abstraction, through the Grundgestalt, its developing variation, and the various operations, they also define the underlying tone of grammar schoolboy music. Schoenberg's harmony book is admired for its daring, yet if music were really taught like that, the grammar schoolboy would move house to an area in which children are taught in a more sensible way. Grammar schoolboy music's like that: radical but reactionary; always ready to spot the main chance for self-promotion, and regarding the locals with disdain, as though they belong in the secondary modern.

8. Grammar schoolboy music loathed one thing in particular: pop music. Not jazz: pop music. Pop music had everything grammar schoolboy music couldn't handle: black people, accents, instant good-time sounds, camp, technology, levity, women, blunt politics, pointless music, obvious words, a good beat. Worst of all, it was the music of the secondary modern. The art school tradition in pop music—eventually punk—was a particularly tough enemy: good-looking, politically astute, addictive, and good enough by most people's standards (not those of grammar schoolboys). Selling by the bucketload, pop music people became dead wealthy, and—for all the apparent dedication to technique—power, and the libidinal ride which money can buy, is a big thing in grammar schoolboy music. There's nothing like the venom a grammar schoolboy can hiss out at music which isn't exactly like grammar schoolboy music's supposed to be. As though money wasn't enough, art-school pop-music concerned itself centrally with negotiations of desire: sex, gender, sexuality. Bad news for grammar schoolboy music, which is the music of difficult divorce, power-based flings with female students, housewives needing to do the washing and watch the kids, while the husband goes away to write a load more grammar schoolboy music.

9. The home of grammar schoolboy music is the university music department. No one else wants it. Grammar schoolboy music is the practice, music analysis the theory. Music analysis aspires to necessitate grammar schoolboy music. In fact, music analysis is also full of grammar schoolboys, except that they didn't have quite the narcissism, self-pity, ambition, or talent to produce grammar schoolboy music. Watch carefully the relation between music analysis and grammar schoolboy music: something's gone wrong there. Music analysis is growing up and wants to go its own way; it's got the language, the accent,

the looks; it's hanging out with other people; and a traumatic divorce charac-teristic of grammar schoolboys is on the cards. Without music analysis, grammar schoolboy music's in trouble deep. No one wants to hear it; what they want to hear is the bits when grammar schoolboy music stops being grammar schoolboy music; and you could have that all the time instead of in just those charitable moments. Keep an eye on it. It could be the end of the century. It could be the end.

References

Adorno, Theodor W. (1976), *Introduction to the Sociology of Music* (orig. pub. as *Einleitung in die Musiksoziologie*, Frankfurt am Main: Suhrkamp Verlag, 1962), trans. E. B. Ashton (New York: Seabury Press).

Bratton, J. S. (1975), *The Victorian Popular Ballad* (London: Macmillan).

Griffiths, Dai (1995), 'Genre: Grammar Schoolboy Music', *Critical Musicology Newsletter* 3, July (Oxford: Oxford Brookes University), n.p.

Harker, Dave (1980), *One for the Money: Politics and Popular Song* (London: Hutchinson).

——(1981), 'The Making of the Tyneside Concert Hall', *Popular Music* 1, 27–56.

——(1985), *Fakesong: The Manufacture of British 'Folksong' 1700 to the Present Day* (Milton Keynes: Open University Press).

Haweis, H. R. (1871), *Music and Morals* (London: Longmans, Green & Co.).

Hebdige, Dick (1979), *Subculture: The Meaning of Style* (London: Methuen).

Hopkins, J. (1971), *Elvis: A Biography* (New York).

Lee, Edward (1970), *Music of the People* (London: Barrie & Jenkins).

Lloyd, Albert (1967), *Folk Song in England* (London: Lawrence & Wishart).

Maróthy, János (1974), *Music and the Bourgeois, Music and the Proletarian* (Budapest: Akadémiai Kiadó).

Mayhew, Henry (1861–2), *London Labour and the London Poor*, reprint of enlarged edn. (London: Frank Cass, 1967).

Middleton, Richard (1990), *Studying Popular Music* (Milton Keynes: Open University Press).

Paddison, Max (1993), *Adorno's Aesthetics of Music* (Cambridge: Cambridge University Press).

Pearsall, Ronald (1972), *Victorian Sheet Music Covers* (Newton Abbot: David & Charles).

Raynor, R. (1980), 'London §VI, 5: Concert Life—Halls', in S. Sadie (ed.), *New Grove*, vol. ii (London: Macmillan).

Ritchie, J. E. (1858), *The Night Side of London* (London: William Tweedie).

Saydisc Records (1983), *Music of the Streets*.

Scott, Derek B. (1989), *The Singing Bourgeois: Songs of the Victorian Drawing Room and Parlour* (Milton Keynes: Open University Press).

Subotnik, Rose Rosengard (1991), *Developing Variations: Style and Ideology in Western Music* (Minneapolis: University of Minnesota Press).

Thompson, E. P. (1968), *The Making of the English Working Class* (Harmondsworth: Penguin).

Westminster Review (1855), 'Ballads of the People', unattributed, vol. 7 (New Series).

Willis, Paul E. (1978), *Profane Culture* (London: Routledge).

Part IV
Music and Criticism

Introduction

Graham Vulliamy argues that distinctions between 'serious' and 'popular' music made on the basis of a 'mass culture' critique confuse 'questions of quality in music with questions of genre' (1977: 195). In the given extract, he reviews ideas associated with mass-culture theory—for example, the passive consumer and the manipulative producer—and shows how such ideas have been used to explain the gap between 'serious' and 'popular' this century and to pronounce on the respective value of each category. Vulliamy asks us to recognize, instead, that a new musical language has developed this century with its own individual aesthetic criteria. This point does not fully answer the accusations of passivity, however. To counter these a popular culture critique is required (rather than a mass-culture critique) that stresses our capacity to *produce* meanings from texts of all kinds.

Lucy Green argues that the lack of musical experience of a particular style makes people deaf to its virtues. This is true even when the listener is extremely competent in other styles, and it explains, for her, Adorno's inability to discover anything worth while in jazz. She has coined the terms 'inherent meaning' and 'delineated meaning' in order to explore questions of style. Inherent meaning arises from 'conventional interrelationships of musical materials', whereas delineated meaning relates to 'a plethora of contextualising symbolic factors' (1997: 6–7). Inherent meaning is what enables us to recognize a time-based assemblage of sounds as music rather than noise. A musical style may delineate a social group, activity, or environment (for example, a club or concert hall), and this may have an effect on our sympathy for that style. Hence, Green stresses that style is not solely to be understood in terms of inhering musical materials, but also in terms of a social experience which is outside of these materials. Green is not alone, of course, in theorizing two modes of musical referring. An overview of intrinsic/extrinsic theories is provided in Nattiez 1990: 111–27.

Developing ideas from David Lincicome's article 'Iterational Systems' (1972: 168–205), Allan Moore suggests that there are different modes of listening or 'listening strategies', and it is 'the mode adopted by the listener that determines what the music will yield' (1993: 25). He is keen to understand exactly what people hear when listening, but stresses that a prior task is 'to determine the possible interpretations that a song or piece of music *affords*' (24). The concept of 'affordance' is one to which he has often returned. Moore's determination to focus on the *music* (the 'primary text') of pop and rock marked his work as unusual at a time when most writing about pop music continued to locate meaning in lyric content alone.

In the section of his book from which this excerpt has been taken, he is discussing ways of considering differences between rock and classical styles. After demonstrating that a simple hearing/listening dichotomy fails to explain adequately how these musics are differently perceived, he moves on to consider different listening strategies as they relate to matters of stylistic competence, and evaluations of musical merit as they relate to function. He stresses that competence is only gained in terms of a musical style, and that a competence in classical styles does not ensure competence in popular styles. Later, more problematically, he equates entertainment with undemanding listening, which raises the question of whether or not some listening strategies are more 'aesthetically worthy' than others.

In the next excerpt, Michel Foucault speaks of a plurality of musics, each 'worth as much as the group which practises it or recognizes it', whereas Pierre Boulez relates value to an economic distinction between that music which is written for profit and that which is not. Boulez also criticizes those taking refuge in the past, and envisages a 'pseudo-culture of documentation'. Foucault turns to the problems of recognition created by attempts to introduce uniqueness into the elements of contemporary music (meaning the post-war avant-garde). Boulez explains that listeners need to rid themselves of laziness and inertia if they wish to understand 'serious music', and asserts that today only popular forms are created according to genres and accepted typologies. His argument here can be related to Adorno's notion of 'standardization': 'In the advanced countries pop music is defined by standardization: its prototype is the song hit' (Adorno 1976: 25).

Boulez's ideal listener is a servant of the text (rather than a producer of meaning) and, like servants of the Victorian household, attracts the familiar charge of laziness. The function of the listener, for Boulez, is to struggle towards an understanding of the complexity of the composer's mind as it is revealed in the composition.

Adorno's demand for structural listening arose from his conviction that it was only in 'the strictness of musical structure' that music could 'assert itself against the ubiquity of commercialism' (1973: 19). However, Rose Rosengard Subotnik, despite her profound understanding of Adorno, argues for a paradigmatic shift from structural to stylistic listening. Structural listening she defines as 'a method which concentrates attention primarily on the formal relationships established over the course of a single composition' (1988: 88). She is intent on disputing the *priority* of structure in communication, however, and not on denying the very notion of structure or 'the value of efforts to give a rational account of the dialectic between medium and structure' (118). Medium is defined 'principally through the presentation of sounds, organized by conventional or characteristic usages, into particular configurations called styles' (88). Her deconstruction of the writings of Adorno and Schoenberg exposes their hidden assumption that 'the terms on which structural listening operates originate . . . in universal conditions of music', rather than from 'our own specific cultural predilections' (100). Nevertheless, she shows that, because Adorno felt his duty as a critic was to expose destructive social values and ideology in art, and because he was convinced that social ideology was embedded in the sound and style of music, he devoted most of his criticism to those aspects of music he held in the least esteem and, in fact, developed criticism 'as a mode of stylistic rather than structural analysis, even when dealing with elements of structure' (109).

Lawrence Kramer takes as his subject the demands of poetry and music in song. A composition may be colonized by a text or, at the other extreme, may appropriate a text, denying it authority, even deconstructing it. The given excerpt contains as a case study Schubert's setting of Goethe's 'Gretchen am Spinnrade'. Kramer's position is distinct from that of Edward Cone in *The Composer's Voice* (1974), especially as regards the latter's notion of the 'musical persona', the controlling presence in the musical composition (see Kramer 1984: 125–31 for a critique of Cone). He furthers his work on music and deconstruction in *Music as Cultural Practice, 1800–1900* (1990) and *Classical Music and Postmodern Knowledge* (1995).

Steve Sweeney-Turner illustrates how the dialectical interpretations that have dominated the critical reception of Peter Maxwell Davies's output can be challenged by hearing the music in deconstructive mode. He outlines the stages of a deconstructive process based on Jacques Derrida's writings in *Positions* (1987: 39–96) and elsewhere. In doing so, he is able to demonstrate that where oppositional structures are constantly being destabilized, dialectical synthesis is unachievable.

On Music and the Idea of Mass Culture

GRAHAM VULLIAMY

The debate over mass culture, entwined as it is with the sociological debate over the origins and consequences of a mass society, has a history which pre-dates the rise of the modern mass media. As Gans (1967) has pointed out, the charges against mass or popular culture have been repeated so often that it is possible to view them as part of an established critique. The main themes of this critique in its contemporary form may be identified from a number of articles in Rosenberg and White (1959) and in Jacobs (1961).

I will begin by defining the key terms as they are used by the mass-culture theorists. Wilensky (1964) identifies high culture by referring to two character- istics of the product: first it is created by, or under the supervision of a cul- tural elite operating within some aesthetic, literary or scientific tradition, and secondly, critical standards independent of the consumer of the product are systematically applied to it. He then continues to identify mass culture as cul- tural products manufactured solely for the mass market, while folk culture is seen as the traditional culture of the people predominant in rural society. Set up in these terms the problem of mass culture, as the critics see it, is that with increasing industrialization and urbanization there is a tendency for the culture purveyed by the mass media to destroy both traditional high culture and folk culture.

The starting-point of the critics of popular culture is that such products are made solely for commercial reasons and consequently they must be standard- ized in the interests of mass production. This mode of production results in a 'separation of the manufacturers of culture from the consumers' (Haag 1961: 58) and the consumers then become no more than passive objects who are unscrupulously manipulated and commercially exploited by the producers of mass culture:

> Mass culture is imposed from above. It is fabricated by technicians hired by businessmen; its audiences are passive consumers, their participation limited to the choice between buying and not buying.   (MacDonald 1959: 60)

It follows from this that the creators of mass culture are denied the expres- sion of true creativity and individuality, which is normally associated with the production of high culture:

'Music and the Mass Culture Debate', in J. Shepherd, P. Virden, G. Vulliamy, and T. Wishart, *Whose Music? A Sociology of Musical Languages* (London: Latimer, 1977), 179–85.

> Popular culture does not grow within a group. It is manufactured by one
> group—in Hollywood or in New York—for sale to an anonymous mass market.
> The product must meet an average of tastes, and it loses in spontaneity and
> individuality what it gains in accessibility and cheapness.   (Haag 1959: 519)

Critics of popular culture see it as leading to a deterioration of both traditional high culture and folk culture, since not only are potential artists lured
away by the lucrative rewards of involvement in popular culture, but also the
products of past and present high culture are actually exploited in the production of popular culture. All the features hitherto attributed to mass culture are
perhaps best summarized by Coser:

> It [mass culture] is distinguished from folk culture and from high culture by its
> standardised mass production, marketability and parasitic dependence on
> other forms of art and culture. It embodies a sharp cleavage between the con-
> sumer [the audience] and the producer. The latter exploits and manipulates
> the former. These characteristics radically distinguish mass culture from other
> cultural forms.   (1960: 81)

There are differences of emphasis and opinion amongst the mass-culture
critics, particularly in the social and political orientation of the critique: both
conservatives and radicals agree in many respects in their criticism of popular
culture, but disagree in their explanations of the causes of the problem. The
conservatives (for example, Haag) tend to be hostile to political democracy or
to political, social, and economic equality. They explain the existence of
popular culture by the inadequacy of its audiences. On the other hand, the radicals (for example MacDonald) argue that it is not the audiences who are at
fault but rather the use of the market mechanism, with all its possibilities of
commercial exploitation, to provide culture in a society characterized by a
'mass' audience. Gans summarizes the differences between the conservatives
and the radicals in the following way:

> The conservatives attack popular culture because they resent the rising pol-
> itical, economic and cultural power of the so-called masses: the socialists,
> because they are disappointed that these masses, once liberated from prole-
> tarianism, did not accept high culture or support socialist advocacy of it.
> (1967: 575)

The Afro-American Tradition in Twentieth-Century Music

A historical perspective on music in the twentieth century suggests the importance of an increasing split between so-called 'serious' music and so-called
'popular' music, together with a corresponding dwindling audience for the
compositions of those working in the 'serious' music idiom. The increasing
failure of contemporary 'serious' composers to communicate with a wide audience is explicitly recognized by the music establishment and has led to considerable debates concerning the problems of communicating the new forms
of music, such as the twelve-tone developments of Schoenberg, which mark
such a considerable break from earlier forms of tonal music. At the same time

the ever-increasing popularity of different styles of 'popular' music throughout this century has been obvious.

This gap between 'serious' and 'popular' music has been interpreted by the music establishment and by many sociologists via the assumptions of the mass-culture critique, so that clear differences have been postulated between 'serious' music on the one hand, which it is assumed results from the unique creative potential of the artist unpolluted by commercial pressures, and 'popular' music on the other, whose purpose is seen as chiefly commercial and aimed at a mass market. Thus Routh (1972), for example, in surveying contemporary British music since the last war, begins by defining a musical artwork as the following:

> The term music is taken to include as many aspects of the composer's work as fall under the heading of art-work. An art-work is one which makes some claim on our serious attention. This implies a creative, unique purpose on the part of the composer and an active response on the part of the listener; it implies that the composer possesses and uses both vision and technique, and that the listener in return is expected to bring to bear his full intelligence. This excludes non-art music, such as pop music, whose purpose is chiefly if not entirely commercial. Pop groups are big business; they are socially significant; there is no question that they form a remarkable contemporary phenomenon—but this does not make the result into an art-work, and to consider it as if it were is an illogical affectation.   (p. x)

That this is the dominant ideology of the music establishment, by which I mean the institutions (such as music conservatoires), music journals, and the composers, performers, and critics dedicated to the European 'serious' tradition in music, hardly needs documenting.

A major tendency of the critics of popular culture in setting up the terms of the debate is to consider 'popular culture' as a homogeneous category whilst high culture is subdivided into many different categories with strict boundaries. Thus, for example, in the sphere of music, 'popular' music is always treated unquestionably as a holistic category whilst 'high culture' music is subdivided into music of the Classical era, the Romantic era, Baroque, the Avant-Garde, and so on. An 'intellectual field' exists to differentiate the good high culture music from the poorer variety, whilst 'popular' music, because it is 'popular' music, is *automatically* assumed to be of inferior quality as music. Following the stimulating work of the 'classical' music critic, Henry Pleasants, I have argued at length elsewhere (Vulliamy and Lee 1976) that such an interpretation is fundamentally misguided, since it fails to recognize the impact of an important musical revolution in this century. The music establishment failed to observe this revolution because it took place in an area of music (jazz and 'popular') which, because of the European culture-specific definitions of music, was not recognized as music at all. The new musical developments came from the Afro-American tradition, springing from the Negro blues and now covering such diverse fields as jazz, rock music, soul and Tamla Motown music, and so on. This tradition has ushered in a new musical language with both musical and aesthetic criteria which markedly differentiate it from music in the European 'serious' tradition. The differences spring from the partial retention of various elements from African musical cultures, such as the use of antiphonal response, varying vocal timbres, the use of improvisation, the emphasis on dynamic polyrhythms, the functional use of music for communal participation, and the oral-aural (as opposed to notated) transmission of music. In addition such Africanisms were moulded by contact with a European musical heritage to produce specifically Afro-American musical characteristics such as rhythmic swing.

What I propose to argue is that in applying the assumptions of the mass-culture critique, critics of 'popular' music during the twentieth century have consistently failed to differentiate between varieties of 'popular' music and in particular have failed to recognize the alternative musical criteria of the Afro-American tradition. The reactions of the music establishment to the growth of jazz have been well documented and illustrate how jazz was dismissed because it did not conform to either the musical or culture criteria of the European 'serious' tradition. This tendency of the music establishment to judge the worth or seriousness of music in terms of 'classical' music standards has led to highly misleading assumptions being made about the nature both of various so-called primitive musics and of Afro-American musical styles. In the latter case, alternative musical criteria derived from an African tradition of music are not recognized, but other standards of judgement, appropriate to composed music concerned primarily with harmonic exploitation, are imposed on an improvised music, which incorporates complex melodic and rhythmic inflections. A case in point is Meyer's well-known attempt to discover what it is that 'makes music great' (Meyer 1959), where he tries to isolate those factors in music which will enable us to compare the greatness of different pieces of music of all types. In fact his reification of 'classical' music criteria involves a basic misunderstanding of styles of music which are not located in the European 'serious' tradition.

It is not only the music establishment which reacted to jazz in this way; so also did a number of sociological critics of mass culture, particularly those like Adorno, himself an accomplished musician, who were associated with the Frankfurt Institute of Social Research. Thus Adorno (1941) analysed jazz and 'popular' music in terms of their submission to the phenomenon of 'standardization' as a result of a highly monopolistic control of the music and entertainment industry concerned to continually 'plug' records in the interests of the profit motive. Unfortunately his concern to highlight the importance of the means of production and to locate his critique of 'popular' music within the Marxist critique of commodity-fetishism blinded him to the fact that his concept of 'standardization' was a reification of musical criteria derived from the 'serious' music tradition, where the main stress is on the harmonic structure and form of music. Viewed from this perspective, the simple standard harmonic structure of most 'popular' songs at that time was indeed limited, but such an analysis like that of Meyer's already referred to, in judging styles of music from 'foreign' musical and cultural criteria, inevitably distorts the essence of such music. To the jazz performer in particular, and to a lesser extent to certain 'popular' music performers, the structure of the song is simply the limits within which the piece of music is actively recreated by the performer via the incorporation of complex rhythmic and melodic inflections and other musical nuances derived from an Afro-American performance tradition in music.

Since the time of Adorno's writing there has been a belated recognition of the jazz musicians' art. The increasing legitimation of jazz [. . .], means that only very rarely is jazz today lumped together with all other varieties of so-called 'popular' music in sweeping condemnations of mass culture. The ideology of the mass-culture critique continues, however, in such a way that, whereas thirty years ago the assumptions underlying the mass-culture critique made it incapable of differentiating between jazz and other varieties of 'popular' music, today similar assumptions make it incapable of differentiating between various type of so-called 'pop' music. Thus Parker (1975) has recently drawn explicitly on the terminology of the mass-culture critique in his analysis of contemporary rock music. Like Adorno, his main stress is on the means of production—as he sees it, a commercial machine, providing rock music of the lowest common denominator in taste which detracts from the folk culture of the people (in this case identified as the folk music and Radio Ballads of Ewan McColl and others). I want to argue, however, that such a structural analysis, stressing as it does simply the role of the production system in music, rides roughshod over a more phenomenologically inclined analysis, which takes more seriously the definitions of the situation of the actors concerned—in this case of various participants in the 'pop' music process.

On Musical Experience

LUCY GREEN

Style is the medium by virtue of which we experience music, and without which we could have no music at all. No piece of music is ever stylistically autonomous. Whether particular individuals hear all music in terms of either the pop or the classical styles alone, or whether they make finer distinctions between late Haydn and early Beethoven, Tamla Motown and Disco, whether such activity is self-conscious or intuitive, it cannot be avoided. This is not only because musical delineations so forcefully and ubiquitously divide styles of music into categories with appropriately related listeners, but also because *we must have some knowledge of the style of a piece of music in order to experience inherent meanings as distinct from non-musically meaningful sound, at all.*

With regard to inherent meaning, a dominant seventh chord in Beethoven, for example, can only be experienced as meaning a tonic chord if we are familiar with tonal harmony in the broad classical style. A chord with exactly the same notes as the dominant seventh would, in a blues, carry no such tonic implication and might well be the final chord of the piece. This is not at all remarkable to familiar listeners, because such a use of this chord is normal within the blues style.

It may appear, from the way I have put it in the preceding paragraph, that knowledge of style as it inheres in music is possessed only by people with at least an A level in music. But this is very far from the case. Such knowledge is by no means acquired only through study, but is learnt through repeated experience of music, an experience granted more readily than ever before by the media and the music industry, and is gained, to varying degrees, by every normal member of society. If not, an individual could not tell a song from the sounds of a cat-fight, let alone distinguish pop from classical music.

Although some styles are more familiar and therefore more readily understood than others, that does not necessarily prevent their recognition. I receive relatively few inherent meanings from Indian classical music, for example, but I can still tell it is Indian. However, the greater the familiarity with style, the more *affirmative* the experience. When we are familiar with the normative stylistic terms of reference in a piece of music, we are able to distinguish disturbance from normality and resolution from disturbance. We can therefore refer back and forth in time, and assimilate foreground events in terms of larger

Music on Deaf Ears: Musical Meaning, Ideology and Education (Manchester: Manchester University Press, 1988), 33–7.

processes, which themselves develop into coherent shapes and become forms on higher levels. If the music surprises us with an unexpected event, we understand it. Although our temporal intentions towards the music may have been negated, we assimilate the negation in terms of a wider field of presence, and thus we enjoy it: without negation, disturbance, difference, at whatever level, no inherent musical meaning could arise, and only through these and through our understanding of them do we relate meaningfully to music. Hence ultimately, our negation is understood in the light of its own affirmation: we are negated only because we understand, to whatever extent, the style of the music; and we are thus *affirmed* in our overall temporal intentions towards the music and in our structuring of self-consciousness. Inversely, if we are unfamiliar with its style, the capacity of a piece of music to structure our intentions towards it is relatively limited. Not being aware of what is and is not normative, we cannot readily distinguish disturbance or its resolution, are unable to hear processes in themselves, and cannot relate them to higher-level forms. We therefore receive few, or merely confused, inherent meanings, cannot engage with the music, are rarely negated and rarely affirmed. At times such an experience is just boring. At other times it is more forceful. . . . Adorno had very little experience of popular forms, and hardly any of jazz. He felt qualified to write about them, because he was an extremely sophisticated musician; but his unfamiliarity with these particular styles deafened him to their virtues, and was a major cause for his disparaging and despairing attitude towards them. A student in her fifteenth lesson of an adult music course, taught by a friend of mine, was played 'Mondestrunken' from Schoenberg's *Pierrot Lunaire*. Admitting to a prejudice against its style, she said that the music would sound no different to her ears were it completely random. Unfamiliarity, no less than bias, had prevented her noticing that the first four bars have four uninterrupted repetitions of a melodic fragment that is heard three more times at the same pitch, once two octaves lower, and is varied, maintaining the same rhythm and melodic shape, throughout. When style is this unfamiliar, we may well find music incoherent or random. Our experience is fragmented, tossed to and fro on apparently unrelenting, arbitrary waves of meaningless movement, journeys to nowhere: such experience is *aggravating*.

We are uplifted, affirmed, bored or aggravated by music's inherent meanings in as many different ways as the diversity of musical style and of our individual understanding and prior experiences imply. However, for analytical purposes I shall refer to this plethora of possible reactions by way of the two poles, *affirmation* and *aggravation*.

As regards delineated meaning, music transmits a delineated style, however vague, to every listener. Although knowledge of style—even if it is highly confused or vague—must accompany every listening experience, we also have such knowledge without even needing to hear music. We know that Tchaikovsky is classical and Dépeche Mode pop; we may know that the former is, more precisely, Romantic and the latter Synthesizer; we switch on Radio 1 if we want pop, Radio 3 for classical music; jazz, ethnic music and folk we have to look for in the programme lists; when asked if we like this or that sort of music we know roughly what is meant, may request more detail in the question, can give some sort of answer; all without hearing any music. The style is none the less delineated. From this secondary delineation of style arise all other delineations, which confront us during listening. Listeners are aware that music asks them to know: whether they have any sympathy for the style; whether they deride, envy, admire or disregard the social group or activity delineated; to know how they see themselves in relation to the music, whether they regard themselves as liking, understanding, dismissing, hating or identi- fying with it. The point is, not that everyone knows the answers, but that the delineated meaning of music automatically poses the questions. It does not categorically demand a response, nor need it infringe upon the consciousness of every individual. But it is always present as a quality of music. We feel posi- tively or negatively towards music's delineations in as many ways as we are affirmed or aggravated by its inherent meanings, and for analytical purposes it is appropriate to conceive of *positive* and *negative* feelings as two poles in between which runs the whole gamut of our possible relations with musical delineations. I shall therefore use these words with this specific, but logical, formal, meaning.

I hope the clumsiness involved in using different words to describe the reac- tions to inherent and delineated meanings, may be forgiven: it will become apparent later why I have to do this. The model then looks like this: we are affirmed or aggravated by music's inherent meanings, and we feel positively or negatively towards its delineations. The relations between these states, quite apart from the states themselves, are manifold and complex, and they form the subject of much further discussion. I shall turn, for the moment, to a summary of my discussion of style.

On one hand, the style of a piece of music *inheres* in its materials. In so far as we can be familiar with style, in so much as we can talk and write about it, analyse its general principles and pick out its particular qualities, style has an objective existence. But it remains an abstract, transcendent category, for style is only ever materially expressed in the inherent meanings of particular pieces of music, which together form a stylistic body. The idioms of these pieces— their norms, disturbances and resolutions, their internal structure and the relations between their parts—form a musical language in which they com- municate. When studying music, for whatever purposes, we can analyse style historically and creatively. When listening, we surmise style as music passes through time, to varying degrees of finesse depending on our age, ability, and prior experience. On the other hand, although we are not usually aware of this, style is also *delineated* by music, for we receive inherent meanings in terms that both lead us to our knowledge of their style, and allow us to relate musical processes to that style as we know it. Hence we do not only refer to style in terms of inherent musical materials passing through time, but music also com- municates its style by delineating it as a social relation existing outside the inherent musical materials.

For each individual, any style has loose boundaries that merge into one or more other styles. However, each is none the less defined by virtue of its dif- ference from others. In this sense, one style is, only because there are others that it is not.

Style is both inherent and delineated, but most importantly, it provides the pathway between the two meanings, making each understandable as it is mediated through the other. Style is what makes musical experience possible, for it both structures our intentions towards inherent meanings and allows us to cognize them in terms of historical delineations of what music is. It is through style that the dual musical experience of inherent and delineated meanings reaches consciousness as a unified, undifferentiated, apparently inseparable whole.

On the Pop–Classical Split

ALLAN F. MOORE

In order to provide a closer focus for the differences in listening strategies, I shall invoke the term 'style', which ultimately contributes to more precise distinctions than just those of 'popular' and 'classical'. Musical competence, in the abstract is a meaningless concept. To take an extreme example, the ability to comprehend the musical relationships present in a work of Mozart is of no help in comprehending the relationships present in the songs of the Aborigines of Arnhem Land (see Jones 1980). Competence is only gained in terms of a style, where it tends to entail the ability to recognize normative from unusual exemplars, and to make predictions of the likelihood of certain events in real-time listening, on the basis of past events within the example under consideration. (This is a simplified account of the conventional position. See Green (1988: 17–25) for further comment.) To be sure, competence in one style may make it easier to acquire competence in another, particularly if they are related, and particularly if the first style has been acquired at an early age, but no more (see Green 1988: 102 ff.). Thus, competence in a 'classical' style does not ensure competence in a 'popular' style, nor vice versa: competence within any style is learnt. This point frequently causes difficulty for those listeners who believe their 'native' style to be somehow 'natural', in opposition to others, which are somehow 'constructed', 'artificial', and even 'contrived'. The observation that we learn a style through familiarity and constant exposure (in the same way that we learn our native tongue) rather than through methodical exposition, does not mean that it was not, at some historical juncture, invented. And, to reiterate, we do learn styles through familiarity and constant exposure, and it is this that I mean here by competence. It is not necessary to be able to explain a style (to be trained in it, perhaps as a performer) in order to have a cognitive competence in it. That competence is demonstrated by being comfortable with particular styles. . . .

We can invoke [another] way to discuss the differences between popular and classical styles by focusing on the musics' functions. The ethnomusicologist Alan Merriam draws upon a long line of thought in both ethnomusicology and cultural anthropology in making a distinction between the use of a cultural practice (see Merriam 1964: 217–18) and the function(s) it serves. Merriam suggests that uses tend to be overt. Parallel to them, he proposes some ten categories of function, stressing that they concern what he calls 'analytical' rather

Rock: The Primary Text (Buckingham: Open University Press, 1993), 25–8.

than 'folk' evaluations. Not all these functions will be relevant to every culture, but they do offer a global perspective.

Merriam's first four categories, although problematic, are probably familiar. The first, 'emotional expression', includes music as a means of emotional release and of evoking specific emotional states. Concerning the second, 'aesthetic enjoyment', he attempts to analyse the Western concept of 'aesthetic', comparing its constituent aspects with views from other literate cultures. He argues that it may not be relevant to non-literate cultures on the grounds that the function of aesthetic enjoyment is predicated upon the existence of a philosophy of the aesthetic (which is not, of course, the way I have used the term above). His third category, entertainment, he treats as self-evident. The function of communication, his fourth, is beset with problems. . . . Merriam's next two functions are also fairly self-evident. Symbolic representation refers to the practice of mimesis, the representation (rather than the evocation) of emotional states, and perhaps the existence of homologies. Physical response includes dance, the encouragement of the reactions of warrior and hunter, practices of possession and the excitation and control of crowd behaviour. His last group of four are less transparent, and less easy to differentiate. He terms them the functions of

> enforcing conformity to social norms . . . validation of social institutions and religious rituals . . . contribution to the continuity and stability of culture [and] . . . contribution to the integration of society.   (Merriam 1964: 224–7)

Merriam's distinction between use and function, and his stress on the difference between 'analytic' and 'folk' evaluations, seems close to arguing that 'use' refers to a folk evaluation (an 'emic' understanding), while 'function' represents the analytic evaluation (an 'etic' understanding). This reading of the situation has been criticized by another leading ethnomusicologist, Bruno Nettl. Nettl argues, with reference to particular cultures, that we need to take account not only of etic statements of function and emic statements of use, but also of etic statements of use and emic statements of function: 'in field research it turns out that informants are quite capable of making "etic" statements, that is, of describing their own culture in "objective" ways that do not give the culture's primary evaluations' (Nettl 1983: 154–5). Nettl subscribes to an alternative ethnomusicological position which claims that music has only one function, which for him

> is to control humanity's relationship to the supernatural, mediating between people and other beings, and to support the integrity of individual social groups. It does this by expressing the relevant central values of culture in abstracted form.   (Nettl 1983: 159)

Although Nettl's position often finds greater favour (it espouses the 'homological' model) . . . Merriam's further distinctions are fruitful in the case of the pop–classical split. To exemplify this, I shall use 'popular classics' (the 'Mozart's Greatest Hits' phenomenon), the post-war 'avant-garde' (Stockhausen, Boulez, Xenakis, *et al.*), and 'pop dance' (what used to be simply disco).

Pop dance music clearly calls forth physical responses (Merriam's sixth function): the explicit nature of the beat and, more particularly, the syncopations in the bass of a song like Cameo's 'Word Up' make it hard not to move some part of the body in time. The physical response called up by some Mozart will depend far more on its performance situation, and is thus a reaction to the performers rather than the music. The applause given it in a concert hall would normally be out of place when listening at home to the recording. On the one hand, the addition of a bass and drums line with a strong rhythmic profile may have turned it into acceptable disco. On the other, it may be hard for such dance music to provide aesthetic enjoyment (Merriam's second function). Both Mozart and Stockhausen are found by some to do this. Stockhausen, however, may only rarely be listened to for entertainment (Merriam's third function), for his music makes strenuous demands on any listener. And so on.

I would suggest that many of the arguments concerning the relative merits of different musics can be resolved into arguments concerning the relative merits of different functions, which thus becomes an ethical rather than an explicitly musical issue. I, for one, have a rather extreme dislike of being 'entertained'; I would always try to argue that the music I use is serving some other function. Thus, an evaluation is more useful if it asks how well a particular function is served. (Stockhausen's music cannot be described as bad merely on the grounds that we cannot dance to it. Nor do we devalue the music of the Clash in noting that it is not used for quiet contemplation.) Even this can depend on other factors: time, place, mood, will. The function a music serves is not an attribute of that music, but is dependent on both the music itself and the user. Two evenings before writing this, I spent time on Tears for Fears' 'Sowing the Seeds of Love', primarily for the teasing reminiscences of the Beatles' 'All You Need is Love', 'I am the Walrus', and 'Hello, Goodbye' it contains. The previous day, I had spent time with the third movement of Tchaikovsky's Fourth Symphony, in order to experience the composer's virtuosic control of orchestral sonority. In both cases, the music functioned aesthetically for me, because of the listening strategy I decided to adopt (I could have used Tears for Fears to dance to, or the Tchaikovsky as a means of emotional catharsis). Neither could have served me as well on the next day. Thus, to acknowledge that we cannot just talk about 'music', that it is necessary to be particular about which music, does not demean any particular style. It is merely a way of acknowledging that no music is suitable in all circumstances, by recognizing that differences in listening strategies and differences of function are not directly congruent to differences of style.

On Music and its Reception

MICHEL FOUCAULT AND PIERRE BOULEZ

MICHEL FOUCAULT. One must take into consideration the fact that for a very long time music has been tied to social rites and unified by them: religious music, chamber music; in the nineteenth century, the link between music and theatrical production in opera (not to mention the political or cultural meanings which the latter had in Germany or in Italy) was also an integrative factor.

I believe that one cannot talk of the 'cultural isolation' of contemporary music without soon correcting what one says of it by thinking about other circuits of music.

With rock, for example, one has a completely inverse phenomenon. Not only is rock music (much more than jazz used to be) an integral part of the life of many people, but it is a cultural initiator: to like rock, to like a certain kind of rock rather than another, is also a way of life, a manner of reacting; it is a whole set of tastes and attitudes.

Rock offers the possibility of a relation which is intense, strong, alive, 'dramatic' (in that rock presents itself as a spectacle, that listening to it is an event and that it produces itself on stage), with a music that is itself impoverished, but through which the listener affirms himself; and with the other music, one has a frail, faraway, hothouse, problematical relation with an erudite music from which the cultivated public feels excluded.

One cannot speak of a single relation of contemporary culture to music in general, but of a tolerance, more or less benevolent, with respect to a plurality of musics. Each is granted the 'right' to existence, and this right is perceived as an equality of worth. Each is worth as much as the group which practises it or recognizes it.

PIERRE BOULEZ. Will talking about musics in the plural and flaunting an eclectic ecumenicism solve the problem? It seems, on the contrary, that this will merely conjure it away—as do certain devotees of an advanced liberal society. All those musics are good, all those musics are nice. Ah! Pluralism! There's nothing like it for curing incomprehension. Love, each one of you in your corner, and each will love the others. Be liberal, be generous toward the tastes of others, and they will be generous to yours. Everything is good, nothing is bad; there aren't any values, but everyone is happy. This discourse, as liberating as it may wish to be, reinforces, on the contrary, the ghettos, comforts one's

'Contemporary Music and the Public', trans. John Rahn, *Perspectives of New Music* (Fall–Winter 1985), 7–11.

clear conscience for being in a ghetto, especially if from time to time one tours the ghettos of others. The economy is there to remind us, in case we get lost in this bland utopia: there are musics which bring in money and exist for commercial profit; there are musics that cost something, whose very concept has nothing to do with profit. No liberalism will erase this distinction.

MICHEL FOUCAULT. I have the impression that many of the elements that are supposed to provide access to music actually impoverish our relationship with it. There is a quantitative mechanism working here. A certain rarity of relation to music could preserve an ability to choose what one hears, and thus a flexibility in listening. But the more frequent this relation is (radio, records, cassettes), the more familiarities it creates; habits crystallize; the most frequent becomes the most acceptable, and soon the only thing perceivable. It produces a 'tracing', as the neurologists say.

Clearly, the laws of the marketplace will readily apply to this simple mechanism. What is put at the disposition of the public is what the public hears. And what the public finds itself actually listening to, because it's offered up, reinforces a certain taste, underlines the limits of a well-defined listening capacity, defines more and more exclusively a schema for listening. Music had better satisfy this expectation, etc. So commercial productions, critics, concerts, everything that increases the contact of the public with music, risks making perception of the new more difficult.

Of course the process is not unequivocal. Certainly increasing familiarity with music also enlarges the listening capacity and gives access to possible differentiations, but this phenomenon risks being only marginal; it must in any case remain secondary to the main impact of experience, if there is no real effort to derail familiarities.

It goes without saying that I am not in favour of a rarefaction of the relation to music, but it must be understood that the everydayness of this relation, with all the economic stakes that are riding on it, can have this paradoxical effect of rigidifying tradition. It is not a matter of making access to music more rare, but of making its frequent appearances less devoted to habits and familiarities.

PIERRE BOULEZ. We ought to note that not only is there a focus on the past, but even on the past in the past, as far as the performer is concerned. And this is of course how one attains ecstasy while listening to the interpretation of a certain classical work by a performer who disappeared decades ago; but ecstasy will reach orgasmic heights when one can refer to a performance of 20 July 1947 or of 30 December 1938. One sees a pseudo-culture of documentation taking shape, based on the exquisite hour and fugitive moment, which reminds us at once of the fragility and of the durability of the performer become immortal, rivalling now the immortality of the masterpiece. All the mysteries of the Shroud of Turin, all the powers of modern magic, what more could you want as an alibi for reproduction as opposed to real production? Modernity itself is this technical superiority we possess over former eras in being able to recreate the event. Ah! If we only had the first performance of the Ninth, even—especially—with all its flaws, or if only we could make Mozart's own delicious difference between the Prague and Vienna versions of *Don Giovanni* . . . This historicizing carapace suffocates those who put it on, compresses them in an asphyxiating rigidity; the mephitic air they breathe constantly enfeebles their organism in relation to contemporary adventure. I imagine Fidelio glad to rest in his dungeon, or again I think of Plato's cave: a civilization of shadow and of shades.

MICHEL FOUCAULT. Certainly listening to music becomes more difficult as its composition frees itself from any kind of schemas, signals, perceivable cues for a repetitive structure.

In classical music, there is a certain transparency from the composition to the hearing. And even if many compositional features in Bach or Beethoven aren't recognizable by most listeners, there are always other features, important ones, which are accessible to them. But contemporary music, by trying to make each of its elements a unique event, makes any grasp or recognition by the listener difficult.

PIERRE BOULEZ. Is there really only lack of attention, indifference on the part of the listener toward contemporary music? Might not the complaints so often articulated be due to laziness, to inertia, to the pleasant sensation of remaining in known territory? Berg wrote, already half a century ago, a text entitled 'Why is Schönberg's music hard to understand?' The difficulties he described then are nearly the same as those we hear of now. Would they always have been the same? Probably, all novelty bruises the sensibilities of those unaccustomed to it. But it is believable that nowadays the communication of a work to a public presents some very specific difficulties. In classical and romantic music, which constitutes the principal resource of the familiar repertory, there are schemas which one obeys, which one can follow independently of the work itself, or rather which the work must necessarily exhibit. The movements of a symphony are defined in their form and in their character, even in their rhythmic life; they are distinct from one another, most of the time actually separated by a pause, sometimes tied by a transition that can be spotted. The vocabulary itself is based on 'classified' chords, well-named: you don't have to analyse them to know what they are and what function they have. They have the efficacy and security of signals; they recur from one piece to another, always assuming the same appearance and the same functions. Progressively, these reassuring elements have disappeared from 'serious' music. Evolution has gone in the direction of an ever more radical renewal, as much in the form of works as in their language. Musical works have tended to become unique events, which do have antecedents, but are not reducible to any guiding schema admitted, a priori, by all; this creates, certainly, a handicap for immediate comprehension. The listener is asked to familiarize himself with the course of the work and for this to listen to it a certain number of times. When the course of the work is familiar, comprehension of the work, perception of what it wants to express, can find a propitious terrain to bloom in. There are fewer and fewer chances for the first encounter to ignite perception and comprehension. There can be a spontaneous connection with it, through the force of the message, the quality of the writing, the beauty of the sound, the readability of the cues, but deep under-standing can only come from repeated hearings, from remaking the course of the work, this repetition taking the place of an accepted schema such as was practised previously.

The schemas—of vocabulary, of form—which had been evacuated from what is called serious music (sometimes called learned music) have taken refuge in certain popular forms, in the objects of musical consumption. There, one still creates according to the genres, the accepted typologies. Conservatism is not necessarily found where it is expected: it is undeniable that a certain conser-vatism of form and language is at the base of all the commercial productions adopted with great enthusiasm by generations who want to be anything but conservative. It is a paradox of our times that played or sung protest transmits itself by means of an eminently subornable vocabulary, which does not fail to make itself known: commercial success evacuates protest.

On Deconstructing Structural Listening

ROSE ROSENGARD SUBOTNIK

Given Adorno's idealization of structural listening, the actual character of his musical writings might seem surprising. His entire output as a music
critic can be viewed as illuminating the irreducibility of the concrete medium
of music. Actually it was only through such criticism that Adorno could fulfil
what he saw as the critic's principal obligation, to expose the destructive values
of society as they manifest themselves in the public and conventional aspects
of music, and to disentangle music from the corrupting power and effects of
institutional ideology. This obligation required him to engage in continuous
criticism of the musical medium (thereby performing much the same
service that he praised in Schoenberg's and Webern's recasting of Bach's
instrumentation).

Adorno scorned the very notion of an actual non-ideological music. Insistence on the non-existence of ideology in music was radically different for him
from a continuing sensitivity to ideology as a force to be resisted, a sensitivity
which he discerned in the uncompromising structural integrity of the late
Beethoven quartets and Schoenberg's music. Certainly he was no less adamant
than Barthes has been in condemning as a lie any attempt by a musical 'sign',
so to speak, to hide its own cultural artificiality, and to present itself as either
a socially and historically isolated object or an ideologically innocent or neu-
tral construct, fit for 'merely' formal analysis. Such self-deceptively non-
ideological analysis was far more consistent with the spirit of Stravinsky's
Poetics, which can be shown to project a wide range of ideologically loaded,
even anti-humanistic subtexts. And, indeed, Adorno's own criticism of Stravinsky's music shows him every bit as sensitive as more recent, unmistakably anti-
formalist critics, such as Eagleton, to the chasm that separates narrowly formal
intentions from a purely formal character, effect, or significance, whether in art
or in criticism itself.

Adorno's constant preoccupation with social ideology, then, led him to a continuous engagement with that layer of music which he least valued, and to
establish an ongoing, relatively explicit connection between his own values and
those of the various cultures represented in the composition, performance, or
reception of the music he discussed. As perhaps the premier practitioner in our

'Toward a Deconstruction of Structural Listening: A Critique of Schoenberg, Adorno, and Stravinsky', in Eugene
Narmour and Ruth Solie (eds.), *Explorations in Music, the Arts, and Ideas: Essays in Honor of Leonard B. Meyer*
(Stuyvesant, NY: Pendragon Press, 1988), 107–14.

century of concrete social and historical criticism, who deplored systems and abstractions, Adorno set an unexcelled example for those figures in current literary debate, such as Said, Jameson, Blonsky, and Eagleton, who likewise stress the concrete social and historical responsibilities of criticism.

Furthermore, precisely because Adorno viewed music as part of an historically open-ended context of concrete social relationships, his principal focus as a practitioner of criticism was not the isolated work but the broader category of style. This, too, encouraged him to develop criticism as a mode of stylistic rather than structural analysis, even when dealing with elements of structure. In fact, what Adorno actually did in his musical writings was stylistic criticism of the highest calibre. By this I mean criticism of a kind that had nothing to do with the mere listing of characteristic musical devices but rather demonstrated the capacity of a rigorously fashioned critical language to analyse style incisively. Adorno's ability to find richly evocative yet succinct and precise metaphorical verbal equivalents for structural and non-structural elements in music, and thereby to characterize persuasively the cultural and historical significance of both individual works and styles, is masterful, even uncanny.

It is sometimes asked whether Adorno really 'knew' music. Frequently he is taken to task for not doing the thing he seems most to require of the listener, structural analysis. Moreover, Schoenberg regularly used charts and diagrams as well as the specialized terminology of academic structural analysis; and Adorno himself identified the ability to 'name the formal components' as a sign of competence in structural listening. Yet his criticism rarely offers such signs. Probably this was because at bottom such techniques smacked too much for Adorno of those anti-intellectual 'proceedings in which general demonstrability of results matters more than their use to get to the heart of the matter' (1976: 195). But did Adorno get to the heart of the matter? I would argue that even if we reject vehemently the conclusions that pervade Adorno's metaphorical observations (a possibility which the unusually honest and explicit presentation of his own values allows), Adorno's thorough familiarity with the music he characterizes as well as the aptness and importance of his metaphors are virtually always confirmed by a reconsideration of the music in question. 'The genuine experience of music,' Adorno wrote, 'like that of all art, is as one with criticism' (152). For Adorno, in fact, no less than for the German Romantics a century earlier, metaphorical criticism of the characteristics, choices, and relationships that embed music in one or another socio-historical context is not a 'supplement', in Derrida's sense, to the possession of detailed structural knowledge but rather the very means of getting to the heart of such knowledge.

Now in a way all of this amounts to saying that the kind of structural knowledge that interests Adorno and the German Romantics alike is culturally concrete, encompassing, or 'replete'. But here it must be explicitly acknowledged that the concept of replete structural listening is itself a concrete, metaphorical account of perception, not a logical principle. Not only does the concept of replete structure itself point to a condition which is characteristic only of music in certain styles, and thus first of all to a stylistic rather than to a structural condition. In addition, this concept depends no less than Stravinsky's chic formalism does for its intelligibility, persuasiveness, and usefulness on a culturally defined, stylistic sensibility in the listener. This stylistic particularity of replete structural listening as a principle helps explain how this concept can readily be misinterpreted by those of us from other cultures, not privy to its stylistic nuance, as justifying far narrower practices of structural listening. But the fundamental sense in which Adorno's concept of structural listening as well as Schoenberg's compositional choices were both governed by needs that were more stylistic than structural in character was something Adorno did not and probably could not recognize—any more than he could assess the degree to which his own aesthetic convictions represented cultural preferences.

Nor was Adorno willing, therefore, any more than Schoenberg was, at bottom, to understand the widespread unresponsiveness to Schoenberg's music relativistically, as the reflection of something other than an immature unwillingness or intellectual incapacity to master the technical demands of structural listening. Grounding structural listening in a supposedly universal rational capacity, Adorno was utterly unable to criticize as 'ideological' the elite social standing and the long years of education that were ordinarily required for the exercise of this capacity. He could not bring himself to characterize either Schoenberg's unpopularity or non-structural modes of listening as functions of legitimate differences among listeners in cultural or stylistic orientation.

This is not to say that Adorno was oblivious to actual characteristics and effects of his or Schoenberg's style. On the contrary, Adorno explicitly considered irreducible stylistic 'difficulty' necessary to the structuring and value of both men's work. From Adorno's standpoint, a 'jagged physiognomy' not only signified the resistance of individual usage to the conventions of ideology. In addition it was needed to preserve the integrity of 'subcutaneous' argument from social 'neutralization'. Such integrity required a refusal by structure to compromise itself by 'smoothing over', as Adorno accused Brahms of doing, or by allowing to be obscured a dehumanizing contradiction between the rational ideals of structure and the ongoing anti-rational force of society, as represented in the musical medium.

Where Adorno's self-critical capacity failed him was both in his attribution of a universal necessity to the social analysis and the convictions that explained such stylistic choices and in his inability to imagine alternative, equally honest, stylistic definitions of, or solutions to, the social problems surrounding music. What drew Adorno to Schoenberg's music was not just its structural idealism but also the ugliness, by conventional standards, of its sound. But while it is true that Adorno valued this ugliness for its 'negative' capacity to scorn the ideological blandishments of 'affirmative culture', it is by no means clear that he would have been similarly drawn to the jagged qualities of punk rock or Laurie Anderson's music, much less that anything could have convinced him to view Leonard Bernstein's choice of the popular route as socially responsible. Adorno was sympathetic to Schoenberg's ugliness because he understood its cultural significance. And he understood this significance because he operated within the same set of concrete cultural assumptions, expectations, conventions, and values that Schoenberg did. He could listen to Schoenberg's music with the advantage of an insider's knowledge not of a universal structure but of a particular style.

Schoenberg, too, was inclined to dismiss objections to his style as signs of a 'childish' preoccupation with pleasures of the senses rather than of differences in cultural orientation; just as form for Stravinsky is sound stripped of meaning, so style for Schoenberg is sound devoid of 'idea'. In emphatically replacing the aesthetic notion of beauty with epistemological notions such as truth and knowledge as the central philosophical problem of music, Schoenberg revealed in his writings the hope of weaning listeners away from sensuous preoccupation. And yet instinctively he recognized the need to draw the listener inside his own stylistic world. Again and again in his writings he explains the numerous 'lost' historical origins of his works, including the tonal system and earlier German compositional techniques, which although literally absent from his works, are nevertheless constituent elements in their conception and significance. One would be hard pressed to find a composer whose work is more fully and clearly characterized by elements in Derrida's concept of the 'trace'—or for that matter a critic whose intelligibility depends more than Adorno's does on a knowledge of absent 'subtexts'. In both cases, these traces and subtexts consist precisely in ideas and values defined in a surrounding cultural context. They are functions not of a literally present structure but of a more open-ended style.

Both Schoenberg's and Adorno's work provides massive evidence of the degree to which the communication of ideas depends on concrete cultural knowledge, and on the power of signs to convey a richly concrete open-endedness of meaning through a variety of cultural relationships. Their work supports the thesis that style is not extrinsic to structure but rather defines the conditions for actual structural possibilities, and that structure is perceived as a function more than as a foundation of style. Even in a crude sense I would argue that if we are forced in musical analysis to grab hold of one end or the other of the dialectic between a style and a structure which are always affecting each other, it makes most sense to define the composer's starting point as his or her entrance into a pre-existing musical style. Certainly such a notion has large currency in our own culture, where its status as a cliché ('the medium is the message') no doubt accounts in large measure for our perception of Stravinsky as more modern than Schoenberg. And certainly for those who begin interpreting either Schoenberg's or Adorno's work from the vantage point of a stylistic outsider, any relatively abstract, structurally rational argument is likely to constitute not the most but the least accessible parameter of meaning.

This is precisely the situation that confronts us with any culturally distant music. Did medieval music, for instance, once define structurally the value and power of individuality? Perhaps it would be most accurate to say that too much distance from the wealth of associations that once informed medieval usages prevents us from answering this question conclusively. To the extent that our perception of medieval culture and its signs remains what anthropologists call 'etic' (that is, external and merely physical) rather than 'emic' (that is, internal and literate), we are not in a position to view individualities of structure as signifying much more than a stylistic aberration. (Why are we so much more inclined to apply the name 'Mannerism' to early than to recent artistic styles?) Certainly the kinds of medieval musical 'structure' that our culture allows us to perceive are nothing like the system of relationships that Adorno's structural listening would have us grasp from within.

Ever since the crystallization of the notion of 'Art' in the early nineteenth century, it has become a truism of Western culture that the proper evaluation of any structure as 'Art' requires the perspective of time. And in a culture that explicitly allows individuals, such as artists, to alter the conventional cultural meanings of signifiers, some time-lapse undoubtedly is required for a full understanding of the altered medium. By this time, however, it has probably already (or more likely, as Derrida likes to say, 'always already') become impossible to understand the full import of those changes at the time they were made, or, hence, to claim an insider's access to arguments structured within that medium. By this point, as Hildesheimer suggests in his biography of Mozart, crucial aspects of an original significance have become unrecoverable (1983: 4, 11–12). The listener is already hearing overtones of intervening knowledge and experience which drown out or 'erase' various responses that could have originally been intended or anticipated, while adding others. This condition of difference and delay, which Derrida has termed 'differance', calls increasing attention over time or distance to the irreducibility of style, both in its concrete physicality and in the ever-changing face it presents to new contexts of interpretation, as a source of signification. In other words, the more culturally distant the music is, the more inescapably aware we become of its style—of its style as a barrier to understanding, and also as a condition of any structural perceptions we may form.

On Deconstructive Text—Music Relationships

LAWRENCE KRAMER

It is often said that the poetic text of an art song loses its own identity to that of the song. The song does not so much express the text as express itself through the text. But there are some texts that it is hard to assimilate in this way, either because they are famous, or difficult, or written by an author of high canonical standing. Such a text is never really assimilated into a composition; it is incorporated, and it retains its own life, its own body, within the body of the music. Moreover, the subsumption of the text by the music is not a *fait accompli* that is given to the listener with the sound of the first note. It must be enacted, must be evolved, within the course of the music itself. What the music expresses in these cases is neither the text, nor itself through the text, but its relationship to the text. The music appropriates the poem by contending with it, phonetically, dramatically, and semantically, and this contest is what most drives and shapes the song.

Confronted with a text that, so to speak, insists on being heard, the art song takes as its generic task the suggestion of an imaginative space that the text is unable to occupy, a dimension of emotion or meaning that the text may imply but cannot quite embody. To do this the song must address itself, not only to the words of the text, but also to the listener's probable interpretation of them, or, more broadly, to the often tacit conventions of understanding through which the text may come to appear as a self-authorizing, self-interpreting whole. A poem judged to be minor or conventional may be known only or mainly through its setting, so that a listener may look at it rather indifferently. A culturally important text, however, will come already invested with a compelling variety of prescripted meanings, associations, and interpretive procedures. In order to incorporate such a text without being colonized by it, the music will have to grapple with the accumulated force of all this preunderstanding. Interpretation is the contested area; possession of the text—which in this context becomes a kind of incantation, a word object that is numinous regardless of what it means—is the reward. 'Possession' is not a casual term here, as anyone who has ever read Heine's line 'Im wunderschönen Monat Mai' by mentally hearing Schumann's music has demonstrated. A song that appropriates a significant text, then, does so by suggesting a new interpreta-

Music and Poetry: The Nineteenth Century and After (Berkeley and Los Angeles: University of California Press, 1984), excerpted and adapted from 127, 145–6, 150–5 by the author.

tion for it, and specifically a sceptical interpretation, one that rewrites the text in some essential way. In other words—slightly exaggerated but only slightly—the music becomes a deconstruction of the poem.

One way for the music of a song to do this is to deny the text's autonomy, and therefore its authority, by denying it expressive support in a crucial way or at a crucial moment. What this often entails is a disparity in one of the obvious formal features that music and poetry have in common: closure, sectionalization, repetition, the differentiation and affiliation of material, and so on. Schubert's 'Gretchen am Spinnrade', a song often taken as paradigmatic of the Lied, provides a striking example of this structural dissonance. In treating Gretchen's broken lament for Faust, Schubert wrote music that is universally admired for its simple yet devastating sadness; most likely—composing the song at 17 on a single October day—he had nothing else in mind. Yet his song has something in mind that Goethe didn't.

As a poem, 'Gretchen am Spinnrade' uses the relationship between its refrain and its non-repeated stanzas to expose a surging emotional rhythm within a lament that seems static, consumed by its own hopeless monotony. Though fairly long, the poem requires full quotation; as a convenience, I have marked its division into three groups of stanzas:

(I) Meine Ruh ist hin,
Mein Herz ist schwer;
Ich finde sie nimmer
Und nimmermehr.

Wo ich ihn nicht hab,
Ist mir das Gab,
Die ganze Welt
Ist mir vergallt.

Mein armer Kopf
Ist mir verrückt,
Mein armer Sinn
Ist mir zerstückt.

(II) Meine Ruh ist hin,
Mein Herz ist schwer;
Ich finde sie nimmer,
Und nimmermehr,

Nach ihm nur schau ich
Zum Fenster hinaus,
Nach ihm nur geh ich
Aus dem Haus.

Sein hoher Gang,
Sein edle Gestalt,
Seines Mundes Lächeln,
Seiner Augen Gewalt,

Und seiner Rede
Zauberfluss,
Sein Händedruck,
Und ach, sein Kuss!

(III) Meine Ruh ist hin;
Mein Herz ist schwer;
Ich finde sie nimmer
Und nimmermehr.

Mein Busen drängt
Sich nach ihm hin.
Ach, dürft ich fassen
Und halten ihn

Und küssen ihn,
So wie ich wollt,
An seinen Kussen
Vergehen sollt!

(Translation given at
end of excerpt)

Each group of stanzas here begins with the refrain, Gretchen's cry of anguish, then continues by spelling out the particulars of her situation. The refrain combines the specific sensation of an absence within the self ('Meine Ruh ist hin') with a free-floating sense of emotional agitation. The continuations refer to both of these elements, first making an implicit equation between Gretchen's absent peace and the absent Faust, then portraying the impact of that double absence on Gretchen's feelings. But this sequence is worked out with telling differences as the poem unfolds.

As the continuations succeed each other, they register the changing nature of Gretchen's agitation. At first, her emotions are invested in self-conscious representations of inner emptiness—a world gone sour, a mind shattered, Faust's absence as a grave. In the second continuation, this gives way to a series of impassioned, alluring images of Faust that slowly accumulate an erotic charge; the third continuation is a more intense, more erotically explicit play of images that seems to absorb Gretchen completely. By the close of the poem, the agitation of grief has become indistinguishable from sexual desire, the imagery of mourning indistinguishable from sexual fantasy. The emergence of this ambivalence suggests an unacknowledged struggle in Gretchen between pain and desire, or more exactly between two kinds of pain: one redoubled by self-consciousness, and one mitigated by desire (an antithesis: other-consciousness). In the end, it is desire that controls the foreground. The missing Faust is restored in imaginary form, so much so that he nearly takes over the poem; and Gretchen's fantasy about him becomes a partial compensation for the absence that calls it forth. The detailed, arousing imagery that envelops the figure of Faust contradicts the closing insistence of the refrain that what is lost—really the part of Gretchen's ego that is identified with Faust—can never be found again. Gretchen reintegrates her 'shattered mind' by spontaneously internalizing the object of her love.

As the persistence of the refrain reminds us, Gretchen's passage from self-alienation to desire is a movement of reinterpretation, not one of difference. The desire acts as a sublimation of the violent misery and ritualized searching—the trips to the window and into the street—by which her 'poor head' is turned/maddened ('verrückt'); sexuality appears as a sublimating, not the sublimated, force where identity is concerned. Goethe articulates this process by giving each continuation an influence on the recurrence of the refrain. The first continuation, barren of fantasy, fixed in the 'grave' of Faust's absence, lasts for two stanzas, suggesting a norm that is also observed by the final stanza-group. The second continuation, in which the threshold of fantasy is imperceptibly crossed, lasts for three stanzas, as if Gretchen were able to defer the outbreak of lament by spinning out the images in which her desire is beginning to find itself. The effect of a deferral is very specific; it is the extra, third stanza that makes the erotic element in the poem explicit for the first time. The climactic cry of this stanza, 'Und ach, sein Kuss!' is the culmination of a series of images that re-creates Faust's body from scattered reminiscences of his gait, figure, smile, and so on. The movement of integration also reverses the imagery of fragmentation attached to Gretchen's mind and body in the first continuation. But the final continuation does even better than this. Not only is it a violent and open expression of sexual fantasy, but it also defers the refrain indefinitely, so that the poem ends with an image of passion, indeed of the 'fading (Vergehen) of the subject' into the other that comes with sexual fulfilment, rather than with the abstract 'nevermore' of barren despair.

Schubert's treatment of 'Gretchen am Spinnrade' is based on a structural dissonance that turns Goethe's pattern inside out. Goethe's lament—the refrain—becomes Schubert's mitigation, while Goethe's mitigation—the pattern of continuation—becomes the basis of Schubert's lament. The curve of anguish traced by Schubert ascends with the curve of sexual desire, and is relieved only by the sense of isolation from the beloved that appears in the refrain. This structural rhythm leads Schubert to make a famous alteration, the repetition of the first couplet of the refrain at the close of the song. For musical as well as dramatic reasons, Schubert wants the song to end with a release of tension; like Goethe, he directs Gretchen's pain toward a sublimation. But Goethe's sublimation is a spasm of desire, while Schubert's is a lapse into resignation. Where Goethe completes a continuous transformation of Gretchen's disturbed peace, Schubert posits an exhausted ebbing of passion. This change, one might add, is not necessarily to Schubert's advantage, though the fierce emphasis of the song on the pain in sexual longing partially compensates for the loss of Goethe's evocation of the mobility of intense emotion.

The structural rhythm of Schubert's song matches that of the poem, with three large-scale crescendos to parallel the three groups of stanzas, but the matched rhythms move in opposite directions. Where Goethe starts with a cry of pain and dilutes it with the flow of images, Schubert starts with a sorrowful whisper and intensifies it almost to a scream. Each section of the music begins pianissimo, with the refrain sung over a D-Minor 'spinning' figure in the accompaniment. The crescendos mount through the continuations—to forte the first time, fortissimo thereafter—while the spinning figure exposes the self-torturing core of Gretchen's grief by imperceptibly shifting the imitative focus from her wheel to her wheeling emotions. The vocal line for the Faust imagery of the second continuation does seem to seek the balm of desire, but there is a poignant inflection at the thought of emotional intimacy—'Seines Mundes Lächeln, | Seiner Augen Gewalt' set to restless harmony—and this prepares the way for an aggrieved conclusion at the remembrance of physical intimacy—'Sein Händedruck | Und ach, sein Kuss!' ('Sein Händedruck' is sung as a d2–f2 oscillation, the melodic pattern that will later dominate the despairing D-minor vocal line of the last stanza.) For Schubert's Gretchen, imagery fails—and worse: it steadily heightens the consciousness of separation. Desire is present, certainly, but it is unable to internalize the images of Faust, impotent to convert the imagery into fantasy.

This pattern produces two crises in the musical design. The first of these comes at the close of the second crescendo, the setting of 'Und ach, sein Kuss!' At this point the spinning figure, which has been continuously sustained since the beginning, is abruptly replaced by clamorous sforzando chords while the voice mounts to an extended cry of pain on 'Kuss', the erotic turning-point of the poem. Gretchen's anguish is marked in the vocal line by an anti-cadential movement from D (the tonic tone) to G on 'sein Kuss'; the G of 'Kuss' is the dissonant tone of the dominant-seventh chord that bursts forth in the accompaniment, and it turns the word into an almost inarticulate protest against frustration and rejection. The overflow of sexual feeling momentarily brings the song to a halt, producing a strong structural disso-nance by breaking continuity; in the poem, the quasi-incantatory rhythm that leads smoothly from stanza to stanza is essential in articulating the always transitional character of Gretchen's feelings. The impression of a sonorous void is heightened as the dominant-seventh chord under 'Kuss' fails to resolve, transforming itself instead into a drawn-out diminished seventh (see Musical Example 19.). The suspension of harmonic motion registers the paralysis of Gretchen's ego.

Several measures of the spinning figure now follow pianissimo, echoing Gretchen's anguish by elaborating on the diminished-seventh chord that con-summates her cry. Twice the figure breaks off after a painful dissonance, a bare minor ninth, as if the emotional and harmonic impasse reached in the second crescendo could admit of no recovery. Then the figure smooths itself out and the refrain returns, exchanging Faust's all-too-seductive image for the vacant shelter of Gretchen's heavy heart. The return is momentarily placating, the more so because its figuration now provides the deferred resolution of the cli-

Ex. 19. Musical Example. Schubert, 'Gretchen am Spinnrade'

mactic dominant-seventh chord. But the music rises inexorably into the third and most turbulent crescendo, this one marked by a thickened texture for the spinning figure and by prolonged fortissimo writing. For a climax, the voice turns to three plangent outbursts on 'Vergehen sollt', the last two capped by melodic leaps at 'Vergehen' that reach a sustained high A over a forzando-laden accompaniment. (The 'open' sonority of these moments supports their stark intensity; each high A forms part of a complex of bare fouths and fifths that momentarily represents the dominant-seventh chord.)

At the same time, the text is successively condensed. First we hear the last two stanzas in full, then only the last stanza—as revised by Schubert to incorporate a rhetorically intensified first line, 'O könnt ich ihm küssen' ('O if I could kiss him'). Finally, the death-driven closing couplet stands alone. The effect of this gesture is to expel, even to exorcize, all of the elements of pleasure and intimacy—the embracing, holding, uninhibited kissing—from Gretchen's sexuality, until all that is left is a hopeless wish for obliviousness. Where the 'Vergehen' of Goethe's Gretchen unifies an evolving sexual fantasy with the image of a swoon, the increasingly shrill 'Vergehen' of Schubert's Gretchen exposes a thwarted and fixated consciousness trying to exhaust itself. Schubert's condensations and repetitions constitute Gretchen's attempt to blot out—more literally to displace—the seductive images that torture her awareness of separation beyond enduring.

With this new impasse, the song reaches its second crisis, one that appears mainly as an unappeased need for psychic defence and aesthetic distance. Nothing is available to limit the fragmentation and depletion of the self except the refrain, with its protective sense of imageless solitude. Yet to bring the refrain back at this point would close the song with a moment of calm, something without warrant in the relentlessly downward curve of feeling throughout. As we know, Schubert brings the refrain back anyway, perhaps partly from a sense that the inevitable return of the music to the tonic would subvert any implication of total collapse. His quiet ending contradicts the statement of the refrain, 'Meine Ruh ist hin', much as the rise of passion in the poem contradicts the numb resignation implied by 'mein Herz ist schwer'. But where Goethe's ending is a closure, the outcome of a process that shapes the whole poem, Schubert's is suspended, rootless. Its arbitrary quality, coupled with its undeniable effectiveness, suggests that Schubert far more than Goethe read 'Gretchen am Spinnrade' as a study in what a later age would call psychosexuality, a kind of subjectivity in which sexuality acts as an independent, often compulsive, sometimes destructive force.

Translation of 'Gretchen am Spinnrade'

> My peace is gone,
> My heart is sore,
> Never will I find it,
> Nevermore.
>
> Wherever I lack him,
> That place is my grave;
> My whole world
> Turns into gall.

My poor head
Is madly turned,
My poor mind
Is shattered.

My peace is gone,
My heart is sore,
Never will I find it,
Nevermore.

Only for him
Do I gaze from the window,
Only for him
Do I go from the house.

His proud step,
His noble form,
The smile of his mouth,
The power of his eyes,

And his talk's
Magic stream,
The touch of his hand,
And ah! his kiss!

My peace is gone,
My heart is sore,
Never will I find it,
Nevermore.

My bosom urges
Me after him,
Ah could I but clasp him
And hold him close

And kiss him
As my heart would choose,
In his kisses
To swoon, to die away!

(Translation by L. Kramer)

On Dialectics versus Deconstruction

STEVE SWEENEY-TURNER

Ever since Michael Chanan's 1969 *Tempo* article connected Peter Maxwell Davies with the philosophical tradition of speculative dialectics, this connection has been virtually the mainstay of Davies's critical reception. If we accept the popular model of dialectics as the resolution (synthesis) of two opposing terms (thesis-antithesis), then we can easily identify a dialectical critique underpinning, for instance, Paul Griffiths's monograph written thirteen years later (1982). In discussing Davies's parody technique, Griffiths begins by highlighting those processes which result in the 'distortion' or 'corruption' of sources, leading to situations of 'ambiguity' or 'contradiction'. Such an account is no doubt authorized by the composer's own terminology of 'distortion', 'ambiguity', 'dissolution', and 'fragmentation', which is found particularly in the sleeve-notes to *Vesalii Icones* (1969). Nevertheless, for both Davies and the authorized Griffiths, the function of these parodic turns is not so much to engender despair in the listener, but rather to lead them to a higher plane of spiritual reconciliation. As Griffiths writes of *Missa Super l'Homme Armé* (1968), its merciless parodies of sacred musical styles are not a 'cheap exercise in blasphemy', but on the contrary raise questions of 'discerning and communicating religious truth'—specifically, it becomes a question of 'distinguishing what is true from its precise opposite' (1982: 64). Again, Griffiths's version is fully authorized by the composer's own accounts; of *Vesalii Icones*, Davies writes that 'the point I am trying to make is a moral one—it is a matter of distinguishing the false from the real—that one should not be taken in by appearances' (1984).

What we see emerging here is a discourse based in oppositional thought, despite the plurality of the music's surface. The way in which Davies suggests we use *Vesalii Icones* is to learn to distinguish between the falsity of plural surfaces and the unitary truth which lies beneath them. One moves from amoral multiplicity to an oppositional morality. As Arnold Whittall has recently commented of such pieces, 'aesthetic satisfaction was the result of appreciating the motive *behind* the oppositions' (1994: 545). In other words, one works through a material world full of sin, as a spiritual *katharsis*—in approaching sin, one dialectically transcends it, achieving a higher synthesis.

'Resurrecting the Antichrist: Maxwell Davies and Parody—Dialectics or Deconstruction?', *Tempo*, 191 (Dec. 1994), 14–15, 16–17, 19–20.

Stephen Walsh's *New Grove* article also hooks into this common currency of dialectical thought: 'At bottom one senses Davies's own uncertainty over relative values, his search for a coherent belief and a coherent style through the conflict between opposed possibilities' (1980: 277). In other words, the whole point of engaging in an oppositional conflict is to achieve a coherent, stable, unequivocal resolution. In this reading, then, Davies ultimately rejects the pragmatic relativity which marks both postmodernism and poststructuralism, embracing a much more traditional concept of value.

However, if we engage in a parallel reading of the composer's sleeve-notes and score of *Vesalii Icones*, various questions regarding the relationship between its parodies and the idea of dialectics will gradually emerge, which complicate received critical wisdom, and ultimately challenge the status of the composer's own reading.

[. . .]

Of the narrative level of [the final] movement, Davies writes:

> In the last dance, 'The Resurrection', the Christ story is modified. It is the Antichrist—the dark 'double' of Christ of medieval legend, indistinguishable from the 'real' Christ—who emerges from the tomb and puts his curse on Christendom to all eternity. Some may consider such an interpretation sacrilegious—but the point I am trying to make is a moral one—it is a matter of distinguishing the false from the real—that one should not be taken in by appearances. (1984)

Here, then, Davies's sleeve-note provides us with the final dialectical closure to absolve the piece of all preceding sins of non-resolution, a closure which is very much in line with the critical positions adopted by Chanan, Griffiths, Whittall, and Walsh.

But—and this is an enormous but—this closure is not provided *within the piece itself*, but is foisted onto it after the event through the guidance of the composer's notes. In the piece as one hears, sees, or reads it, the *Antichrist's* de-cadence triumphs, and in two ways: (1) the displacement of all teleological attempts; (2) the irreverent 'mocking' of the image of Christ's purity. Significantly, the actual triumph of the Antichrist in this period of Davies's music is indicated by Whittall: 'the aural effect was of confrontation not synthesis' (1994: 545). If, then, the *aural* affectivity of the piece does *not* lead to synthesis, then it is clear that the received wisdom of the neo-Hegelian schema outlined at the start of this article is something imposed upon the music after the event: we are either expected to read the composer's notes (and its attendant authorized derivatives), or to actively interpret this spiritual message from the evidence of the piece in the fully theological, hermeneutic sense of interpretation.

If, as Umberto Eco has written, 'we have to respect the text, not the author' (1992: 66), then what would happen to our reading of *Vesalii Icones* if we suspend the theological dialectic achieved by its interpreters (including its composer), and return to what Whittall lets slip as its 'aural confrontation'? This will not involve 'appreciating the motive behind the oppositions', as he and Davies allege, but will involve allowing the piece to play out its multiple *aural* specificities in a space prior to (perhaps even fully aside from) such 'appreciation'.

Both the move against theological hermeneutics as a model for textual critique, and the swerve away from the Hegelian tradition of speculative dialectics, are two of the crucial projects of philosophical *deconstruction*, first defined as such by the Parisian philosopher Jacques Derrida in the late 1960s/early 1970s. His classic texts *Of Grammatology* (1967), *Writing and Difference* (1967), *Dissemination* (1972), and *Margins of Philosophy* (1972) amount to one of the most significant *re-workings* (deconstruction does *not* obliterate) of the Western philosophical tradition carried out in the century. In particular, they engage with one of the crucial problems of Parisian philosophy at that time—*how to avoid the dialectic.* The motivation for the swerve from Hegel had many resonances (not least political), but for current purposes it will be necessary to simplify to the point of risking absurdity.

Deconstruction begins with the idea that in a dialectical system, the initial term (thesis) effectively commands the entire project—it is only through producing its own shadow that the antithesis is produced (like Adam's spare rib producing Eve). In a very precise structural way, the antithesis is a derivative property of the thesis. Given that the thesis creates and defines its opposition to the antithesis, it is no wonder that the resultant synthesis can be read as effectively a purified repetition of the thesis. Dialectics, then, can be read as a powerful means of appropriating the force of an opposing term, and using the power of that opposition in order to reinstate one's initial term even more forcefully. On the other hand, deconstruction attempts to break out of this unitary closure, and play instead within the space of the provisional and the multiple. Closure is suspended, and in this we can see the first connection which *Vesalii Icones* has with Derrida's philosophy (and let us not forget Derrida's interest in Nietzsche's 'transvaluation of all values' in *The Anti-Christ*, or Nietzsche's description there of spiritual closure as an 'imaginary *teleology*').

It is also necessary to note that deconstruction is a mode of reading an extant text, and that this process effectively has three stages (always allowing for the important fact that in practice, these stages often do not follow in strict sequence, and will inevitably interrupt each other):

(1) *engage* with the text—in effect, one quotes or rehearses its structure, and in so doing identifies the conceptual oppositions on which the structure is based;

(2) *reverse* the hierarchical structure of the text's oppositions, thus destabilizing them *from within*, but without breaking the structure as such;

(3) *displace* the hierarchical structure which previously bound the terms within a static or dialectical opposition, exacerbating the internal destabilization achieved in the stage of reversal (note that the terms of the opposition are not annihilated—only the *hierarchical* structure which bound them).

From this, we can easily see that *Vesalii Icones* could be said to be deconstructive on many layers at once—quoting specific pieces and stylistic traits from various traditions whether medieval, Romanticist, or popular, and focusing on various levels of their structures in order to perform inversions (reversals) and displacements of their terms. Further than that, the intertextuality of the piece extends so far as to include deconstructive approaches to analytical techniques as well as compositional elements—a truly poststructuralist transgression of traditional boundaries.

Reading through Davies's notes on the piece and the critical tradition which stems from it, it is significant that all of these features are very openly acknowledged. Often the terminology surrounding Davies's parody technique is remarkably Derridean, from the composer's own 'distortion', 'ambiguity', 'dissolution', and 'fragmentation' already noted, to his idea of 'a series of images which are "infiltrated" or "corrupted" from within', to Griffiths's reading of it as 'depicting at once identity and inversion' (1982: 55–6). As Derrida writes, one 'operate[s] according to the lexicon of that which one is delimiting' (1982: 17); in other words, one 'borrows from a heritage the resources necessary for the deconstruction of that heritage itself' (1978: 282).

And if Whittall is right about Davies's technical (if not intentional) emphasis in this period on 'confrontation, not synthesis', then we can also align him with Derrida's preference for speaking more of 'conflicts of force than of contradiction' (1987: 101). If *Vesalii Icones* really did operate according to a dialectical programme, then we would expect there to be contradictory forces as such—textual elements which were in strict metaphysical opposition to each other. What we actually have, as Davies himself admits, is a situation where 'clearly separate identities emerge rarely' (1984)—a scene where multiple elements may occasionally be in *conflict* with each other, but which are never stable enough to establish the kind of oppositional structures which are prerequisite of dialectical synthesis. Where such oppositions and syntheses are attempted, there is always already a number of other terms in play which can divert such a directional plan. The insistent lack of closure, and the vast array of technical devices which are brought to bear on source materials to ensure an ever-present reversal and displacement of any teleological end, force the piece well out of dialectical territories, and towards the deconstructive field. In this, its modernity exceeds that of its reception.

References

Adorno, Theodor W. (1941), 'On Popular Music', *Studies in Philosophy and Social Science* 9, 17–48 [in English]; repr. in S. Frith and A. Goodwin (eds.), *On Record* (London: Routledge, 1990).

—— (1973), *Philosophy of Modern Music* (1st pub. Frankfurt, 1948), trans. Anne G. Mitchell and Wesley V. Bloomster (London: Sheed & Ward).

—— (1976), *Introduction to the Sociology of Music* (orig. pub. as *Einleitung in die Musiksoziologie*, Frankfurt am Main: Suhrkamp Verlag, 1962) trans. E. B. Ashton (New York: Seabury Press).

Chanan, Michael (1969), 'Dialectics in the Music of Peter Maxwell Davies', *Tempo* 90, 12–22.

Cone, Edward T. (1974), *The Composer's Voice* (Berkeley: University of California Press).

Coser, L. (1960), 'Comments on Bauer and Bauer', *Journal of Social Issues* 26.

Davies, Peter Maxwell (1984), notes to *Vesalii Icones* (Unicorn-Kanchana).

Derrida, Jacques (1978), *Writing and Difference* (London: RKP).

—— (1982), *Margins of Philosophy* (Brighton: Harvester).

—— (1987), *Positions* (London: Athlone).

Eco, Umberto (1992), *Interpretation and Overinterpretation* (Cambridge: Cambridge University Press).

Foucault, Michel, and Boulez, Pierre (1985), 'Contemporary Music and the Public' (orig. pub. in *CNAC magazine* no. 15 (May–June 1983), Centre national d'art et de culture Georges Pompidou), trans. John Rahn, *Perspectives of New Music*, Fall–Winter, 6–12.

Gans, H. J. (1967), 'Popular Culture in America', in H. S. Becker (ed.), *Social Problems: A Modern Approach* (John Wiley).

Green, Lucy (1988), *Music on Deaf Ears: Musical Meaning, Ideology and Education* (Manchester: Manchester University Press).

—— (1997), *Music, Gender, Education* (Cambridge: Cambridge University Press).

Griffiths, Paul (1982), *Peter Maxwell Davies* (London: Robson).

Haag, E. van den (1959), 'Of Happiness and Despair We Have No Measure', in Rosenberg and White (1959).

—— (1961), 'A Dissent from the Consensual Society', in Jacobs (1961).

Hildesheimer, Wolfgang (1983), *Mozart*, trans. Marion Faber (New York).

Jacobs, N. (1961) (ed.), *Culture for the Millions* (Princeton).

Jones, Trevor (1980), 'The Traditional Music of the Australian Aborigines', in E. May (ed.), *Musics of Many Cultures* (Berkeley: University of California Press).

Kramer, Lawrence (1984), *Music and Poetry: The Nineteenth Century and After* (Berkeley: University of California Press).

—— (1990), *Music as Cultural Practice, 1800–1900* (Berkeley: University of California Press).

—— (1995), *Classical Music and Postmodern Knowledge* (Berkeley: University of California Press).

Lincicome, David (1972), 'Iterational Systems', *Journal of Music Theory* 16, 168–205.

MacDonald, D. (1959), 'A Theory of Mass Culture', in Rosenberg and White (1959).

Merriam, Alan P. (1964), *The Anthropology of Music* (Evanston, Ill.: Northwestern University Press).

Meyer, Leonard B. (1959), 'Some Remarks on Value and Greatness in Music', *Journal of Aesthetics and Art Criticism* 17:4, 486–500.

Moore, Allan F. (1993), *Rock: The Primary Text* (Buckingham: Open University Press).

Nattiez, Jean-Jacques (1990), *Music and Discourse: Toward a Semiology of Music*, trans. Carolyn Abbate (Princeton: Princeton University Press).

Nettl, Bruno (1983), *The Study of Ethnomusicology* (Indianapolis: Indiana University Press).

Parker, C. (1975), 'Pop Song, the Manipulated Ritual', in P. Abbs (ed.), *The Black Rainbow* (Heinemann Educational Books).

Rosenberg, B., and White, D. (1959) (eds.), *Mass Culture* (The Free Press).

Routh, F. (1972), *Contemporary British Music* (MacDonald).

Subotnik, Rose Rosengard (1988), 'Toward a Deconstruction of Structural Listening: A Critique of Schoenberg, Adorno, and Stravinsky', in Eugene Narmour and Ruth Solie (eds.), *Explorations in Music, the Arts, and Ideas: Essays in Honor of Leonard B. Meyer* (Stuyvesant, NY: Pendragon Press), 87–122.

Sweeney-Turner, Steve (1994), 'Resurrecting the Antichrist: Maxwell Davies and Parody—Dialectics or Deconstruction?', *Tempo* 191 (Dec.), 14–20.

Vulliamy, Graham (1977), 'Music and the Mass Culture Debate', in J. Shepherd, P. Virden, G. Vulliamy, and T. Wishart, *Whose Music? A Sociology of Musical Languages* (London: Latimer), 179–200.

——and Lee, Edward (1976) (eds.), *Pop Music in School* (Cambridge: Cambridge University Press).

Walsh, Stephen (1980), 'Davies, Peter Maxwell', *New Grove*, vol. v.

Whittall, Arnold (1994), 'The Bottom Line', *Musical Times*, Sept.

Wilensky, H. (1964), 'Mass Society and Mass Culture: Interdependence or Independence?', *American Sociological Review*, Apr.

Part V
Music Production and Consumption

Introduction

When considering the production and consumption of music, it is worthwhile reading the thoughts of Adorno: one of his hardest hitting polemics on this subject is the article 'On the Fetish Character in Music and the Regression of Listening' (1978; originally published 1938). It was not just Adorno, however, who became agitated at the impact records and radio were having on musical life; Constant Lambert, in *Music Ho!* of 1934, was another among the many writers in the 1930s who were aghast at the massive increase in the mechanical reproduction of music. At this time, much of the BBC's radio output did not fall under the responsibility of the Music Department but of the Variety Department. Thus, an opposition was set up between what was regarded as 'real' music and what was not. The serious versus popular binarism was mapped onto an audience who were consequently thought of as being either 'high brows' (those who listened to symphonies and operas) or 'low brows' (those who preferred dance bands and cinema organs). Paddy Scannell has studied the implications this division had for the BBC Music Department, such as the perceived need to educate and 'improve' the taste of the general public. In the given excerpt the citations beginning 'WAC' refer to index numbers of files held at the BBC Written Archive, Caversham, Reading, UK.

In *The Recording Angel*, Evan Eisenberg is concerned to distinguish recording from live music, and to claim that the former, what he calls 'phonography', deserves to be considered an art-form (a collective art like film) rather than being denigrated as the poor relation of the latter. It becomes an art-form by exploiting its creative potential to manipulate sound, freeing it from social frames such as public concert performances. Eisenberg is clearly influenced by Walter Benjamin's famous essay 'The Work of Art in the Age of Mechanical Reproduction' (1936). Consider, for example, Benjamin's remark, 'mechanical reproduction emancipates the work of art from its parasitical dependence on ritual' (1968: 224). In the selected extract, Eisenberg discusses jazz records, arguing that they 'not only disseminated jazz, but inseminated it', making reference to Louis Armstrong's experiments in the studio and Jelly Roll Morton's 'construction of dazzling phonographic montages'. It is instructive to keep in mind Lydia Goehr's critique of the work-concept while reading this excerpt, especially when Eisenberg cites André Hodeir.

Bach may not have thought he was composing 'musical works', and most jazz and popular music (like the majority of the world's musical practices) may not be conceived in this way, but Lydia Goehr shows, nevertheless, that the work-concept has dominated Western musical criticism and assessments of musical value since around 1800. She points out that the label 'musical work' can be used to evaluate as well as classify, and that these two senses may be conflated under the influence of a 'conceptual imperialism' that encourages the packaging of all music into 'works'. The *Werktreue* ideal, the need for performers to be true to the composer's intentions in the work, developed in tandem with this concept. Without accurate scores this was not possible; yet, in the eighteenth century an accurate score had not been especially desirable, since improvisation was still a major feature of music-making. During the next century, however, when the mass production of sheet music became a reality and copyright laws were being introduced to combat theft and plagiarism, a complete and detailed score became a necessary means of asserting ownership. In the given excerpt, Goehr explains how the work-concept is often used in a *derivative* manner, being applied to any music that approximates the condition expected of a musical work, or being borrowed by musicians to describe their musical output even when the work-concept is foreign to their music-making.

In discussing the music business, Peter Wicke has several illusions to dispel. For example, even 'rebel rock' functions in the ideological as well as economic interests of capital without any need for crude manipulation, since 'The more marked the musician's individualism, the more convincingly the capitalist order appears as the true basis of individual self-realisation and the more convincing the motive for purchasing his record as an expression of the consumer's same individualism' (1990: 115). In the given excerpt, Wicke is concerned, first, to show that the music industry only *appears* to give people what they want (in fact, it is primarily guided by what people are able and willing to pay for), and, second, that competition is about product presentation, which entails successfully creating a context for the record (for example a frame of reference indicating its importance) that will draw in eager consumers apparently as free agents.

Peter Martin shows how the music business's development and its attempts to control its market has been undermined by technological innovation, since this has generally posed threats to established ways of profiting from music. Disruption caused by new technology can have a transforming effect on business: Martin gives as examples network radio and cassette players. Power struggles in the industry therefore have to be given due consideration alongside other sociocultural factors when accounting for the emergence of new directions in popular music.

Jacques Attali's basic thesis in *Noise* is that music is prophetic: changes in music herald social changes. For example, he writes, 'The present economic crisis [1977] and efflorescence of our decadence were preprogrammed in Viennese music [at the end of the nineteenth century]' (81). In another example of what Nattiez has dubbed 'Pythian sociology', he refers to 'The renaissance of violence in our cities, which the pop music of the 1960s so prophetically announced' (130). Attali contends that music is used as part of a panoply of power (even among birds). When it comes to cultural theory, he inclines towards Adorno and 'mass culture' critique: he speaks of 'standardized products' and reasons that 'it is necessary to ban subversive noise because it betokens demands for cultural autonomy' (6–7). He is drawn to structural homologies: 'We can, for example, toy with the idea that it is not by chance that the half-tone found acceptance during the Renaissance, at precisely the same time the merchant class was expanding' (10). He adopts a humanist notion of musical meaning—'Jazz expressed the alienation of blacks' (103)—and a modernist, evolutionary interpretation of the development of musical style—'music evolved toward a pure syntax' (35). He also has leanings towards *kulturpessimismus*: 'there is glaring evidence that the end of aesthetic codes is at hand' (11).

He describes four networks, each entertaining specific relations with money: (1) *sacrificial ritual*, where music is part of ceremony; (2) *representation*, where music becomes a spectacle (e.g. at a concert hall); (3) *repetition*, where music becomes mass produced (e.g. as records); and (4) *composition*, a Utopian vision of a time when music would be a self-transcendent, yet self-communicating, non-commercial activity. Rather confusingly, Attali also uses (2) above to mean music represented by its score, music as representation or symbol of social order (e.g. the orchestra), and music being *re*-presented (i.e. re-performed). His other notion of representation—music as spectacle—is more than a little indebted to 1960s 'situationism' (the situationists made much of the argument that art had been reduced to the spectacle of a commodity). Attali is concerned with music *itself* as representation (i.e. music as spectacle) rather than with the way representations (e.g. of nobility, anger, seductiveness, etc.) might be constructed within musical styles.

John Shepherd has, for a number of years, been steadily elaborating theoretical models in order to understand how power (the 'force of social structures') is mediated through music. He identifies the moment of consumption as a crucial (though not exclusive) point for the negotiation of meaning. In theorizing processes of negotiation, he draws on the work of French sociologist Pierre Bourdieu and on Gramsci's theory of hegemony. Like Bourdieu, Shepherd is keen to test his theories, and has undertaken fieldwork in Montreal, examining moments of individual consumption against the background of a statistical consumption study. The emphasis on subjectivity, dialectical interplay, 'expressed intentionalities', and empirical research sets Shepherd apart from the poststructuralism and deconstruction camp.

In many discussions of music and postmodernism (especially of music video and postmodernism) there has been both a tendency to forget about such notions as the arbitrary character of the linguistic sign, and a temptation to neglect the pitfalls of logocentrism. As a consequence, music has often been conceived of as unique among artistic practices in being incapable of forging stable signifier–signified relationships; in other words, music is regarded as possessing nothing but 'empty signs'. It is a source of wonder that some otherwise radical film theorists have been prepared to accept the most conservative notions about musical communication and meaning. In the final excerpt, however, Andrew Goodwin is not concerned with postmodernist semiotics, but rather with contradictions in postmodernist theories as they relate to issues of aesthetics and 'cultural capital' (a term coined by Bourdieu). Goodwin is able to tease out the incoherence in postmodernist theory while, strangely, leaving an impression that modernist theory may have been coherent. He argues that the postmodernist debate intersects popular music at five distinct levels: MTV, the music itself, technology, 'structures of feeling' (a concept from Raymond Williams), and 'postmodern rock'.

At each level he finds problems—the increased rigidity of MTV programming, the failure to account for the current state of popular music, the use of sampling technology to invoke history and authenticity, the concern to identify reading formations that celebrate pastiche rather than identify postmodern texts, and the emergence of postmodern rock as a sales category. Goodwin resists the common postmodernist assertion that the categories of high art and mass culture have collapsed, remarking that art/pop distinctions are made within pop itself: not all pop, that is, fits comfortably into one side of a high/low opposition. It is interesting to see that, in the manner of Dai Griffiths, Goodwin has found a consumer label for minimalist compositions—'college student music'.

On Music and its Dissemination

PADDY SCANNELL

From Musical Appreciation to Musicology

Since the nineteenth century there had been a growing middle-class concern to educate the people and to promote social harmony by weaning 'the horny handed sons of toil' away from 'vicious indulgences' towards more rational, moral, and peaceable forms of recreation and leisure. Musical education and appreciation formed one part of this pervasive social movement. In Sunday Schools and the emerging system of national elementary education new teaching methods (the tonic sol-fa) encouraged group singing, whose effects reached beyond the classroom into the great Victorian revival of choral singing which, by the end of the century, had an extensive network of regional and national festivals and competitions. The growth of the works brass bands, with their competitions and festivals, was a parallel part of this movement. In the later part of the century a 'music for the people' campaign was one strand in the missionary work of those philanthropic middle-class settlements in the working-class ghettos of the great cities, designed 'to bring beauty home to the people'. Cheap musical concerts, expecially on Sundays, in places like Ancoats, Manchester or the East End of London, aimed to bring high-class music at a low price within the reach of the lower orders and to encourage their taste for such rational recreation.

Thus the musical appreciation movement has a well-established history long before the coming of wireless. Broadcasting, the BBC argued, was the final step in the 'true democratization of music'—the means through which 'the shepherd on the downs, or the lonely crofter in the farthest Hebrides and, what is equally important the labourer in his squalid tenement in our but too familiar slums, or the lonely invalid on her monotonous couch, may all, in spirit, sit side by side with the patron of the stalls and hear some of the best performances in the world' (*BBC Yearbook* 1928: 85). This concern with putting fine performances of great music within reach of all was the main aim of musical policy in the days of the Company through to the end of the twenties. Its effect is hard to gauge, but the initial impact of radio (so difficult for us now to imagine) should not be underestimated. Thus a 'listener-in' from Whitstable in 1923: 'in these little provincial towns, whose chief items of amusement consist of two or three picture houses, a local struggle on the part of the amateur societies and

'Music for the Multitude? The Dilemmas of the BBC's Music Policy 1923–1946', *Media, Culture and Society*, 3 (1981), 244–7.

strong sea air, a feast of good [radio] music *is* appreciated' (*Radio Times*, 12 October 1923).

It was recognized that the ordinary listener, who had probably never before heard a Beethoven symphony, needed help to appreciate this feast, so from the earliest days musical teachers and critics were engaged to explain the meaning of music. The BBC was fortunate in its choice of Percy Scholes and Sir Walford Davies. Both had the knack of explaining musical form simply and clearly and without condescension. Sir Walford Davies, who inaugurated Schools broadcasting in April 1924 with a musical talk, soon established his reputation as a great popular evangelizer of music and as an accomplished broadcaster. His series, *Music and the Ordinary Listener* (commenced January 1926), was extremely popular with listeners (cf. Briggs 1961: 262, 284, 254). Scholes was a prolific writer, with an encyclopaedic knowledge of musical history. His book, *Everybody's Guide to Broadcast Music* (Scholes 1925), described in clear and easy language the elements of musical form with advice on how to listen to opera, orchestral, and chamber music. Scholes drew on his ample correspondence with listeners, and his eminently readable book contains valuable evidence of the difficulties and prejudices of listeners at the time in relation to broadcast music.

In the very first month of its new charter and licence the Corporation launched *The Foundations of Music* (3 January 1927), a fifteen-minute programme broadcast five times a week in the early evening, which was to run continuously for the next ten years. The idea for this programme came from Filson Young, appointed as 'critical adviser' to the BBC by Reith in August 1926 and who maintained this curious post until his death in 1937. The series started life as an attempt painlessly to provide the ordinary listener with a systematic introduction to the shorter compositions for solo instruments and small ensembles by those masters who had laid down the foundations of music. For Filson Young the original idea was entertainment for the musical and unmusical alike—'a quarter of an hour's pleasant sound, like the bubbling of a fountain, which might be listened to attentively or drowsed over at the end of a tiring day' (Filson Young to Eckersley, 30 November 1934).

By 1934 the Music Department had become restive with the programme and wanted to give it a complete overhaul. The standard repertoire of 'the present fashion in classics' had been exhausted. Bach—Mozart—Haydn, Beethoven—Schubert—Mendelssohn and Schumann—Brahms had all been 'done' but in a very inconsequential manner in which one week had been pitchforked in after another without any idea more than rough contrast (Boult to Dawnay, 11 November 1934). It was now proposed to present the *real* foundations comprehensively and systematically in due chronological order, paying attention to the historical founders of any school or style of composition, including many minor ones hitherto neglected. Properly speaking this scheme needed a five-year plan, and it was proposed to start with the foundations of English music in the sixteenth century played on the original instruments of the period with the assistance of the Dolmetsch family and the advice of two leading authorities on the music of this period, Sir Richard Terry and Professor E. J. Dent.

This new departure roused the wrath of Filson Young, who complained that this flood of sixteenth-century music appealed only to the very narrowest minority of cultivated musicians and to the general public not at all. Its effect would be to render the series, hitherto so important to 'the humble listener', almost completely sterile. But the Music Department replied that the idea was 'an amazing example of historical development such as had never before been available to students in any country, arranged and sponsored at the microphone by the greatest experts in the world'. In the autumn of 1935 two weeks were devoted to the Italian Madrigals of Peter Phillips. This was claimed as the most important moment in the history of the programme, since it rediscovered one of the key figures of the madrigal period whose work had completely escaped the attention of modern researchers. Particular stress was laid on the prestige this would win for the department. By the end of 1935 Boult was declaring that the series had never been of such value to the world of music. It was assisted by eminent musicologists, it had enhanced the BBC's musical reputation at home and abroad (winning praise from musicians and critics in Paris and Prague), and had become the object of close attention from truly musical listeners (Boult to Graves, 25 November 1935: for all these details cf. WAC R27/106).

The changing tune of this series is one of the clearest indicators of an internal shift of emphasis in the Music Department—a move away from trying to educate the ordinary listener in the appreciation of good music, towards winning the approbation of the knowledgeable musical world. It does not imply a whole-scale abandonment of that early ideal, but it does reveal that for the Music Department prestige and the validation of its activities was tending to be sought from the serious musical public and from musicologists, with whom the department felt a greater collective affinity.

Promenade and other Concerts

In 1927 the BBC took over responsibility for sponsoring and financially guaranteeing the Promenade Concerts. The Proms, which began in 1895, had already become a unique musical institution under the inspired direction of Sir Henry Wood. Their special success lay in their appeal to a much wider audience than the usual concert-going public. There were three reasons for this. They were considerably cheaper than the usual subscription concerts; their social atmosphere was relaxed and informal; and thirdly it was Wood's particular genius, in building the programmes for these eight-week festivals, to blend together the established classics and popular favourites (which formed the unchanging basis of the overall programme) with more adventurous material old and new, British and foreign. The Proms drew in, year after year, people interested in music but who would never have dreamt of attending a standard orchestral concert. For most of them the Proms have always meant a broadening of musical experience. Wood succeeded in combining the familiar with the unfamiliar, demanding and undemanding orchestral music in such a way as to keep good faith with his audiences while maintaining an excellent box office record.

In spite of this the Proms were in severe financial difficulties by the mid-twenties for orchestral concerts (like opera) have always needed patronage, and their sponsors (Chappell's, the music publishers), having lost £60,000 in three years, decided to pull out. It was an inspired decision by Reith that the BBC should assume responsibility for these concerts, a move which Wood greeted with gratitude and relief: 'with the whole hearted support of the wonderful medium of broadcasting, I feel that I am at last on the threshold of truly democratizing the message of music and making its beneficial effect universal' (Cox, 1980: 88). Throughout the thirties decisions about the Prom programmes rested largely with Wood, with the BBC exercising only a light control over their content. They recognized that they had backed a winner. The Proms have remained the most successful attempt at the democratization of music in this country.

The Music Department had less success in its own efforts at organizing public concerts for simultaneous transmission to the listening public. When the BBC Symphony Orchestra was formed (1930) Boult knew that it could not be confined to studio performances. To bring out the best in performance, to maintain the morale of players, a live audience was essential. To augment its prestige and sustain its standards the orchestra must give regular public concerts not just in London, but in the provinces and abroad. This was bitterly opposed at first by the music profession as unfair competition and strenuous efforts were made. led by Sir Thomas Beecham, to cage the orchestra in the studio. These pressures were rightly resisted and after a few years they faded away. In fact the Symphony Orchestra stimulated the formation on a full-time basis of other orchestras, and undoubtedly improved the general standard of professional orchestral playing throughout the country. But the BBC's public concerts never quite caught on as the Proms had done.

At the end of their first season of public concerts Boult felt moved to suggest that the title of the concerts and the name of the orchestra should be changed, and the word 'National' substituted for 'BBC'—'I am repeatedly told outside that it is the expression "BBC" that helps to keep people away. Why I cannot imagine!' (Boult to Nicoll, 17 March 1931, WAC R27/431). When in 1934 the Department met with the administration to discuss the Five Year Plan for music it was agreed that the Proms were immensely more successful than any other concerts undertaken by the BBC. This could not be explained by the personal charisma of Sir Henry Wood. Their atmosphere was less stodgy, their programmes less formal and the prices were lower than the BBC's own concerts. The need to include more standard and popular works was strongly emphasized by Roger Eckersley, Director of Entertainment, and there was unanimous agreement that the BBC's own concerts should be made more like the Proms, including prices (Meeting of 18 October 1934, WAC R27/100).

On Phonography

EVAN EISENBERG

In 1917 the first jazz records appeared. They were cut by a white group, the Original Dixieland Jazz Band. (According to Johnny St Cyr, Freddie Keppard had the chance to record first but refused, saying 'he wasn't gonna let the other fellows play his records and catch his stuff'. The story rings true: Armstrong recalled that in New Orleans Keppard 'used to keep a handkerchief over his valves so nobody could see what he was doing'.) In 1923 Jelly Roll Morton and King Oliver started recording, and two years later Louis Armstrong, who had played second cornet in Oliver's Creole Jazz Band, began his series of Hot Five records for Okeh.

Records and radio were the proximate cause of the Jazz Age. Because of them the white audience was no longer limited to gamblers, gangsters, and doomed young musicians (I mean outside New Orleans; in New Orleans jazz had long been played at genteel fraternity dances). Intellectuals and society matrons who hesitated to seek the music out in its lair played the records. Distinguished composers in Europe heard the records and understood that the popular transcriptions of 'jazz' and 'blues' and 'ragtime' they had seen were wan facsimiles. In the pages of the *Nation* and the *New Republic* the latest Armstrong records were analysed by classical-music critics like B. H. Haggin. It was not that being on record conferred respectability; since Edison's day plenty of junk had been recorded, and its junkiness had only been confirmed by repeated listening. But it turned out that the best jazz was anything but junk. As Haggin later wrote, recording 'makes it possible to hear and discuss' improvised jazz performances 'as one does a piece by Haydn or Berlioz'. And the respectability achieved by the records was passed along to the live music, so that by the end of the twenties black jazz bands could be heard in the stuffiest hotel ballrooms.

All this is well known. But I will argue that records not only disseminated jazz, but inseminated it—that in some ways they created what we now call jazz. It is important to remember, first of all, that numbers were often 'composed' just before a recording session. As record companies did not like to pay royalties unless they had to, published tunes were avoided; but if one of the musicians came up with a tune, that came under his flat fee. So even regular performing bands, when they recorded, often put aside their well-worn, worked-out routines and threw together fresh ones. A skeletal tune, all ribs and riffs, left plenty of room for powerful new muscle. Armstrong said of Oliver, 'When he started makin' records, he started bein' a writer. Ha ha ha!' The same was true of

The Recording Angel: Music, Records and Culture from Aristotle to Zappa (London: Pan Books, 1988), 118–23.

Armstrong and several of his Hot Five players. Classics like Oliver's 'Snake Rag' and Armstrong's 'Cornet Chop Suey' were concocted in this way.

Oliver's Creole Jazz Band records are densely and somewhat rigidly contrapuntal in the New Orleans style, with infrequent breaks and less improvisation than we like to think. Armstrong's Hot Five sides move with startling rapidity from this style to what we now think of as jazz—music with a four-four swing and long, improvised solos that lag behind and dart ahead of the beat like street urchins at a parade. Most of those solos are Armstrong's; the rest of the Hot Five, although top-flight New Orleans men (except for Lil Hardin Armstrong, who was none of these things), barely keep up.

The Hot Five was almost exclusively a studio band. Armstrong played with and led various Chicago dance bands in those years, but it was only in the studio that he could experiment freely with the light-textured, daringly improvised music that was in his head. The very first cut, 'Gut Bucket Blues', shows Armstrong's keen sense of the medium. As the players solo he introduces each by name, urging each to 'whip that thing' or 'blow that thing'—evoking both a presence and a place, New Orleans. The flip side, 'Yes, I'm in the Barrel', begins with a riveting three-note riff, anticipating the sort of 'hook' that will later be standard equipment for a pop single. In case this fails to catch us, Armstrong plays a swaggering minor-blues oration over it, daring us to try and turn him off. We can't, and in any case it's too late. In an instant the key has turned major and the whole band is in step, playing with a buoyancy that carries all before it, with Ory's slide trombone to nudge the laggard. The dark drama of the prelude is back within two measures and keeps coming back, as in a march under heavy clouds; if Dodds's clarinet solo dissipates it somewhat, Armstrong's lead condenses it again. The style would almost be pure New Orleans were it not for the dominance of Armstrong's lead. That dominance is far greater on records made a few months later, such as 'Heebie Jeebies', which contains the first recorded scat and was Armstrong's first hit, and 'Cornet Chop Suey', in which Armstrong surrounds his wife's white-rice solo with exotic breaks.

Armstrong was a shy man. Part of the attraction of his first Chicago job, James Lincoln Collier suggests, was that he 'would be nestled down behind the large and forceful figure of Joe Oliver'. Although by 1925 he was getting used to asserting himself on-stage, he did so more by singing and clowning than by seriously playing his horn. In the recording studio, Armstrong was insulated from both the danger of failure and the lure of easy applause. The atmosphere was casual; producers assumed, as Collier puts it, that black music was 'crude stuff' and 'required few niceties of direction'. So here, as Ellison might say, Armstrong was really invisible, and freely 'made poetry out of being invisible'— 'never quite on the beat'. And here it was easy for him to deploy the full weight of his horn.

And he may have sensed that it was not only easy, but necessary. The ensemble music of New Orleans was fine so long as people could see the band, could see who was playing what and when, could watch the bustle of the stationary parade. Records were different. Of the records Armstrong had played on so far, those on which he accompanied Bessie Smith had been more compelling (and had sold better) than the ensemble records of Oliver and Fletcher Henderson. Perhaps Armstrong had learned that a powerful personality could hold a record together, welding a succession of pretty sounds into a compelling whole.

The principle involved here is not limited to jazz; in a sense, it is the same principle that suggests a forward balance for the soloist in a concerto recording. In a wider sense, it is the same principle that required, for phonography to get off the ground, figures like Armstrong and Caruso—figures I call icons of phonography.

Any new art, but especially one that is also a new medium, relying on technology to bridge distances in space and time, needs icons. For if the audience is being given something, it is also being deprived of something: a human presence. What I mean by icon is someone with a personality so powerful that he seems to be present when he isn't; someone so in command of his art that he turns its disadvantages into advantages; someone, preferably, whose person has the look of cartoon—a mask-like, symbolic quality. The great icon of film was Chaplin. With him film ceased to be a novelty or a dumb mimic of drama. Its two great disadvantages, the lack of sound and the lack of live actors, became advantages. A child could draw the Tramp from memory; an intellectual could find in the Tramp the soul of cinema, which was the soul of machine-age man.

Similarly, with Caruso the phonograph ceased to be a toy, although it remained a blind and short-winded mimic of opera. But even that blindness could be an advantage—surely the easy caricature (sometimes self-drawn) of Caruso that the record listener knew was more endearing than his short, fat self in some ridiculous costume. And the phonograph's limited playing time meant that one heard only the juicy arias, not the dry recitative. Caruso had, in Gaisberg's words, 'the one perfect voice for recording', and his mild hamminess helped make up for the lack of visible gesture. In 1924 Compton Mackenzie wrote:

> For years in the minds of nearly everybody there were records, and there were Caruso records. He impressed his personality through the medium of his recorded voice on kings and peasants . . . People did not really begin to buy gramophones until the appearance of the Caruso records gave them an earnest of the gramophone's potentialities . . . There are three things in this life that seem to store up the warmth of dead summers—pot-pourri and wine and the records of a great singer.

With Armstrong the phonograph began to do a job more remarkable than storage. It ceased to be a mimic; if anything, live music and paper-composed music would now mimic records, especially Armstrong's. Anyone could imitate his ballooning cheeks and gravelly voice, and any critic could recognize in him the voice of the phonograph, the voice of invisible man. So it is no accident that when one thinks of a stack of old 78s one thinks first, depending on one's predilections, either of Armstrong or of Caruso.

But the most powerful creative influences on a new art are not always the most powerful personalities in this sense. In film Eisenstein made his effect not by self-projection, but by painstaking and daring construction of the film object. In phonography Jelly Roll Morton played a similar role. His pianism on the classic Red Hot Peppers records of the twenties shows discretion remarkable in a man who wore a diamond in his tooth and claimed to have invented jazz. What is even more remarkable is his construction of dazzling phonographic montages in whole takes, without the aid of tape—as if Eisenstein had done the steps scene in *Potemkin* without a splice. That these masterpieces were, except for their skeletons, really composed in the studio is made clear by the recollections of the Red Hot Peppers themselves (who were not a permanent performing band, but simply the best New Orleans men available for a given session). Morton's records rely less on the power of his personality than on the power of his constructions: the dazzling succession of riffs, breaks, and bitter-sweet harmonies is what carries the listener along. Future phonographers, in popular and classical music as well as jazz, would need one power or the other to succeed.

Morton embodied the phonographic impulse in one of its purer forms. 'There is nothing permanent in the entertainment business,' he told Alan Lomax. To Morton not even records seemed permanent. But at least they were hard evidence of his greatness. They could be perfect, as a stage show rarely could be; and Jelly Roll was a perfectionist, as dandy in his art as in his dress. Although he composed on paper and believed that his 'little black dots' contained the secret of jazz, he knew that to bring his music to life he needed musicians, New Orleans improvisers who knew what to put between the written notes. His genius as a phonographer lay in making his musicians put their musical imaginations at the service of his own—in making them spontaneously prove, like reagents in a flask, his calculations. The Red Hot Peppers records are the prototype for a school of phonography that includes Ellington, Monk, Mingus, Zappa, Miles Davis, and the Beatles—master builders who would mean much less to us if their work had been done only on paper.

When splicing did become a possibility, jazz musicians resisted it; as improvisers they believed, even more passionately than old-fashioned classical musicians, in the spontaneity of the long take. Bands like Basie's and Ellington's achieved great fluency on-stage, which they duplicated in the studio. What critics have called the greatest jazz album ever made, *Kind of Blue*, consists, according to Bill Evans's liner notes, of first-take improvisations on sketches that Miles Davis had put before his players only moments before; Evans likened this virtually 'pure spontaneity' to that of Japanese ink drawing. Ornette Coleman's *Free Jazz* was an even bolder experiment, a collective free improvisation recorded in one thirty-six-minute take (here a record validates 'experimental' music by recording the results). On the other hand, some of Monk's mock-Gothic constructions were impossible for his superb players to achieve without splicing. And now Davis himself, like many younger jazz musicians, uses the multi-track techniques of pop without qualm.

Jazz people love and hate records. Like anglers, they talk about the ones that got away—the legendary players like Buddy Bolden, the glory days ('Joe Oliver's best days are not on records,' said Armstrong), the sudden numinous solos that were not caught. They sometimes complain that on record their improvisations sound fossilized. 'I have always found it difficult to listen to my past recordings,' Stan Getz said. 'They have felt too close, too painful and too frustratingly irrevocable.' But Earl Hines recalled that when 'Weather Bird' first came out, 'Louis and I stayed by that recording practically an hour and a half or two hours and we just knocked each other out because we had no idea it was gonna turn out as good as it did.' In general love has the upper hand, partly because records are the only solid proof of a jazz musician's greatness—or, for that matter, of the greatness of jazz. They make jazz 'legitimate', in part by giving scholars and critics something to cite instead of swapping nightclub stories. In André Hodeir's *Jazz: Its Evolution and Essence*, 'the words *work* and *record* are used interchangeably', and this is common practice. In jazz the record is the work. Even in bebop, which made a cult of spontaneity, records were respected as permanent works of art; Charlie Parker's alternate takes for Savoy have come to be as treasured for their endless invention as Picasso's studies and series. In every sense, records are the conservatory of jazz: its school, its treasure-house and thesaurus, its way of husbanding resources.

On the Musical Work-Concept

LYDIA GOEHR

The musical work-concept found its regulative function within a specific crystallization of ideas about the nature, purpose, and relationship between composers, scores, and performances. This crystallization shaped and continues to shape a standard or 'establishment' interpretation of the work-concept and of the practice it regulates. It continues also to motivate our classification of examples of musical works.

When we use the work-concept or any other open concept, we use it with an understanding revealed in our beliefs, ideals, assumptions, expectations, and actions. We can, however, use it in different ways. At least two of these ways ground a distinction between original and derivative examples. Original examples are not those produced first, but those produced directly and explicitly under the guidance of the relevant concept. We classify examples as derivative, by contrast, when we classify them as falling under a certain concept, even though these objects were not brought into existence with that concept in mind or within the specific part of practice associated with it. Whether an example is original or derivative is not something decided independently of how we *use* the concept. Thus, we should talk first of an open concept as having an original and derivative arena of employment and only then of its extension in terms of original and derivative examples.

The original use of an open concept tells a familiar story about conceptual use. Derivative use is more complicated, for there are different sorts of such use. Given the musical work-concept, one may look first at how far the activities of musicians producing music of a non-classical sort have approximated none the less to the condition of producing musical works. One may look at how work-associated concepts have gradually been taken over and how musicians have then begun to speak of their production in terms of works.

When non-classical musicians borrow work-associated concepts (and only when they do, for they certainly do not always have an interest in doing this), they adopt an understanding sufficient to sustain the functioning of these concepts. In the romantic eyes of the classical musician, they more or less successfully impose the appropriate categories upon their practice. They act in what classical musicians consider to be the right way and in a way they themselves presumably find satisfactory and rewarding. The concepts come to be employed in a non-classical setting in much the same way as natives incorpor-

The Imaginary Museum of Musical Works: An Essay in the Philosophy of Music (Oxford: Clarendon Press, 1992), 253–7.

ate into their understanding any concepts introduced to them by foreigners. Without exposure to foreign concepts, native musicians probably remain oblivious to them. It is on this assumption that we say that the use of the concepts is foreign to the native's own practice, and that if the concepts are used at all, they are used derivatively.

Or one can look at how musicians steeped in the romantic view interpret non-classical types of music according to their own conceptual framework. This would be more like persons who, entering into a foreign cultural context, make use of their native linguistic or social apparatus to acquire what is for them a sufficient grasp of unfamiliar customs. Work-orientated musicians can effectively choose to regard music in terms of *works* if they believe they can, with the relevant understanding, act successfully or usefully in relation to the music regarded in this way. In general, they extend the concept's employment when they infer its presence in a cultural setting which, without that inference (or interference), would not acknowledge its presence.

Hence it is possible for musicians to look at a practice, one, for example, in which the music of Bach or Palestrina was produced, and to classify the music derivatively as works. This is possible because they can identify composers, represent the music in adequate notation, specify determinate sets of instrumental specifications, etc. In the same manner, it is possible for classical musicians to identify the same features when listening to transcriptions, improvisations, aleatoric pieces, or even blues songs, and to talk thereafter of the music in terms of works. In all these cases, the use of the work-concept is derivative.

The assimilation of work-associated concepts into different kinds of music is not uniform. Some kinds of music stand in closer conceptual proximity to work-music than do others: the eighteenth-century sonata stands in closer conceptual proximity than the Indian *raga*. Some kinds of music are regulated by ideals that conflict with the *Werktreue* ideal. Jazz is an obvious example. It is likely, finally, that derivative works, precisely because they are derivative, fail to comply perfectly with the beliefs and expectations associated with the work-concept. Notations (or transcriptions), if existing at all, will not always be as precise as Beethoven would have liked. If they are, that often indicates that one has been rather lenient with the ideal of fidelity to the original music—the recent ethnomusicologist's complaint. When, however, we confront such imperfectly complying examples, we do not exclude them from falling under the concept. To do so would defeat the very idea of their being derivative.

When an example falls under a concept it is less a matter of its having the appropriate properties than of its being brought to fall under the concept by a user of that concept. If the relevant features are lacking in the first place, they can be assigned to the example so that it can be regarded in the right way. If this is not possible in any adequate manner at all, the attempt fails. Only then do we exclude the example from falling under the concept. This procedure functions because of the *connection* obtaining between a concept's original and derivative uses. The connection is a conceptual dependency of the latter on the former, understood in terms of the aims and beliefs of musical agents, how and why an agent wants to use a concept in a given way.

Thus, to use a concept derivatively one attempts to match a 'foreign' example with an original example. The match can be more or less successful. Often the match is triggered by a desire that the foreign example replicate original examples. The dependence of derivative on original use can vary in character and complexity. But it always has to do with the particular understanding implicit in a given person's involvement in the practice.

Though derivative examples are dependent upon original examples, it is possible, none the less, for the former to affect one's understanding of the latter. Derivative examples might bring something new to the understanding of the concept under which they now fall. When derivative use affects the meaning of the concept in any of these ways, we react accordingly. Sometimes we decide or sometimes we come to accept (as participants in a practice) that we must expand or modify the meaning of the concept itself. And sometimes that persuades us to redefine the scope of the concept's original and derivative use. Neither of these reactions is problematic. On the contrary, it is precisely the possibility of expansion and modification of conceptual meaning (seen here in terms of the interplay of original and derivative use) that confirms the desired *openness* of many of our concepts.

This general view of conceptual use leaves open three more possibilities. First, a musician in 1810 and one in 1990, for example, might both function under the regulation of the work-concept, but because of possible modification of meaning, they might be working with a different understanding and with a different range of original and derivative examples. Whether or not this is the case, there is a dynamic and diachronic relationality, in addition to our affirmation or rejection of the past, linking together the successive stages of the concept, all of which preserves the concept's identity over time.

Second, to talk of original and derivative examples falling under a given concept does not mean this is the only way to classify the examples. It is possible to interpret and perform Beethoven's 'Spring' Sonata, say, in accordance with the ideals of a tribal rain dance. We would then be obliged—in the context of the corresponding practices—to describe the music not as an original example of a work, but as a derivative instance of a rain dance. If this example is too extreme, consider the reconception involved in our listening to classical works that have been jazzed up, used in films, or ranked in the Top Twenty.

Finally, one may speak of an object falling originally or derivatively under more than one concept. Musicians might deliberately produce music that fails to fall neatly under a single concept. Many musicians have recognized the limitations, say, of producing music solely under the dictate of romantic ideals and have chosen to employ notions associated with other types of music. Numerous composers have made use of folk-music and jazz, in order to make statements not fully comprehensible within, or explained by, a romantic aesthetic. To what extent, if at all, the work-concept has remained central to their musical production has differed from case to case.

On the Economics of Popular Music

PETER WICKE

The starting-point for the marketing of any product is the definition of its market, for a 'market' only exists as a fact in economic categories. In capitalist language *marketing* has now become a technical term. Which needs represent a marketable demand and therefore form a 'market' is decided and defined by the industry according to its criteria, i.e. profit. 'What people want' is only of interest to it if this desire is linked to an ability to pay and is likely to provide the highest possible sales for its product. For example, around 1980 the sharp rise in youth unemployment in the late seventies, particularly among working-class teenagers, led to a clear market shift away from the former towards teenagers from the lower middle-classes. The musical needs of working-class teenagers ceased to be marketable because of their decreasing disposable income and willingness to buy, in spite of the fact that, in purely quantitative terms, this social group offered far more potential record buyers. This shift had far-reaching consequences, for the musical needs of lower middle-class teenagers not only have a quite different structure, but in this social group television also plays a dominant role in involvement with music. This led directly to the development of the pop video. Thus it is not the teenagers who decide which music is pressed on record, but the industry, which decides on the basis of which music sells most records. Of course before this the industry has already investigated musical needs and classified them in order to discover whether, according to its criteria, they represent a demand for the sale of records which is coupled with the ability to pay. If we simply look at the process in relation to the music, then it seems to be the exact opposite, as though records were sold because teenagers wanted this music and no other. John Beerling, BBC programme controller, once explained: 'You know how things are marketed these days. You bring in an import, hold it back for a while and then sell enough to get it in the charts. It doesn't always mean it's universally popular' (quoted in *New Musical Express*, 14 November 1985).
[. . .]

But marketing is only one aspect of the commercialization process. The other and more important one is *promotion*, the presentation of the product through advertising, image-building, and through the media of radio, television, and the press. Harry Ager, Vice-President, Marketing, for PolyGram, once put it like

Rock Music: Culture, Aesthetics and Sociology, trans. Rachel Fogg (Cambridge: Cambridge University Press, 1990), 128–9, 131–4.

this: 'If pitching is 70 per cent of baseball, promotion is 70 per cent of the record business' (Bernstein 1979: 60). For a long time the over-production of records had led to a situation in which it was impossible for record buyers actually to make their choice from all of the new releases. If around one hundred thousand songs appear on record in the USA and Britain every year, then a daily uninterrupted twelve-hour listening marathon would still not be enough even to listen to this whole crazy amount of music inside the 365 days available. Paul Hirsch once calculated that of all the singles released, just 23.7 per cent are played more than once on radio, and 61.6 per cent are never played at all, which, in view of the importance of radio in the music business, means these sell very few copies (1973: 32). Thus for the record companies everything depends on bringing as many as possible of their record releases to the attention of the vast range of potential buyers. Just heaping a large number of new releases onto the market is not enough to optimize the firm's percentage share of the yearly hits. Walter R. Yetnikoff, President of the CBS Recording Group explained the process:

> Things are considerably different than a few years ago, when the philosophy was to throw a lot of products against the wall and see what sticks. That approach is too expensive today. Now, every album that goes out has a complete marketing plan—with full details on advertising, airplays, discounts for the trade, personal appearances by the artist, sales targets and national and regional breakdowns.   (Blaukopf 1982: 17)

In the meantime enormous sums of money are spent. Roy Carr did some research using the example of WEA International, the overseas representative of Warner Communications: 'WEA, to quote just one of the big firms, considers that it needs to invest at least $250,000 in order to give a new release a fair starting chance. And even a superseller like the Bee Gees' 'Spirits Having Flown' needs a promotional spend of $1 million in order to realize maximum sales' (quoted in *Sounds* 11 (1979/8), 41). Of course, this goes far beyond the actual production costs. This is naturally not based on the naive idea that high expenditure on advertising will convince people of the necessity of buying this particular record. It is much more a matter of competition on the plane of product presentation, where the number of competitors declines with increasing expenditure and therefore the company's market share grows. It is quite impossible to persuade someone to buy a record, let alone to force them to do so. But the more a particular record is brought to the attention of the buying public, the less likely it becomes that it will not be bought simply because it is unknown. Thus an extensive system of product presentation has grown up in the music industry which gives the record a secondary and incorporeal existence in the media combine of radio, television, film, the music press, and fan magazines, and, since 1981, video, posters, and poster advertising. An image of the record is projected into the consciousness of its potential buyers, a process which achieves far more than merely pushing the competition out. The music too is integrated in this image and is not played on the radio or television merely for its own sake. The aim is to build up a context around the record, using the media, which makes the potential buyer feel that it is important. He will not buy the record just because of this, but this process makes sure that, from the immense selection available, only those new releases come to his attention which are made to seem important by vast expenditure. In this process there are no moral or other limits to the imagination of the promoters, the end literally justifies the means. The fact that the expenditure is admittedly worth it and that its result is completely calculable was confirmed by Geoff Travis (boss and owner of Rough Trade Records, a distinctive independent New Wave label with a middling commercial scope) with the following facts: 'If we succeed in getting a group and their song onto the BBC television programme "Top of the Pops", the sales figures will go up by around £50,000 in the following fortnight' (interview with author).

As Paul Hirsch determined, since a record only has a life of around 60 to 120 days as far as the music industry is concerned, and sales over longer periods are an exception, the image conception is primarily concentrated on the personality of the musician or the collective 'personality' of the band, for their commercial viability is normally an order of magnitude higher. Charlie Gillett pointed out that: 'for most record companies what's important is to produce and sell an *act*, an image, and not just a record—in the long run it's easier to run a star with assured sales than to have to work on a series of one-offs' (1974: 41). If the band has a stable image, this can be carried over onto each of their records which considerably reduces costs. But this stable image can be even sharper than a group image, and therefore more effective, if it is linked to a single musician, usually the band's lead singer. The result of this is an unparalleled star cult, and the concentration of capital in the music industry has given this factor increasing weight. Using larger and larger sums of money each record company tries to chase the others from the battlefield, out of the consciousness of the potential buyer.

But the ideological mechanisms which are set in motion are far more important than the media spectacular with all its comic side effects. The whole apparatus of promotion is constructed so that it creates a field of reference which draws in the listener as an active participant, thereby influencing him in a very subtle way. He himself must find the record presented to him so important that he recognizes its existence and possibly even buys it. The repeated playing of the record on the radio, press comments, interviews with the musicians, television appearances, and the rest of the circus tend to lead to the conclusion that this record must be important, and this is the buyer's own conclusion. He is not persuaded to feel like this, nor directly forced to, rather the rules of the whole system rely on his free, voluntary, and active participation. But by doing this, without being conscious of it, he is placed in a social role in which he behaves primarily as a record buyer and not—as he himself believes—as a recipient of music. It was not the music which made this record more important to him than the many other nameless ones, but the frame of reference in which the music industry placed it. Only later does he look at the record from the musical point of view and possibly even buy it. Instead of trying to exercise a direct influence on his behaviour, to direct him and dictate to him—an attempt which would in any case end in failure—the music industry continually flexibly arranges things around him so that his 'free' decisions always benefit it. The industry does not control his decisions but does control the results. However he behaves, things are arranged so that the result is always the same—profit. And as a part of this process he is tied into a context which makes him feel that the music industry is realizing his interests and not vice versa. The mechanisms of the music business reconstruct social reality in his mind in such a way that it seems to correspond to his interests. At the same time, these mechanisms reflect social circumstances back to him from such a perspective that they become an expression of a style of behaviour that conforms to the system. Jon Landau developed this point very vividly using the example of the star cult:

> Its only demand on the intellect is that we should accept what is, in fact, a flagrant lie: good versus evil, impossible romances between the mighty and the humble, the visible triumphs of zeal, hard work and steadfastness over dishonesty and laziness, or whatever. Of course, these assertions are nothing more than the myths and lies of culture. And the star cult, with whose help these lies are lived out on our behalf, is the greatest of all lies. For through this cult we are taught to identify with the supermen who act out these fantastic images and through this to make these images credible, attractive, motivating and erotic. We are taught that the unreal existence which they represent is possible, not that we ourselves are not qualified for it.   (1975: 177)

Riches and fame through one's own efforts—this is the ceaselessly repeated credo of the star, which turns social class barriers into individual barriers to achievement.

The mechanisms of the rock business speak a language that everyone understands, but in a voice that no one can hear and identify. They have no identifiable subject and this is what makes their effect so insidious. They give to the music which comes into contact with them a meaning which the listeners ultimately adopt as their own.

On Changing Technology

PETER MARTIN

Just as the record industry has been shaped by the need to cope with its volatile market, so its established practices and institutions have been constantly undermined by technological innovations which not only offer new and better ways of doing things but—as we shall see—have generally had the effect of increasing consumers' choice at the expense of the industry's ability to control its market. Indeed, the music business began to assume its modern form as an unanticipated consequence of the development of recording in the 1880s, and the threat which this posed was soon apparent to piano-makers and retailers, music teachers, sheet music publishers, music hall and vaudeville artists, proprietors and so on. The new gramophones and phonographs were important, too, in creating a mass market for music and entertainment.

Somewhat paradoxically, however, the new mass market was different in character: music was no longer a necessarily public, communal experience, but could be heard at home, divorced from the settings in which it was originally produced. Sound recording, then, gave a powerful boost to the 'privatization' of experience which many have held to be a fundamental aspect of twentieth-century culture. Moreover, the chance to buy recordings gave individuals, in principle, an unprecedented degree of control over their own musical environment: this ability to choose from a range of cultural options has also been seen as an important component of modernity. According to Schafer:

> The three most revolutionary sound mechanisms of the Electric Revolution were the telephone, the phonograph, and the radio. With the telephone and the radio, sound was no longer tied to its original point in space; with the phonograph it was released from its original point in time. The dazzling removal of these restrictions has given modern man an exciting new power which modern technology has continually sought to render more effective. (Schafer 1977: 89)

Nor should this power be thought of as confined to the sphere of domestic entertainment. 'We should not have captured Germany', wrote Adolf Hitler, 'without . . . the loudspeaker' (Schafer 1977: 91).

The development of recording techniques threatened the structure of the nineteenth-century entertainment business, but the new record companies

Sounds and Society (Manchester: Manchester University Press, 1995), 256–60.

were themselves challenged in turn by the rise of cinema and then radio. Later upheavals were brought about by television and tape-recorders, with the latter giving people an unprecedented ability to make their own recordings. Nor is there any likelihood that the pace of change will slacken: in recent years, the 'compact disc' has brought to an end the forty-year reign of the twelve-inch LP (with considerable consequences for production, distribution, and marketing), and in turn discs and tapes have been threatened by technologies which can deliver high-quality sound via cable direct to potential consumers (thus eliminating the need for the established pattern of product marketing and distribution). Within studios, the advent of synthesizers has blurred the established distinctions between musicians, composers, engineers, and producers—to the point where they may well disappear. And recording technology has advanced well beyond the point where the main purpose is to 'record' a 'performance'. According to Brian Eno: 'There's been a break between the traditional idea of music . . . and what we now do on records . . . It's now possible to make records that have music that was never performed or never *could* be performed and in fact doesn't exist outside of that record' (Eno 1983: 16). Beyond that, of course, it is now apparent that the recording studio itself is not longer necessary for the production of good-quality recordings.

The list of possible innovations, many simply using already existing technology, could be extended; indeed, the development of the music business provides countless illustrations of Marx's insight into the ways in which changes in the 'forces of production' ultimately act to undermine existing 'social relations of production' (Marx 1976). In the present context, however, the point to be emphasized is the idea that this constant stream of technical innovations has been a perpetual source of disruption and disturbance in the music industry, posing a persistent threat to the established ways of exploiting musical materials to yield a profit. In fact, composers, publishers, and record companies have waged a never-ending war in order to protect or establish copyrights on their material and collect royalties from its use.

For present purposes, the essential points are, first, that new technology has presented a constant threat to established interests in the music business, and, secondly, that the outcomes of the ensuing struggles for control have had a major effect on the nature of the music which becomes available to the public. Two examples must suffice. The first concerns the American Society of Composers, Artists, and Publishers, formed in 1914 as a means of actually collecting the royalties from public performances which had been legally established in 1909. By the 1930s the combined effects of recession and the rise of network radio had resulted in sharp falls in the sales of records and sheet music; to ASCAP members, radio was 'the business that killed music through repeated use' (Sanjek 1988: 188). Naturally, radio stations did not see things that way, and indeed were reluctant to pay ASCAP any royalties at all, on the grounds that their use of ASCAP music was valuable free publicity. Moreover, a substantial number of musicians and songwriters, operating in fields such as country music, blues, and jazz, had always been excluded from ASCAP membership by the publishing, theatre, and movie interests which had come to dominate the Society. In 1939 the National Association of Broadcasters organized a rival society, Broadcast Music Incorporated, to publish alternative, non-ASCAP, music.

Matters came to a head early in 1941, when the radio stations refused to accept a doubling of ASCAP royalties; from then on, only non-copyright and BMI music was broadcast. To the chagrin of ASCAP, the listening public got along without them very well. 'The ASCAP–BMI dispute', writes Shepherd, 'sowed the seeds for the decline of Tin Pan Alley as the major force in the production and marketing of white popular music . . . the way for rock 'n' roll was undoubtedly prepared through broadcasts of country music and "cover" versions of rhythm and blues' (Shepherd 1982: 134–5). By October of 1941, ASCAP conceded defeat, and a transformation in the power structure of the music business was under way. Thus a technological innovation—in this case national network radio—first can be seen to have presented a threat to established interests, then generated a tremendous upheaval in the industry, the outcome of which was a radical transformation of the character of the music made available through the media. In this case, too, it is evident that, as Peterson has argued, the emergence of rock 'n' roll is better understood as a result of specific alterations in the structure and power relations of the music business than as a reflection of more nebulous social or cultural changes (Peterson 1990).

A second example of the disruption which can follow the introduction of new technology is provided by the case of the portable cassette player. It would be difficult to exaggerate the contribution which cassette technology has made to the proliferation of music as an aspect of social life in the late twentieth century. But the popularity of cassette players was viewed with great suspicion by the record companies, and when their sales started to slump in the late 1970s it was 'home taping' which was blamed. By this time, writes Sanjek in a telling phrase, the music industry was 'preoccupied' with 'public larceny and its cure' (1988: 593). Moreover, it is apparent that in countries with weak copyright laws (or none at all) 'pirated' cassettes constitute a major sector of the music business. Record company interests have tried, in general with little success, to strengthen the copyright laws, or to have a levy imposed on sales of 'blank' tapes. As Frith puts it: 'if copyright laws express the tension between the need to spread culture and the need to reward authors then each new invention this century has increased the possibilities of public access while threatening authors' rewards' (1987: 71).

However, and this is the thrust of Frith's argument, the relentless process of technological innovation has *again* transformed the situation, with the effect that:

> record companies' primary interest is no longer selling records to domestic consumers, but packaging multi-media entertainment, servicing programme-greedy satellite and cable companies, providing Hollywood soundtracks, seeking sponsorship deals, coming to terms with advertising agencies. (1987: 72)

It is evident that these sorts of business activities are likely to be more attractive to record company executives than pandering to the whims of

14-year-olds; exploiting the rights they already hold, rather than trying to cope with a hugely unpredictable market and constantly changing technology. Frith's conclusion is uncompromising: 'For the music industry, the age of man-ufacture is now over. Companies (and company profits) are no longer organ-ised around making *things*, but depend on the creation of *rights*' (1987: 57).

Despite the new freedom of choice provided by cassette technology, then, it has been argued—just as by Adorno—that such freedom is essentially illusory: the bombardment of electronic messages to which we are all subject is not a response to genuine human needs and values but is rather determined by the interests of huge multinational media corporations in their endless quest for profits and market share. Interpretations of popular music have thus tended to reflect either an optimistic view, which sees in new technology the means of democratization and empowerment, or a pessimistic one, regarding the indi-vidual in 'mass' society as little more than a docile consumer. It is possible, of course, that these contrasting views may reflect different aspects of the same situation. As we have seen, the modern music business exhibits certain char-acteristics of a 'dual economy' in which dominant, high-tech, mass production can coexist with small-scale, specialized, and participatory projects. Indeed, as Lopes (1992) has suggested, such contrasting modes of organization may coexist within the same company. It may be, then, that the worst fears of the 'mass society' theorists will not be realized, just as it may be too optimistic to suppose that technology will lead to an era of human emancipation.

On Musical Reproduction (Exchange-Object and Use-Object)

JACQUES ATTALI

Records and Radio

Until 1925 the record was very little used; the waxes were of bad quality and transmission was only possible by placing the microtransmitter close to the phonograph's acoustical horn, resulting in very bad transmission. In 1925 these two disadvantages were overcome by electrical recording, the use of better waxes, and the invention of the pickup, permitting direct transmission from the record. In the beginning, there were no problems associated with using records: record producers freely distributed their products to the various radio stations. But two or three years later, complaints against the use of records for radio broadcasting began to be made; they were first voiced by music writers, music publishers, performing artists, and above all record manufacturers.

The *authors* said nothing at first, thinking that radio broadcasts gave them good publicity. But later, they began to fear that the public would lose interest in performance halls and that record sales would fall as public broadcast cut into private consumption. The *music publishers* saw one of their markets shrinking. They were the ones who sold the scores to radio musicians, a declining market. Moreover, music publishers had an interest in record sales; at that time, they held reproduction rights that they exercised against record manufacturers. The *performing artists* saw one of their places of work disappearing. The *record manufacturers* also feared a decline in record sales. They held rights to the mechanical reproduction of works under copyright, which they acquired either from the author or the publisher. In the second case, which was the most common, their reproduction rights were strictly limited to reproduction by mechanical means; they were not given general reproduction rights, which remained in the hands of the publisher. Thus it was impossible for the record manufacturers to oppose radio broadcast, which, as already noted, was considered a form of representation: they could neither invoke copyright law nor claim unfair competition to prevent their product from being used. We will see later on that this problem has yet to be resolved even today.

Noise, trans. Brian Massumi (Minneapolis: University of Minnesota Press, 1985), 96–101.

Exchange-Object and Use-Object

Reproduction did not have a dramatic impact on the economic status of music until sixty years after its introduction. The existing copyright laws, which defined a musical work as something written and attributed an exchange-value to its representation, provided no answer to these questions: Can a phonograph cylinder be considered a 'publication' protected as such under law? In other words, does sound recording entail a right for the person whose work is recorded? What share of the exchange-value of the recording should go to the creator? Will he continue to be a rentier, as he was under representation? What compensation should be given for playing a record, in other words, for the representation of repetition, the use of the recording? How should the performers and companies who made the recording be compensated?

These questions were not unique to music: at least as early as the beginning of the nineteenth century, the problem of ownership rights over the reproduction of a work was posed for all of the arts, and more generally for all productions for which there exists a technology permitting the replication of an original. These questions became central when competitive capitalism and the economy of representation catapulted into mass production and repetition.

In France, the law of 19 July 1793, did not make it clear whether income from reproduction should go to the creator of the original or to the person who buys his work. However, this issue took on considerable economic importance in the course of the nineteenth century; it was decided on a case-by-case basis, depending on the balance of power between creators and merchants. Painting is a case in point: Watteau died in poverty while the engravers of his works made fortunes; Léopold Robert, on the other hand, in one year sold a million prints of *Les Moissonneurs* (The Reapers), the original of which was bought for 8,000 francs; Gérard made 40,000 francs from his *Bataille d'Austerlitz* (Battle of Austerlitz), which it cost Pourtalès 50,000 francs to have engraved; Ingres, an able manager of his financial interests and glory, ceded the reproduction rights for his works for 24,000 francs (Reinach 1910).

In France, a law of 16 May 1886, regulated the specific case of 'mechanical instruments', or recording without prior representation or a pre-existing score—barrel organs, music boxes, pianolas, aeolian harps—which had made considerable headway as substitutes for bands at dances. The rights belonged to the industrialist and not the musician: 'The manufacture and sale of instruments serving mechanically to reproduce copyrighted musical tunes do not constitute musical plagiarism as envisioned under the law of July 19 1793, in combination with articles 425 ff. of the Penal Code.' Royalties could be collected only when these machines were used for public representations.

The manufacturers of these machines unsuccessfully cited this text to support their refusal to pay royalties to the authors of songs they reproduced, insisting on the private nature of the use to which these instruments were put. A decision of 15 November 1900 returned a guilty verdict against a café owner who installed a pay music box in his establishment (*Gazette des Tribunaux* 2, No. 3, 1901). But can this same reasoning be applied to records, equating them with scores?

In this period, the compensation performers and authors obtained, in the absence of texts, varied widely and was in some cases considerable. In 1910 Mme Melba and Tamagno received 250,000 and 150,000 francs respectively from the Compagnie des Gramophones; Caruso made a fortune on his recordings beginning in 1903.

The courts had a hard time settling on an interpretation of the law. The civil court of the Seine district, in a ruling of 6 March 1903, authorized the recording of music without payment of any royalties. Then a decisive ruling was issued on 1 February 1905, by the court in Paris: its motivation is very interesting, since it was one of the last attempts to maintain the fiction of representation in repetition, of the written in the sonorous, in order to equate the record with the score, which requires a specialized knowledge to be read:

> Finding that disks or cylinders are impressed by a stylus under which they pass; that they receive a graphic notation of spoken words, that the thought of the author is as though materialized in numerous grooves, then reproduced in thousands of copies of each disk or cylinder and distributed on the outside with a special writing, which in the future will undoubtedly be legible to the eyes and is today within everyone's reach as sound; that by virtue of this repetition of imprinted words, the literary work penetrates the mind of the listener as it would by means of sight from a book, or by means of touch with the Braille method; that it is therefore a mode of performance perfected by performance, and that the rules of plagiarism are applicable to it. (*Le Droit*, 5 March 1905)

An astonishing text: it equates the record with the score. Written reproduction determines the record's exchange-value and justifies the application of copyright legislation. It should also be noted that in this judgement sound reproduction is considered a popular by-product of writing, anticipating a time when specialists would decipher the recording directly.

The problem of compensating authors and performers was passed over in silence by legislators for a long time: in his fascinating report of 1910 to the Chamber of Deputies, Th. Reinach does not once refer to the case of music. Then, little by little, the principle of copyright was established for records. Authors and certain performers became the recipients of rent, a result of laws or court judgements on the mechanical reproduction of their works.

The parallel to writing was pursued, and institutions were established to regulate this industrial production on behalf of those receiving rent. These associations, similar to author's associations, enforced payment of royalties to the authors. Performers, and publishers of the works. In effect, repetition poses the same problems as representation: rent presupposes a right to industrial production, in other words, a right to monitor the number of pressings and number of copies sold, to which the royalties are proportional. And it also presupposes the confidence of the authors, who totally delegate the management of their economic rights to experts working for associations whose function it is to valorize their works.

The author's associations thus played a decisive role in determining the relations between music and radio. In law, the radio broadcast of a work was deemed a public performance on 30 July 1927 (by decision of the criminal court of Marseilles), and consequently the law of 1791 became applicable. There was a fleeting attempt to develop another position. L. Bollecker, in a 1935 article in the *Revue Internationale de Radioélectricité*, makes a distinction between radio broadcasting, which consists in transmitting waves through space, and reception, which consists in transforming those waves into sounds. In this view, only reception is representation, and it is generally private (it would only be public if the loudspeaker were public). Radio broadcasting, for its part, would be a new form of publishing. An extraordinary fantasy of spatial writing, the marking of space. Bollecker, however, was not followed: since waves are not *durable* and are *immaterial*, radio broadcasting remained a form of representation.

The opposition to the use of records on radio was resolved in France by a contract between SACEM and the private stations concluded in 1937. After that, radio stations had to pay for representation and reproduction rights.

The performers and publishers would continue to be excluded. They were recognized as having no claim. The difficulties associated with the evaluation of copyrights and related claims in representation resurface here, because the multiplicity of sale and listening sites make it difficult to collect payment.

In addition, there arise specific obstacles to monitoring recordings, because free access is taken to a new height: today it has become possible for each listener to record a radio-broadcast representation on his own, and to manufacture in this way, using his own labour, a repeatable recording, the use-value of which is a priori equivalent to that of the commodity-object, without, however, having its exchange-value. This is an extremely dangerous process for the music industry and for the authors, since it provides free access to the recording and its repetition. Therefore it is fundamental for them to prevent this diversion of usage, to reinsert this consumer labour into the laws of commercial exchange, to suppress information in order to create an artificial scarcity of music. The simplest solution would be to make such production impossible by scrambling the quality of the broadcast representation, or by truncating it, or again by taxing this independent production, financing royalty payments on these unknown recordings through a tax on tape recorders—this is done in Germany. The price of music usage is then based entirely on the price of the recorder. But the number of recordings could increase without a change in the number of tape recorders. We could then conceive of a tax on recording tape, which would mean paying music royalties in proportion to the exchange-value of non-music.

This problem of monitoring recording already announces a rupture in the laws of the classical economy. The independent manufacture of recording, in other words, consumer labour, makes it more difficult to individualize royalties and to define a price and associated rent for each work. It is conceivable that, at the end of the evolution currently under way, locating the labour of recording will have become so difficult, owing to the multiplicity of the forms it can take, that authors' compensation will no longer be possible except at a fixed rate, on a statistical and anonymous basis independent of the success of the work itself.

At the same time, usage becomes transformed, *accessibility replaces the festival.* A tremendous mutation. A work that the author perhaps did not hear more than once in his lifetime (as was the case with Beethoven's Ninth Symphony and the majority of Mozart's works) becomes accessible to a multitude of people, and becomes repeatable outside the spectacle of its performance. It gains availability. It loses its festive and religious character as a simulacrum of sacrifice. It ceases to be a unique, exceptional event, heard once by a minority. The sacrificial relation becomes individualized, and people buy the individualized use of order, the personalized simulacrum of sacrifice.

Repetition creates an object, which lasts beyond its usage. The technology of repetition has made available to all the use of an essential symbol, of a privileged relation to power. It has created a consumable object answering point by point to the lacks induced by industrial society: because it remains at bottom the only element of sociality, that is to say of ritual order, in a world in which exteriority, anonymity, and solitude have taken hold, music, regardless of type, is a sign of power, social status, and order, a sign of one's relation to others. It channels the imaginary and violence away from a world that too often represses language, away from a representation of the social heirarchy.

Music has thus become a strategic consumption, an essential mode of sociality for all those who feel themselves powerless before the monologue of the great institutions. It is also, therefore, an extremely effective exploration of the past, at a time when the present no longer answers to everyone's needs. And above all, it is the object that has the widest market and is the simplest to promote: *after the invention of the radio, that incredible showcase for sound objects, solvent demand could not but come their way.* It was inevitable that music would be instituted as a consumer good in a society of the sonorous monologue of institutions.

The use-value of the repeated object is thus the expression of lacks and manipulations in the political economy of the sign. Its exchange-value, approximately equal today for every work and every performer, has become disengaged from use-value. Ultimately, the price bears no direct relation to the production price of the record itself, to the quality, properly speaking, of the recording. It depends very heavily on the process of the production of the demand for music and on its fiscal status, in other words, on the role assigned to it by the state.

On the Negotiation of Meaning

JOHN SHEPHERD AND JENNIFER GILES-DAVIS

1. (*a*) Meaning is not immanent to the musical text itself. Here the musical text is defined as 'the aural combination of music *and* words' (Frith 1983: 63), but separating out the hard, literal content of the words.

(*b*) Conversely, meaning is not completely arbitrary in its relationship to the musical text as defined. It is not something that is externally visited upon the text regardless of the text's inherent qualities. There are, it could be argued, powerful iconicities between meaning and musical texts.

Meaning, in any situation, is thus a consequence of an intense dialectical interaction between text, other adjacent texts (lyrics, images, movement) and social, cultural, and biographical contexts.

2. In approaching this dialectic, there is no privileged point of meaning—no privileged moment in the process of production of consumption when meanings can be definitely read. There is an absence of a privileged point of meaning for two, principal reasons:

(*a*) The different intentionalities that producers and consumers bring to bear on musical practices are specific to concrete conjunctures of social, cultural, and biographical processes. Intentionalities are in other words socially located in a differential and variegated manner.

(*b*) A 'piece' of music, even if it can be assigned some kind of 'centre of gravity' with respect to meaning, also has a biography of its own during which this supposed 'critical mass' can shift. It is arguable, for example, that music of the 1960s as currently featured on North American AM radio's 'nostalgic' formatting of 'music of the 1960s, 1970s and 1980s' now carries a significantly different 'meaning' for the generation that grew up with it than it did in the 1960s.

However, the moment of consumption is the moment on which producers and consumers alike tend to focus, and, for this reason, that moment has been chosen as the point of analysis here. Such prioritization of the moment of consumption for purposes of analysis should not, however, be interpreted as conferring on that moment a privileged status in terms of the location and negotiation of meaning.

3. In the consumption of music, there is clearly an interplay between major structural forces, the formation and reproduction of specific cultural realities in relation to those forces, and the way those forces and identities are negotiated as a consequence of individual biographical processes, processes them-

'Music, Text and Subjectivity', in *Music as Social Text* (Cambridge: Polity Press, 1991), 175–7.

selves which are intensely social in their mediation. Such negotiation can be reproductive or non-reproductive in its consequences. The interplay between structures, cultures, and biographies presupposes a theorization of processes of negotiation. The most successful attempt at such a theorization, which takes into account the full force of social structures at the same time as remaining sensitive to the ability of individuals to strategically engage the lived consequences of such structures, occurs in the work of Bourdieu in the form of his concept of the habitus. The habitus, according to Bourdieu, is

> the strategy-generating principle enabling agents to cope with unforeseen and ever-changing situations . . . a system of lasting, transposable dispositions which, integrating past experiences, functions at every moment as a matrix of perceptions, appreciations and actions and makes possible the achievement of infinitely diversified tasks, thanks to the analogical transfer of schemes permitting the solution of similarly shaped problems. (Bourdieu 1977: 72)

This habitus operates according to a coherent logic, a logic of practice deriving from the internalization of objective social conditions through successive processes of socialization. The analysis of this 'cockpit' or 'nerve centre' of human action and response, in relation to the consumption of music as to any other arena of human activity, begs the question of appropriate methodologies. It has been argued (Shepherd 1986), in the context of the analysis of people's use of music, that a combination of quantitative and qualitative methods is appropriate:

(a) The play of major structural forces and related cultural identities can be discerned through quantitative and statistical methods. It is possible, in other words, to obtain a reasonably reliable map of who listens to what without, however, obtaining much reliable information as to why these listening habits occur and how they relate to major structural forces and related cultural identities.

(b) This latter information can be teased out through qualitative methods such as in-depth interviews. These methods can also reveal non-reproductive moments and some of the reasons that lie behind them.

4. The consumption of music is rich and complex in an intertextual sense. It can be argued that there are four textual channels of meaning with music: sound, words (the 'content' of lyrics), images, and movement. In relation to the 'same piece of music' these channels may be contradictory in terms of the intentionalities with which they are implicated (Frith and McRobbie 1979). The consumption of some channels by individuals may be reproductive while the consumption of others may not. This means, in terms of hegemonic theory, that the negotiation of hegemony through popular music may be complex in an intertextual sense.

5. Finally, the nature of the interplay of textual processes and processes of subjectivity is important, and has been insufficiently examined. These processes are not extrinsic to one another. An analysis of consumption processes in popular music demonstrates that, in the same way as contextual, intertextual, and textual processes are interpenetrative (that is, the meaning of

220 John Shepherd and Jennifer Giles-Davis

music is simultaneously extrinsic and intrinsic), so are processes of textuality and subjectivity.

All five of these considerations dictate that the development of theoretical protocols take into account the expressed intentionalities of actors without, however, eliding the dialectical presence of the technical features of music implicated in processes of meaning construction. Indeed, it is instructive that the expressed intentionalities of actors themselves bring into play the question of the *specificity* of musical texts. Some insight as to this dual importance of the expressed intentionalities of actors in constructing theoretical protocols *which have specific reference to music as text* can be gained by reference to fieldwork undertaken in Montreal in 1986 and 1987. This fieldwork examined moments of individual music consumption as experienced and interpreted by four English-speaking, middle-class girls.

On Popular Music and Postmodernism

ANDREW GOODWIN

In recent debates about postmodernism, it is often quite casually assumed that we are now living in an era where distinctions between art and mass culture have collapsed. Popular music is sometimes used to establish this argument, and in postmodern writing on pop the elision of high art and pop culture is usually taken for granted. A central problem in these accounts, as I will show, is the conceptual tension that exists between postmodernism's insistence on eclecticism in contemporary culture, and its focus on the apparent conflation of art and mass culture.

Much of this work suffers from two debilitating limitations. First, it often misreads the argument about cultural capital as though the presence or absence of particular aesthetic discourses could be discerned through the identification of timeless historical features, instead of undertaking a conjunctural analysis of the mobilizing categories of cultural power. As Andrew Ross has reminded us, via Bourdieu: 'Cultural power does not inhere in the contents of categories of taste. On the contrary, it is exercised through the capacity to draw the line between and around categories of taste; it is the power to define where each relational category begins and ends, and the power to determine what it contains at any one time' (Ross 1989: 61). Within the field of contemporary popular music, the processes of selection, exclusion, celebration, and denigration are used by critics, fans, and the musicians themselves in ways that continue to sustain the operation of forms of cultural capital. In particular there remains a tendency to identify as 'serious' those acts who subvert and undermine the conventions of the pop song, often in ways that are classically modernist. This process operates *within* generic categories as well as across the whole field of pop, so that art/pop distinctions can be made (and *are* made, by fans and critics), respectively, in mainstream pop (Pet Shop Boys/New Kids On the Block), soul (Prince/Michael Jackson), rock (Sonic Youth/U2), heavy metal (Metallica/Def Leppard), and rap (Public Enemy/MC Hammer). The briefest of conversations with almost any fan of one of the above acts would confirm that arguments about art versus trash remain rampant within today's pop.

Secondly, postmodern theory establishes its categories too easily, by defining discourses of art and mass culture through the use of extremely limited terms of reference. A standard strategy is the presentation of two bipolar

'Popular Music and Postmodern Theory', *Cultural Studies* 5:2 (1991), 178–82.

opposites which are held to signify art, on the one hand, and mass culture, on the other. The writer will then show how they have increasingly converged, thus magically bringing the truth of postmodernism to light. What is usually missing are all the various genres of pop music which lie *outside* the binary opposition, and which may run counter to the analysis.

John Stratton's (1989) account of three key moments in rock history and their relation to aesthetic categories pays much closer attention to musical meanings and is more historically specific in its arguments than Jameson's early typology (1984). Yet it, too, contains a curious flaw. Stratton identifies a convergence of popular and high cultural discourses in rock's third 'moment', *circa* 1975–9, when a 'postmodern' aesthetic (Stratton's description) of minimalism in form, combined with excessive affect, straddles both popular culture (the punk rock of the Sex Pistols, for instance) and the art-music of Brian Eno, Laurie Anderson, and Philip Glass. This makes sound musicological sense, but its usefulness is diminished by the sociological realities of pop consumption. Eno, Anderson, and Glass *are* consumed as high-art, with the exception of Eno's work with the pop group Roxy Music (and even there he was portrayed as the freakish, arty boffin, to Brian Ferry's populist neo-Sinatra), and Anderson's freakish 1983 hit single 'O Superman'. For many pop fans, Eno is known as someone who helps to produce the rock group U2 (and perhaps Talking Heads), not as an avant-garde or postmodern composer. In that area his work is closely associated with art-rock; so much so that a recent musicological account of Eno places his solo work firmly in a tradition of 'progressive rock' (Tamm 1989)—a category which should be (as I will demonstrate later) anathema to postmodernism. Musicologically, Stratton's account is persuasive; sociologically it demonstrates the limits of text analysis (however well-grounded historically) when confronted with the actual practices of pop consumption.

What the postmodernists frequently miss in their accounts of popular music are the continuing presence of the categories of the popular and the artistic. There are, in a sense, two Brian Enos: Eno the avant-garde musician and Eno the popular record producer—and the audience for *both* Enos is probably infinitesimal. Scholars accustomed to listening to Laurie Anderson, Philip Glass, and even Talking Heads run the danger of greatly overestimating their impact in pop culture, and—most importantly—the crucial elements of cultural capital that attach to them.

It seems to me almost redundant to have to point out the sociological specifics that place, say, Philip Glass in the category of art-pop, but in this context it seems important to spell out the details: Glass does not produce music which is recognizably like a pop song; lyrics, where they are used, deviate from the conventional modes of address of pop and the structural and (poly)rhythmic content of his pieces deviates from rock convention. For instance, while much has been made of the superficial resemblance between the music of Philip Glass and rock through their shared emphasis on *repetition*, this misses the point that Glass's music takes this technique to extremes that are rarely deployed in pop. Because he defies the recognized forms of rock and pop music, Philip Glass albums are usually found in record stores under headings such as 'Classical', 'Jazz', and (a telling insult) 'New Age'. His concerts take place in halls associated with classical and modern music performances, rather than rock clubs or stadia. In solo performance, the staging of his music reflects the 'serious' conventions of the venue (e.g. the absence of dramatic use of lighting, stage set or visual effects). When the Philip Glass Ensemble performs its operatic works, the staging is highly visual—but the conventions are those of the art-rock 'concept' performance (Pink Floyd, Genesis, etc.), not a rock and roll show. Glass (1987: 3–26) himself makes the influence of modernist artists like Beckett, Brecht, Pinter, and Godard quite explicit here—influences that are also very clearly at work in the performances of Laurie Anderson. The behaviour of the audience is in either case reverential and distanced, listening attentively to the music, rather than moving, cheering or singing along. Artists like Glass, Eno, and Laurie Anderson in fact occupy a space within contemporary pop that reproduces the position of progressive rock and art-rock in the 1960s and 1970s. It is music for college students and middle-class graduates who have the cultural capital to decode the significance of its heightened use of repetition, its minimalism, and its shifting of attention away from the pop star and towards multi-media contextualization. The music may share an abstract principle with rock and roll (a basis in the use of repetitive structures), but its sound and staging hardly resemble that world at all.

I want now to develop these criticisms, by making two points, which operate at discrete levels. First, empirically speaking, each of the different attempts to substantiate the legitimacy of postmodern theory operates by bracketing out vast areas of contemporary pop that contradict the theory. Secondly, and more fundamentally, each of these approaches establishes the category of post-modernism by setting up binary oppositions from within extremely limited (and quite divergent) fields of reference. Categories of the postmodern which are constructed around oppositions such as punk/pop, authenticity/artifice, rock/New Pop, modernist rock/postmodern pop, and so forth each leave out too much—indeed, the *absences* are precisely what allows each account to seem coherent. (This problem in its turn derives partially from the fact that analysts have tended to focus on just one or two aspects of the debate about postmodernism, thus generating entirely different, and sometimes contradict-ory, positions using the same conceptual field. The problem, in other words, is that the conceptual field is itself unstable.)

A way out of this confusion is suggested, in my view, by Susan McClary's (1989) careful analysis of avant-garde and postmodern musics. McClary's definition of the postmodern is tight and focused, centering on art-music which abandons the 'difficulty' of high modernism (e.g. Schoenberg) in favour of popular, pleasurable devices such as tonality, melody, and simpler rhythms. It thus represents an account of the postmodern which (reasonably, if un-usually) relates that category to modernism itself. For McClary, the quintes-sential postmodern composers are Philip Glass, Steve Reich, and Laurie Anderson. Her account offers a definition of postmodern music which has the merit of being clearly argued and coherent. However, in revealing the limited appeal of postmodern music (none of these artists are mass sellers) amongst audiences for 'serious' music, McClary's arguments undermine a central tenet of postmodern theory—the notion of a convergence of art and mass culture.

The confusion arises because postmodern theory has mixed up two different issues—the identification of eclecticism (which pervades rock and pop) and the collapse of distinctions based on cultural capital (which remain pervasive, especially *within* the field of rock music, as Frith and Horne (1987) have shown). When this mistake is laid over the misapprehension that modernism operates in the field of pop music just as it does in 'serious' modern music, the result is conceptual chaos. Whatever its inroads in the visual codes of television (Brechtian devices in prime-time programming, modernist jump cuts in soap-powder commercials, etc.), the much neglected *aural* codes of music are a different matter. While modernist techniques are accepted by the gate-keepers of high culture, in the marketplace of commerce the sounds of dissonance are not so welcome. Today's rap music, like punk rock before it, encounters extraordinary difficulty in gaining airplay and media exposure precisely because its *sounds*, as much as its sentiments, are not conducive to a commercial environment. The music is, in classic modernist tradition, *disruptive*. It would be interesting to consider further the reasons for this disjuncture between visual and aural modernism in the marketplace. For my purpose here, I simply wish to note the pertinence of Georgina Born's comments:

> It is odd and significant that music is so often cited as the success story of post-modern reintegration . . . Effectively, these cultural theorists collude in asserting that the postmodern *rapprochement* has been achieved . . . It is not only by ignoring the hegemonic 'other' of powerful, contemporary high culture, and failing to deconstruct its rhetoric of *rapprochement*, that writers have arrived at their optimistic and utopian postmodern perspectives. The assertion that modern music culture is moving beyond the modernist/populist divide to achieve a postmodern synthesis or reintegration must be based on empirical study . . . rather than making facile assertions, it is necessary to analyse real socio-economic and aesthetic differences that exist. (1987: 70)

References

Adorno, Theodor W. (1978), 'On the Fetish Character in Music and the Regression of Listening' (orig. pub. in *Zeitschrift für Sozialforschung* 7, (1938)), in Andrew Arato and Eike Gebhart (eds.), *The Essential Frankfurt School Reader* (New York: Urizon Books, 1978), 270–99,

Attali, Jacques (1985), *Noise* (orig. pub. as *Bruits: Essai sur l'économie politique de la musique*, Presses Universitaires de France, 1977), trans. Brian Massumi (Minneapolis: University of Minnesota Press).

Benjamin, Walter (1968), 'The Work of Art in the Age of Mechanical Reproduction' (1936), in *Illuminations*, trans. Harry Zohn, ed. and with an introd. by Hannah Arendt (New York: Schocken Books), 217–51.

Bernstein, Peter (1979), 'The Record Business: Rocking to the Big Money Beat', *Fortune*, 23 Apr.

Blaukopf, Kurt (1982), *The Strategies of the Record Industries* (Strasbourg: Council for Cultural Cooperation).

Born, Georgina (1987), 'On Modern Music: Shock, Pop and Synthesis', *New Formations* 2.

Bourdieu, Pierre (1977), *Outline of a Theory of Practice*, trans. Richard Nice (Cambridge: Cambridge University Press).

Briggs, Asa (1961), *The Birth of Broadcasting*, vol. i (Oxford: Oxford University Press).

Cox, David (1980), *The Henry Wood Proms* (London: BBC).

Eisenberg, Evan (1988), *The Recording Angel: Music, Records and Culture from Aristotle to Zappa* (London: Pan Books; 1st pub. New York: McGraw-Hill, 1987).

Eno, Brian (1983), 'Excursions in the Electronic Environment', *Downbeat*, June.

Frith, Simon (1983), *Sound Effects: Youth, Leisure and the Politics of Rock 'n' Roll* (London: Constable).

—— (1987), 'Copyright and the Music Business', *Popular Music* 7:1.

—— and Horne, Howard (1987), *Art into Pop* (London: Methuen).

—— and McRobbie, Angela (1979), 'Rock and Sexuality', *Screen Education* 29, 3–19.

Gillett, Charlie (1974) (ed.), *Rock File* 2 (St Albans: Panther).

Glass, Philip (1987), *Music by Philip Glass* (New York: Harper & Row).

Goehr, Lydia (1992), *The Imaginary Museum of Musical Works: An Essay in the Philosophy of Music* (Oxford: Clarendon Press).

Goodwin, Andrew (1991), 'Popular Music and Postmodern Theory', *Cultural Studies* 5:2, 174–90.

Hirsch, Paul (1973), *The Structure of the Popular Music Industry* (Ann Arbor: University of Michigan).

Hodeir, André (1956), *Jazz: Its Evolution and Essence* (New York: Grove Press).

Jameson, Frederic (1984), 'The Politics of Theory: Ideological Positions in the Postmodernism Debate', *New German Critique* 33, Fall.

Landau, Jon (1975), 'Der Tod von Janis Joplin', in F. Schöler (ed.), *Let It Be* (Munich: Carl Hanser).

Lopes, P. D. (1992), 'Innovation and Diversity in the Popular Music Industry, 1969–1990', *American Sociological Review* 57.

McClary, Susan (1989), 'Terminal Prestige: The Case of Avant-Garde Music Composition', *Cultural Critique* 12, 57–81.

Martin, Peter (1995), *Sounds and Society* (Manchester: Manchester University Press).

Marx, Karl (1976), Preface to *A Contribution to the Critique of Political Economy* (1857–8) (Peking: Foreign Languages Press).

Peterson, R. A. (1990), 'Why 1955? Explaining the Advent of Rock Music', *Popular Music* 9.

Reinach, Th. (1910), cited in Report No. 3156 to the Chamber of Deputies, 1 Mar.

Ross, Andrew (1989), *No Respect: Intellectuals and Popular Culture* (New York: Routledge).

Sanjek, R. (1988), *American Popular Music and its Business*, vol. iii (New York: Oxford University Press).

Scannell, Paddy (1981), 'Music for the Multitude? The Dilemmas of the BBC's Music Policy 1923–1946', *Media, Culture and Society* 3, 243–60.

Schafer, R. M. (1977), *The Tuning of the World* (Bancroft: Arcana Editions).

Scholes, Percy (1925), *Everybody's Guide to Broadcast Music* (Oxford: Oxford University Press).

Shepherd, John (1982), *Tin Pan Alley* (London: Routledge).

—— (1986), 'Music Consumption and Cultural Self-Identities: Some Theoretical and Methodological Reflections', *Media, Culture and Society* 8:3, 305–30.

—— and Giles-Davis, Jennifer (1991), 'Music, Text and Subjectivity', in *Music as Social Text* (Cambridge: Polity Press), 174–85.

Stratton, Jon (1989), 'Beyond Art: Postmodernism and the Case of Popular Music', *Theory, Culture & Society* 6:1.

Tamm, E. (1989), *Brian Eno: His Music and the Vertical Color of Sound* (Winchester, Mass.: Faber).

Wicke, Peter (1990), *Rock Music: Culture, Aesthetics and Sociology* (orig. pub. as *Rockmusik: Zur Ästhetik und Soziologie eines Massenmediums*, Leipzig: Verlag Philipp Reclam jun., 1987), trans. Rachel Fogg (Cambridge: Cambridge University Press).

Brief Explanatory Notes on Theory

In the 1970s and 1980s writers on culture will usually be found adopting one of the theoretical models described below. In their 'pure' form, these models give rise to arguments that are distinct in their emphases and which sometimes provoke radical disagreements (for example, about whether or not cultural artefacts are capable of communicating an inner human essence, or whether class is a more important issue than patriarchy). In the 1990s a more eclectic mix of theories has been seen. Postmodern theory has, in the main, developed ideas from semiotics, poststructuralism, and deconstruction.

Structuralism and Poststructuralism originate in the Swiss linguist Saussure's theory that the pre-given structure of language organizes your feelings. By extension, all cultural forms may be said to have pre-existing systems of signification. Hence, structuralists ask, 'How does the *organization* of this cultural form *construct* meaning?' The link between a *signifier* (e.g. a word) and a *signified* (what the word means) is established by convention and so it may be understood differently by different social groups (e.g. the word 'wicked'). Because conventions are ideological rather than natural, it follows that where a sign is present, ideology is present. Structuralists make use of semiology (study of signs) to analyse connotations of signs and how they have been assembled into meaningful forms (*signifying practices*); in so doing, they stress that it is not sufficient to look at what is signified without looking at what is not signified (hence, fondness for *binary oppositions*: e.g. 'hot' is only understood in relation to 'cold'). Poststructuralists recognize that a term is not only understood in relation to another, but can be privileged over another in metaphysical oppositions (e.g. 'masculine' over 'feminine'), and that texts offer particular *subject positions* (i.e. they embody assumptions about the person they are addressing). This leads to deconstruction, where hidden assumptions behind texts are exposed, and dialectical reasoning is challenged.

Cultural Sociology seeks to interpret the way individual *experience* is *expressed* through cultural forms. Membership of a certain social group will influence and condition consciousness, and culture is an expression of this consciousness. There is an obvious relationship to the 'vulgar Marxist' determinist notion of a *superstructure* of ideas built over and reflecting a particular economic *base*, but differing in the recognition that *social being* (experience) influences rather than determines cultural consciousness, thereby allowing culture a *relative autonomy* (it is neither completely autonomous nor completely determined). The emphasis is therefore on how the values of a dominant cultural group are *mediated* rather than *reflected*. Moreover, a subordinate group may resist and/or evade meanings disseminated by a dominant social group, and may engage in hegemonic negotiation. As theorized by Gramsci, hegemony is the process by which a dominant class persuades a subordinate class to accept its moral and intellectual leadership. Only one class exercises hegemony, but has to do it by *negotiation* (such negotiations can achieve a *hegemonic bloc*, an alliance of power). Hegemony relies on winning consent, not imposing consent; however, if it fails, coercion becomes necessary. For hegemonic negotiation, areas of exchange are needed between dominant and subordinate classes; popular culture is thus a favoured arena.

Feminism regards *patriarchy* as a feature of all societies, and thus explores male dominance of culture, as seen, for example, in *fraternalism* and in the gender stereotyping of artistic forms. Feminist scholars are keen to analyse *discourses* (domains of language use—medical, legal, literary, religious, etc.) for the 'truths' they construct. Psychoanalytic theory brings to feminism ideas from Lacan and Kristeva on the construction of the subject within the symbolic order of language. There is much concern with the body, pleasure, and questions of sexuality and desire, and this has been a feature, too, of recent gay and lesbian scholarship. There remains a concern in some quarters with the question of whether or not *essential* feminine qualities exist independently of class or social process. Many feminists today, however, consider gender, as well as sexuality, to be culturally constructed.

Index